J. M. (James Mason) Hoppin

Greek art on Greek soil

J. M. (James Mason) Hoppin

Greek art on Greek soil

ISBN/EAN: 9783741177743

Manufactured in Europe, USA, Canada, Australia, Japa

Cover: Foto ©Thomas Meinert / pixelio.de

Manufactured and distributed by brebook publishing software
(www.brebook.com)

J. M. (James Mason) Hoppin

Greek art on Greek soil

GREEK ART ON GREEK SOIL

BY

JAMES M. HOPPIN

PROFESSOR OF THE HISTORY OF ART IN YALE UNIVERSITY

" Willst ben Dichter bu verstehen
Musst in Dichter Lanbe gehen "
GOETHE

BOSTON AND NEW YORK
HOUGHTON, MIFFLIN AND COMPANY
The Riverside Press, Cambridge
1897

PREFACE.

THIS volume is the outcome of two visits to Greece, one in the spring of 1895 and the other as far back as the time of the Bavarian king Otho, affording an opportunity for comparing impressions of quite wide-apart experiences, and noting the changes that have taken place.

While treating of a country that never loses its charm, and having something to say of this Greek land and its people, the aim of the book is to give a fresh picture of Greek art, though the theme be as familiar as the song of Homer; yet it is worthy of endless study as the source of organized art drawn from the principles of nature.

These notes are, indeed, but scanty gleanings of an inexhaustibly rich field, and they embody only the author's own personal observations. They may contain errors, but they are true to actual impressions.

If art is the expression, the flowering of a people's genius and real spirit, this is true, in especial, of Greek art, which lay at the centre of all the manifestations of the life of the Greek people, and still remains the best record of that life.

The author would acknowledge aid derived from works like Furtwaengler's *Masterpieces of Greek Sculpture*, Collignon's *Histoire de la Sculpture Grecque*, Schuchhardt's *Schliemann's Excavations*, Mrs. Jane E. Harrison's *Mythology and Monuments of Ancient Athens*, Percy Gardner's *New Chapters on Greek History*, and Dahl's *Excursions in Greece*; also from books of travel such as Col. Leake's *Morea* and Snider's *Walks in Hellas*, as well as guidebooks, English and German.

NEW HAVEN, January 1, 1897.

CONTENTS.

LIST OF ILLUSTRATIONS

CHAPTER I.

THE LAND OF GREECE.

John Winckelmann, who stood in a rank with Lessing and Goethe, and who still remains the subtlest critic of art, in his "History of Ancient Art" that was written a hundred and thirty years ago, made some capital errors in his estimate of Greek sculpture, setting up statues which belonged to Greek art in its decline, as if they were perfect works. In this he was excusable, and excusable also for not recognizing the supreme merit of Pheidias, because Greece in his time was comparatively unvisited by scholars and artists; though, by a fortunate chance, a French artist, Jean Jacques Carrey, had been in Athens previous to the destruction of the Parthenon in 1687. He made sketches in red chalk of the sculptures on the pediments of the Parthenon, that are now invaluable as enabling us to define and posit these groups, and especially those that were afterwards destroyed. But Winckelmann drew his knowledge of Greek art from Rome, from art-collections in Italy and Germany, and he made a skillful use of the materials that these afforded him; yet he would have infinitely enlarged his æsthetic and critical vision, had he seen the Acropolis. Other German writers since Winckelmann have taken advantage of a better acquaintance with Greece itself, and do not greatly err in this matter; and it is one of the excellencies of the most recent of them and, perhaps, of the highest living authority in this department of knowl-

edge, Furtwaengler, that he made a careful study of
Greek sculpture on Greek soil, in the environment of
place and scene in which this art was created.

In the field of painting, who, we would ask, could
sympathetically know Giotto's frescoes in the upper
church of Assissi, or the religious pictures of the
Umbrian school, who had not first made a pilgrimage
to that Umbrian land, which was the home of early
Italian painting, and where the hills over which St.
Francis walked still glow and palpitate with the life
of religious poetry and the spirit of monkish meditative art ?

In this, then, and the succeeding chapter, I would
say in a plain, straightforward way, something of the
land of Greece and of the people who live there ;
for the people who live on the soil, and the very
earth, the sun and atmosphere, the geography, the
language, the racial derivations and peculiarities,
the political events which have occurred, tell us of
those influences, subtle though they be, which originate and color a nation's art, while, of course, there
ever remains the unknown factor of genius.

The best-hated man in Greece since he published
his book in 1847, has been the German author, Dr.
Philip Fallmerayer, who, in his "History of the
Morea during the Middle Ages," declared and proved
to his own satisfaction that modern Greeks, established in their national existence in 1832, are *not*
Greeks, are not lineal descendants of the old Hellenic
race, but Slavs. This has awaked a tempest of criticism and aroused the wrath of the modern Greeks
against the writer. His undeniably learned reason-
ings have been met and mostly done away by the
labors of more accurate investigators, who have shown

that modern Greeks, with a confessedly large admixture of alien blood, may claim the name of Greeks. These scholars maintain that the Greek germ not only exists undestroyed and indestructible, but that the Greek element has absorbed other races, and that Greeks of the present day may be held to be " a modification of the ancient Achaian, Dorian, Ionic and Etolian, in a word Hellenic populations, though greatly affected by the changes wrought through war and conquest."

I speak now of the Hellenes, not of the prehistoric people who inhabited Greece, and no Greek scholar would or could affirm who these were, be they called Aryans, Pelasgians, or Hittites; and speculation seems now to run to the theory that they sprang from European centers and themselves emigrated into Asia, and made and mixed with the Aryan stock. Who, truly, were " the brass-greaved Achaians " whom Homer calls Greeks, and makes splendid as the rulers of Mycenae, Argos and Sparta? Agamemnon and Menelaos arose from Greek soil and represented a veritable Greek civilization, or one on Greek earth, existing before Homer and from which he drew; and the Achaians, who were pre-Dorians, are held to be one of the four original Greek races—but these are vexed questions about which scholars are disputing.

The two racial factors in Greek art, were, originally, the Dorians and Ionians, the one bringing strength and the other beauty into Greek art; but since those vastly early days, Macedonians, Gauls, Romans, Goths, Normans, Venetians, Slavs and Turks have swept over Greece and left their stamp on the people, but none of them have utterly stamped out and destroyed the primitive race. It is true that in the bloody wars of the Diadochoi, successors of Alexander,

Greece was fearfully depopulated, and down to this day it has not recovered its former population, but the Greek is a tenacious race like the Hebrew and other strong races that have influenced the world, and the survival of race is one of the best established laws of ethnic science; and so true is this in relation to Greece, that Professor Jebb says : ''The central fact of Greek history, from the earliest age down to the present day, is the unbroken life of the Greek nationality.''

There are said to be at present chiefly three races, or classes, of people, who inhabit Greece, clearly distinguishable from one another, the Wallachians, Albanians and Greeks, the last being the germinal or unifying one, which is especially the case in the central regions of Phocis and Boeotia about Mt. Parnassos, where ten old Hellenic names of towns and villages are found for one that is Slavic, or foreign.

The first of these, the Wallachians, who are affiliated in their Thracian ancestry to the Greeks, came into Greece from the southern slopes of the Carpathian mountains, in several streams of invasion in the Middle Ages, sometimes securing permanent foothold and being sometimes driven out by succeeding invaders ; and they are now represented by the nomad population of the regions about the foot of Mt. Olympos in northern Greece, largely shepherds with no very settled place of abode ; and the traveler meets them on the sterile hills and in the narrow valleys, clad in sheepskins, stalwart but savage-looking men, driving their flocks to pick up the scanty pasturage.

The second class, the Albanians, form a more marked and diffused element, comprising as they do the land-possessors, agriculturists and soldiers, the bone and muscle of the state, who came also from the

north, descendants of the ancient Illyrians, mountaineers of those rugged countries of Albania and Epirus
who, in unsettled times, swarmed into Greece, meaning to stay there, and who, though not exactly Greeks,
are more closely allied to them than the Wallachians
in speech, blood and traditions, and have become
Greeks and formed the most vigorous fighting element
in the war of Independence, and would do so in any
other war that should arise.   They brought new blood
into the degenerate Greek race.   You see these striding with haughty carriage about the streets of Athens,
dressed in their jaunty red caps with long tassels,
snowy fustanellas, embroidered jackets, close-fitting
white leggings splaying over the foot, and large shoes
upturned at the toes, with a tuft of wool at the extremity, an armory of silver-mounted pistols and daggers in their belts, and swinging big rosaries, which,
like their petticoats, are not quite in keeping with
their martial character.   They are handsome fellows.
" The mountains are his palaces," the Palikari says,
and when he comes straight down from them he is as
ragged, lean and wolfish as we imagine Walter Scott's
highlanders to have been when they strolled into the
streets of Perth ; but the Albanian grows into an
orderly soldier, farmer and citizen.   He is a stay-at-
home man, who gets all he can and keeps all he gets.

The third class are, in some of their traits, more
properly, Greeks, who, in Athens especially, and sometimes with good cause, boast of their pure blood ; for
Athens and Attica were more exempt from the Slavic
invasions that occurred between the 6th and 14th centuries, than other provinces.   They are, morally and
intellectually, children of Odysseus, man of many de-
vices and who saw many cities ; they are the traders,
merchants, sailors, commercial travelers, shop-keepers,

stock-brokers, money-changers, dragomen, rich men
(if there be such), as well as intermeddlers in all arts,
students, artists, professional men, and, above all,
politicians. They have the versatility of the Greek
character, and I shall have occasion to speak of yet
another simpler type who possess still stronger claims
to pure Greek blood.

It is a weighty argument in favor of the theory of
Hellenistic survival, or the continuous nationality of
the Greeks, that they speak Greek, as they have
always done. Latin continued to be spoken in Italy
till the middle of the 13th century A. D., and this
was in a few exceptional Italian provinces; and yet
Greek has been the language of Greece from the
earliest days until now, and even Romaic, the vernacular language, comes, in some respects, nearer to
classic Greek than Italian does to Latin, although
greatly barbarized. In construction, and very widely
in pronunciation, modern Greek departs from classic
Greek, the moods, case-endings and inflections being
swept away, so that the resemblance between the two
is, in many instances, wholly artificial, but it is nevertheless, at base, Greek, with the same alphabet and
forms. It is a debased idiom from a similar root,
so that it may be built up again into the same language. It is, in fact, as it has been called, Neo-
Hellenic. It grew out of loose conversational usages
of the earlier language, but not until the fifteenth or
sixteenth century did the popular spoken tongue become fully developed, while the literary language
remained unchanged to the time of the taking of
Constantinople; and even the Phanariot and literary
language continued the same. In Greek schools now
the grammar of classic Greek is used, and children are
taught to read Xenophon and other classic authors.

The better the people the better the Greek they speak ; while the written tongue, the language of books and periodicals, even of newspapers is, approximately, the same with that of Homer. Corruptions, of course, have come in, but even as far back as Alexander's day, the Attic dialect had undergone great changes.

With the unification and improvement of the language thus constantly going on, a Greek scholar would have no difficulty in learning to read modern Greek books and newspapers. Two or three months' study at Athens with this object in view, would make him master of the written tongue. Foreign phrases have been introduced to describe foreign and new things, and many dialects have poured in, as in the Greek-speaking population of Constantinople the Turkish, and in the Ionian isles the Cypriote and Italian, and in Athens the Albanian, French, German, Italian, English and a medley of other dialects, but the living language which you hear in street, market-place, shop, house and senate-chamber, on the dock and road, is sonorous Greek. You may, indeed, hear " mitéra " for " μητέρα," and " yinæka " for " γυναῖκα," but this is not such a very wide difference. The streets of Athens have the names of Hermes, Æolus Athene, Lysocrates, Piraeus. The land is classified in nomarchies bearing the old familiar titles of Attica, Bœotia, Phthiotis, Phocis, Akarnania, and so on. It is Greece. You are at home with its spirit, and are not shocked in your classic associations, as you would be, probably, in Syria, in your religious feelings. You take your Plato and walk in the locality of the Akademe, meeting, it may be, some Greek acquaintance with a name quite familiar in the " Dialogues," and with a salutation of the still beautiful χαῖρε. You ride or drive a few miles to the north, over the plain of

Attica, until you come to the deme of Pœania (still so called), under the shadow of Mt. Pentelikon, and there you are at the birthplace of Demosthenes, where his paternal acres lay, for which, when a young man, he contested in the courts, and brought himself before the public eye. In half an hour's stroll outside of Athens, you seat yourself to take breakfast on the stoop of a little vine-trellised coffee-house (καφενῖον) in a grove of olive trees, where Sophocles' villa, in its olive grove, stood. You say to your guide δός, φερε, δειξε—give, bring, show. The railway, indeed, that you get aboard, is the σιδηρόδομος, the steel-way, and, if an American, you may hear America called Βάσιγκτων ἡ γῆ —the land of Washington. Greek was never a dead, but has been a debased, language, a prince in beggar's clothes. A century, or nearly a century ago, since the Greeks have waked up to something like new intellectual life, the question of a common language began to be mooted, and this served to bring the scattered elements of the Greek race together ; and I draw from a little book by a native Greek Professor, the fact, that three views are held on this question. Opinions, in a word, have formed themselves into three parties : 1. those who contend that the common language of modern Greeks has been settled by the Greek people as they commonly employ it, the popular tongue spoken by Greek-speaking people, not only in Greece but in Constantinople and the Turkish empire, and all over the Levant. 2. They who think that the vulgar tongue is too poor (it certainly did have a marked decline in the Byzantine and Middle Age periods, and through the period of Turkish domination) and that classic Greek should be restored as the common language. 3. They who also think the vulgar tongue to be inadequate for the scientific development of the nation, on account of its want of regularity in grammatic properties ; but as the complete restoration of classic Greek is impracticable in all relations and wants of modern life, a middle theory should be adopted, viz: that a common language be formed which does not depart substantially from the vernacular, or so far as to be unintelligible to the people, but that it shonld be corrected on the model of ancient Greek, and enriched by its wealth and power as a language. This is the opinion of the most thoughtful, and is the prevalent one at Athens, tending to banish vulgarisms, barbarisms and local dialects, such as the Wallachian, Roumanian, Cypriote and Constantinopolitan, to give a philosophic base to grammar and style, and to strengthen and elevate the language ; and, as has been said, the best people now speak the best Greek, above all write it, so that the written language more and more approaches the ancient ; and there is a strong tendency, partly pedantic and partly genuine, to restore classic Greek in all its purity. But everything one wants to say on everyday matters of business, travel, literature, politics, art, poetry, from Homer to telegraphs and telephones, can be said in modern Greek ; and, at all events, it is Greek that is spoken in Greece, however diversely it sounds from the classic tongue. While Latin has ceased to be a spoken language, Greek is a living one, and it is an almost miraculous fact that this should be so, considering the great changes and upheavals that have occurred. Professor Jebb, from whom I before quoted, says : "It has been the unique destiny of the Greek language to have had from prehistoric times down to our own, an unbroken life. Not one link is wanting in this chain which binds the new Greece to the old."

In addition to language, the Greek people are inspired

by the old names, traditions and monuments. They
live among them. They are proud of them. If they
do not know as well as a learned archæologist does,
what a classic ruin is, they are to a degree reverent of
it. They point it out and talk about it as something
that belongs to their land, even the most ignorant
among them. A Greek workman, when I happened
to remark of a rich altar of Pan standing near the
theatre of Dionysos, that it should be protected, said,
" Yes, sir, that is true ; Mr. Pan was a much respected
gentleman, and ought to be better treated." He was
right, for the ground in front of the theatre was in a
neglected state, and I have been pleased since to see
that it has been decided to fence it in and further protect this Dionysiac precinct. The Greek, peasant and
learned, is aware of the importance of such monuments, and is in dead earnest when he execrates the
Turk for maltreating and destroying ancient works of
art. He knows his unique heritage, and the fact of
the genuine interest taken by the Greek government
in archæologic research for the last forty years (the
National Archæologic Society was founded in 1858),
and the brilliant results of this society's labors, prove
it. The modern Greek has his eyes open, and, like
the Japanese, is keenly sympathetic to old traditions
and new ideas. He is sensitive and acute, and if he
would discuss politics less at the café, and work more
on the field, he would be a worthy sort of man as he
is a shrewd one.

I am but one witness, and inclined, like other wit-
nesses, to build large theories from a small number of
observations, but I confess to a prejudice in favor of
Greeks, and of a nation bearing their name and speaking their tongue. I desire (letting their boastfulness,
dirt, fleas, sour wine and such small things go) to be

DIONYSIAC THEATRE FRIEZE

a little blind to their faults, and to see their good qualities, or those traits which belong to a higher humanity, rather than those which lower and separate it. The Greeks have ardent aspirations that no disappointments have been able to quench, and "their very vanity is towards intellectual progress." The spark of Greek intelligence yet glows. They expect to be a nation, and are preparing for it. Education has had a development that could not be the case in a dull people. Knowledge is the Greek's passion. Education was broached, among others, by the patriot Admantius Korais, who, at the beginning of the century, as did also the poet Rangabé, began to write and teach of the need of education to prepare the people, sunk as they were in semi-barbarism under four hundred years of Turkish misrule, for liberty. He thought that the remodeling of the nation was no hasty work but required the thoroughly invigorating power of education, and that national enlightenment must precede national regeneration.* He was a reformer of the Greek language, and was born of Greek parents in Smyrna 1748, dying in 1833. He insisted on the union of literature with science in education, and especially the study of Homer, as an influence to raise the popular mind, and from him and those like him came that extraordinary impulse from which sprang the Hetairas (Literary Societies) and the great multitude of schools all over Greece.

In addition to the University and Polytechnic School at Athens, there is, throughout all the provinces, what may be called a graded system, consisting of the elementary or demotic schools, the Hellenic or grammar schools, and the gymnasia, which resemble the French lycées. The instruction in the higher

* M. Constantinides.

schools and the University, is, to be sure, predominantly technical, but every child in Greece can have the benefit of free public instruction. They aim to be an educated people, to acquire that knowledge which gives leadership in affairs, and they have already reaped the advantages of this, and won through the East and in the Turkish empire the place of instructors, officials and agents in every business and profession that demands intelligence. Where knowledge is needed the Greek is found. The idea of a universal education has been overdone, but it is sinning in the right direction. The old Athenian Prytanæum would have sanctioned it, if the Dorian Ephorate would not. In so small a land the professions are naturally overstocked, and there are more candidates than work to supply them with. This creates a class of small savans and literary men, but the students are trained to be doctors, lawyers, civil engineers, classical scholars and archæologists, the last having their material at hand ; and, as I shall have occasion to remark, the Greek museums of antique art are the best arranged in the world, appealing to eye and mind without need of commentator. The modern Greeks can appreciate art if they do not produce artists, though this remains to be seen when they are freed from the anxieties of national embarrassment. The Greek is keen in apprehension but lacks steadiness of application. He has, as is well known, marvelous talent for trade, which makes him the Yankee of the Mediterranean. He is sharper at a bargain than the most crafty Oriental, and, for this reason, the modern Greek has been accredited, as was of old the countryman of him who was "subtle of wit and of guile insatiate," with a streak of dishonesty, and this may have some foundation in fact; but as far as my limited experience goes I have had no reason to doubt the integrity of the Greek, although he is, like Demetrius the silversmith, not apt to yield up his own interests in a given case. I once sent a message from the island of Syros when in quarantine there for fourteen days, to Athens, for a mosquito-net, by a Greek dragoman, who, seeing the note was addressed to a hotel that was rival of the one to which he was attached, slipped round the corner and tore it up. Of course the message was not delivered.

But the Greek is not everlastingly on the lookout for his own advantage; he is, on the contrary, and as a general rule, brusquely outspoken, and is, also, like Odysseus, a natural story-teller and bard. He is never at a loss for words and eloquent words. On the deck of a small felucca running before a gale in the Gulf of Corinth, I heard a young Greek sailor (my guide acting interpreter) sing with kindling eye his legends of war and love, accompanied by short interludes on a kind of guitar, his voice now harsh and loud, then soft and low as a woman's; and an undercurrent of pathos, of pathetic cadence, ran through his lyrics, coming down as they do from the sombre days of the Turk, who, when driven out of Greece, left desolation and despair behind him; and this vein of melancholy runs through the character as well as songs of the modern Greek, so that he is more ambitious than hopeful. Some of these songs have a ring of honest feeling, as in this prose translation of a rude little lyric composed by the soldier-poet, Armatole Sterghio;

"Though the Dervens' strongholds have fallen, and the Moslem has seized upon them, Sterghio lives and cares for no pashas.

"While it snows on the hills, and the plains bloom with flowers, and the heights have ice-cool streams, we will not bend the knee to the Turk.

"Let us go and camp where the wolves have their abode, in the caves of the mountains, on the heights and rugged cliffs. Slaves live in the towns and crouch to the Turks, while we have for our dwellings solitudes and desert ravines.

"Better live with the wolves than with the Turks."

This spirit of melancholy does not, however, spoil the deeper joyousness of the Greek's temper, for he is gay on occasions, and in merry-making on festival days that occur so often, be they religious or secular, and of which, like the old Hellene, he is extravagantly fond; then he is free as a bird, and, like the ancient Greek, is child of the sunshine and air, changing as suddenly as the moods of the Greek sky, from clear to storm, from a hospitable friend to a suspicious foe, and his knife is prompt to his hand. It is stated that crimes in Greece spring from quick temper aggravated by the fierce heat of the climate, far more than from any deliberate cause.* The shining rocks and hills of Greece, now as formerly, do not breed a bad and vicious race. When I was at Olympia, I found the solitary inn there in a state of disorder, arising from the circumstance that two or three days before, the inn-keeper, in a sudden fit of passion, had mortally stabbed a guide and fled to the mountains, and his family were in constant apprehension of his capture and their own imprisonment. But the Greek in a good cause as well as bad is no coward, and a fiery courage seems to run in his veins. The achievements of the Greeks in their modern wars equal anything in their ancient story; since, whatever other Euro-

* Greece under King George, p. 167.

pean nations did in aid of the Greeks, they wrought out their own independence, and showed themselves worthy to be free.

The Greek is a good seaman, having special aptitude for all kinds of marine service, and his proper place would seem to be on the deck of his antique-shaped bark, such as you see scudding before the wind off every headland of the coast, and he meets the sea in his ocean-bound land everywhere, no part of it being more than forty miles from the sea ; and it is estimated that Greece "has a sea-line in proportion to its area seven times as great as that of France, and twelve times as great as that of England."* The sea has been the main resource of Greece, especially when we reckon in the Ionian and Ægean islands and Crete as belonging to Greece.   The ancient Ionians if not the Lacedæmonians, were lovers of the sea.   Tritons, amphitritons and dolphins gambol gracefully through Greek sculpture, even as they do on the lovely friezes of the choragic monument of Lysikrates at Athens, and the temple of Poseïdon in Bithynia carved by Skopas.   The sound of the sea reverberates through all ages of Greek literature, and its voice, like that of the mountains, is the voice of freedom.

* Sergeant's New Greece.

CHAPTER II.

THE LAND OF GREECE.

The Greek is a man admirably fitted to be a sailor, and he lives in sight of the sea that runs around and into all his land. The sea is his pathway to freedom, power, and enlarged thought and life. The intrepid deeds of Kanares, with his terrible fireships, will not soon be forgotten. They struck dismay into the heart of the foe. The Greek, at present, is building up again a respectable commerce, and doing the carrying-trade of the Eastern Mediterranean. The Greek marine consists of some one hundred and twenty steamships, and seven hundred and fifty sailing vessels, and yet Greece should be, on her own account, a far more important commercial nation than she is, when we consider how Athens, at the height of her power, was the center of the marine activity of the Mediterranean, and how splendid was the commerce of Rhodes immediately after the period of Alexander; but now the entire wealth of the country in cereals, currants, olives, fruits, wines, marbles, minerals, pottery and many other products agricultural and industrial, is most inadequately maintained, and but twenty per cent. of its good though light soil is brought under cultivation, the husbandry itself being of an obsolete kind, with the wooden ploughshare shaped like that of Triptolemos.

The government is a poor nurse of commerce and industries, seeming to have but feeble power to foster national activities and internal improvements, and has been called "a system of bureaucracy and narrow centralization." It may be honestly inclined, as it has been under the leadership of Tricoupis, who was a life-long student of English administrative methods, to do better things, and has not been without its efforts in this direction. Dyannis, the successor of Tricoupis, has much of his administrative ability and more popularity, but not the moral power, the firm will, that steered the Greek ship of state through so many dangers and difficulties. The country is bankrupt, with a forced depreciated currency, and unpaid loans saddled on it by foreign governments from the beginning of its new existence. The public debt (the interest of which is paid by a process of legerdemain) now amounts, it is said, to 820,000,000 francs. There is six times the amount of silver in circulation to that of gold. The paper money looks like rags, if it be not so in fact, and you tear a bill in two in order to halve it. In spite of this financial lowness, the state maintains a standing army of more than 20,000 men. Yet it were well for us to recognize the fact, that notwithstanding the pressure on his government by monarchical powers, the Greek is, at core, a genuine republican. His political creed is an antique inheritance, which his land, name, and the air he breathes, nourish. The democratic principle, native to the Greek, is another argument for his persistent nationality. He is an enthusiastic lover of popular government, and he has abolished all orders of nobility. The voting in Greece is by eptarchies, and every voter may give as many votes as there are candidates, exercising his independent choice, of which he is extremely jealous, cherishing the right of ballot, and, it is said, "more Greeks to the thousand have votes than is the case of

2

the citizens of any other country." The Athenian is
as disputatious, restless, liberty-loving and genuine a
democrat, as he was in the days of Kimon and Kleon,
though there is no consistency or cohesion in his
political system, that has been characterized as ''a
monarchical democracy." There is a royal court at
Athens, and there has to be one, for any government
to exist at all. There is, therefore, an aristocratic
circle as well as a monied circle, and a literary or educational circle, though these are well-mixed, for a
stiff spirit of personal independence exists among the
people. Your donkey-driver feels himself as good as
his employer; and yet, it is remarkable with how
little bluster the popular principle asserts itself in
everyday life. The Greek, while he idolizes rich
travelers, as he supposes all to be who visit Greece,
especially Americans, is not toadyish, but preserves
an erect and almost fierce bearing. He is polite
when treated politely, and more naturally so, I think,
than the Italian peasant. He has his virtues as well
as faults, and the pity of it is (not an original
remark) that the modern Greek has been over-blamed
and over-praised. This is a misfortune. He has
suffered both from his friends and his enemies, not
being strong enough to stand alone. But the Greek
is not an intractable radical or a reasonless anarchist,
and he has few popular vices. Inclined though he
be to demagogy, he is not factious, nor is he intemper-
ate, being a water-lover and coffee-drinker, nor profli-
gate, nor irreverent, and he is even religious, up to a
certain point.

The Greek respects his church, as the orthodox
church, the official church, the Greek church, without having very much to do with it in a higher and
more spiritual sense. He is baptized, confirmed,

married, and buried, by it. It is a church strong tra-
ditionally as conserving the orthodox faith, though
its priests are, in a great measure, ignorant and
poorly paid, but, as a general rule, they are moral in
life, and the bishops are sometimes passably learned,
while there are no Chrysostoms. Its six hundred mon-
asteries are picturesquely perched on almost inaccessi-
ble cliffs, to which one has to be drawn up by a bucket,
as the apostle, reversing the process, was let down by
a basket, from the wall of Damascus. But these
establishments have been reduced in number to about
one hundred and fifty ; and the austere but indolent
life led within their walls has been charmingly portrayed in paintings of the Hungarian artist Bida. I
passed a night in a Greek monastery where, though
in such ascetic surroundings, I was treated in quite a
princely fashion. I greatly enjoyed the worship of
the Greek church, that is, its music and ritual, which
retain the fresh devotional flavor of centuries, and,
in fact, the Greek ritual is older than the Roman Catholic. In the new gorgeous Russian church at Athens,
to whose service you are summoned by the sound of a
deep-toned bell, the voices of the priests, who are
picked men for their musical gifts, are of great depth
and richness of tone, and these are mingled with more
youthful voices clear and soaring, the chorals being
especially beautiful.

The Greek church, in point of efficiency and intelligence, is more sleepy than, and not equal to, the Roman
Catholic, but in some respects, having had more to do
with Nicæa than Trent, is purer, discarding purga-
tory, not claiming infallibility, allowing marriage of
the lower priestly orders (a Greek unmarried monk
was the most influential person in carrying this point
at the Council of Nice), not deifying the Virgin,

worshiping only poor paintings. It does not admit good painting or sculpture into the churches, though this may be a doubtful claim to merit, and recalling Goethe's remark, that miraculous pictures are always poor ones. There are some things in belief and practice which are common to Greek and Protestant churches, so that here is a possible ground of union, as, indeed, the Anglican church claims. On the other hand there is a hostile feeling towards the Roman Catholic church, and the Pope's inclination to tolerate or recognize the Greek church, is not reciprocated by the Greeks themselves, any more than it was at the time of the Council of Florence in the middle of the 15th century, when a serious attempt at union between the Eastern and Western churches was made. But the Greek church is a venerable church, coming down as it does from the Apostle of the Gentiles, and though mingled with gross superstitions and puerile forms, remains pure in some of its doctrines; and from its not being a rich and powerful church, or from its being rather homely in its circumstances and priest-hood, its spirit is humble, and for this reason it lives in the life and affections of the people. One fre-quently sees the grave village "Papa" leading about his rustic flock in the museums at Athens, carefully explaining to them, as they seem to listen with rever-ence to his words, the various objects. The worship within the churches, to the stranger who cannot fol-low it, is exclusively addressed to the *ikons* of saints, and to the Virgin, and seems to have no sort of refer-ence to God or the people; yet this is not true, for the chants are exceedingly spiritual and uplifting, and the words of the Greek gospels have new beauty and power when thus repeated in the land where their noble language was born.

Greece is a rich field for the study of old Byzantine, as well as older classic, art ; and the most ancient Byzantine church in Athens, the "small Metropolis," is a jewel of a Lilliputian cathedral, with *narthex* or vestibule, *conche* or apse separated from the body by the *templon* with its three doors, the holy table, the queer little silver-gilt pictures of the Virgin and Saints, rich colors and mosaics, begemmed screens and golden hanging lamps, just as in the biggest church in the land. Many Byzantine churches in Greece occupy the sites of the old classic temples, so that these have been sacred places from time immemorial. The priests, with black robes and tall felt hats, whose tops spread out like inverted flower-pots, and their flowing beards, are a marked feature in town and country, often acting as pedagogues leading about small boys, and though not so conspicuous as the priests of Italy, yet more reverend and picturesque ; and in the grim funeral processions at Athens, where the dead body is borne uncovered in the coffin through the streets, just as in the days of Perikles, the priests going before and after chanting in deep voices the solemn service of the dead, breaking into the circle of busy life as with the voice of the tomb, these make an impressive though ghastly spectacle.

Much has been said of the physique of modern Greeks, and it has been asked if they compare with their ancestors in beauty? This was, undoubtedly, the realistic source of Greek art, for there can be no question that the ancient Greeks were a beautiful race, and one classic writer says that he saw forms in the palæstra, equal to any statue, in symmetry. It is not to be thought that the ancient Greeks, though a superior race, as if lighted down from some fairer planet, were all as beautiful as Greek statues. They

showed every type of face and form, from Achilles
to Thersites ; they had stout bodies and lean bodies ;
they were tall and short ; they had round faces and
oval faces ; and in Greek sculpture, you see these
differences, as in nature ; nor were they all fair, but
commonly of a brownish white, the women having
lighter complexions, as may be seen in the paintings
on Greek vases.   One also recalls the picture of Pene-
lope in the Odyssey : " Her fair face first she, Athene,
steeped with beauty imperishable, such as that wherewith the crowned Cytherea is anointed, when she goes
to the lovely dances, and she made her taller and
greater to behold, and made her whiter than new-
sawn ivory."*   The present race may have greatly
degenerated, but modern Greeks are a good-looking
people, dark and active, with well-made forms, though
they are much smaller than we imagine the old Greeks
to have been, developed as they were by athletic exercises and war ; and yet there are exceptions here.
My guide was a Herakles in stature and strength, and
with a cuff of his open hand, like the buffet the black
knight bestowed on the Clerk of Copmanhurst, he
sent a Corinthian horse-dealer reeling across the
room ; and the peasants and country people of the
Peloponnesos are robust, striding on like giants over
the hills, fierce-looking, neither greeting nor expect-
ing greeting.   But the Greek, if not large-sized, is
wiry, with straight regular features, black hair and
flashing black eyes ; he seems made for activity more
than strength—a Teucer rather than an Ajax ; but in
temperance, chastity, and homely refinement, he is
superior to the Italian or the French.

Among the women, you would not see a Helen
"having eyelids where the graces sat," and for whose

* Butcher and Lang's translation.

transcendent beauty, the sober burghers of Troy thought it worth the while to fight a woful decade. You would not be apt to see a beautiful woman, in the ordinary phrase, nor, indeed, would you see many women at all, except on festas, as the spirit of Oriental seclusion still obtains in Greece ; but there are handsome women among the peasants. In the mountains their dress is a long white woolen gown with red and bright trimmings, being worn easily and freely like the Greek himation, so that you can imagine you behold the Homeric woman sitting at the well, or walking across the market-place. Blondes with golden hair and blue eyes (an ancient Aryan type) are often seen, and vigorous forms that are models of physical health. But the faces of Greek women, though regular in features, are not notably intellectual ; and yet there are exceptions, as was the daughter of Botsares, whom I met in Greece, who was noted for her great charm of manner and fine dark eyes, that looked as if they could kindle with indignation at meanness or injustice. But a Greek woman rarely possesses, like the sister of Tricoupis, a talent for affairs, or cherishes aspirations to be a power in the State ; nor is she apt, like Madame Schliemann, who is wealthy and manages her property with shrewdness, to be a leader in society, or at the head of philanthropic and patriotic movements. Madame Schliemann was an Athenian girl, whose name was Kastromenos, and was chosen to be helpmate of the great Dr. Schliemann, because she believed in his theory of the realness of Homer's poems, and could repeat for his amusement long portions of the Iliad. She would, indeed, represent a woman of the best class, in looks, dignity and intelligence. Her young daughter is named Andromache, and her son Aga-

memnon; and her white marble house on University
Avenue, studded with statues of gods and goddesses,
and named, with pardonable vanity, "The Palace of
Ilion," is, perhaps, the finest in the city. Doubtless in case of another war with Turkey, we would
see the Spartan spirit in the women, as was shown
in the war of Independence, though the weight of
ages of suppression is not easily thrown off; but it
is not probable that there ever will be an eleventh
muse, to follow Sappho, termed the tenth muse.

Love of country inspires Greeks high and low,
and, I believe, it is a genuine feeling, though it
shows itself in sentiment more than in action; but
the great names of Botsares, Kanares, Miaoulis, Kol-
katrous, Ipsilantes and others, live and burn in the
people's hearts, more passionately than the names of
Washington and our revolutionary heroes, live in
American hearts.

The modern Greek, as was said, has been over-
praised and over-blamed, and this has worked to produce in him the opposite sentiments of vanity and
despair, so that, at this time, under the pressure of
national disgrace arising from enormous unpaid loans
and a depreciated currency, he has lost a tithe of his
natural vivaciousness and audaciousness; and what,
indeed, has modern Greece realized from promises
and pledges such as those of the Treaty of Berlin,
and earlier treaties, that gave to her territory and
power, and then dashed her down to poverty ? England has been Greece's best friend, and is so still, but
she has been a selfish, calculating, ungenerous and
disappointing friend, failing signally in great crises.
Yet we may hope that Greece, from native impulse,
will, in spite of these heart-breaking disappointments,
show herself self-reliant and energetic (she was

ready enough to fight in the Crimean war though it
would have been in a false position) and that she will
eventually wrest from her old foe the Doric isle of
Crete, Macedonia, Albania, Thrace, and all her ancient territory, which was larger than her present one,
and may become a state and a civilization worthy of
her name.   Greece is the pivot of European politics.
Her art, or what she owns within her borders and which
points to perfection, is a power ; her land, still there
in mid-Mediterranean with its mountains and valleys
almost the loveliest land under heaven, is a power ;
and although our classical enthusiasm is put to a
strain by modern Greeks, I, for one, am Philhellenist
enough to believe that Greece has a bright future,
that her light cannot be put out in the midst of the
nations.   This little book is a humble *envoi* of such a
hope.   In the vast changes which must soon occur
in the East, her opportunity (the old Greeks had
a divinity named "Opportunity" to which they
sacrificed) may come. : If the Ottoman Empire in
Europe, sustained alone by outside pressure, were
hard beset by one or all of the great Christian
powers, and if the Turk were hurled out of Europe
back to his native Tartar deserts, the Greeks, who
are a nation in European Turkey outnumbering the
Turks three to one (1,996,000 to 700,000), as the
natural inheritors of the Turks who robbed them,
may gain possession of Constantinople, which belongs to Greece as a Hellenic foundation.   Greek
chants may then once more rise under the dome of the
Hagia Sophia that was built by a Greek Emperor, out
of materials plundered from temples of Athene at
Athens, and Artemis at Ephesus ; though this is a vis-
ionary picture, when, in reality, a colossal power like
Russia, coldly antagonistic to Greece at heart, though

of the same Orthodox Church, lies like a giant ogre
in wait to seize upon Constantinople. As northern
races inevitably gravitate south, a little country like
Greece could not interpose to prevent it. If Greece
had the spirit and hope of ancient Greece, she might
raise a barrier against Russia, but for how long? Yet
Greece, Greece in idea, must prevail. The world now,
as in St. Paul's time, is "Greek and barbarian," and
Greece has her last word in the contest of light and
darkness, barbarism and culture, ever going on.

There is a well-known prophecy that when a Constantine shall wed a Sophia, the Greeks shall possess
Constantinople; and this concurrence of names has
already occurred in the case of the present crown-
prince and his wife. However that may be, and this
mere conjunction of names is of no consequence, yet
when 'Constantine,' or the embodiment of Christian
power, shall be united to 'Sophia,' or wisdom, enlightenment, freedom of thought and reason, Greece
shall have her day of triumph. The moral of Greece
does not die, and from its spirit rises a new world.
The new art, the new thought, the new life, the new
love, are Greek ideas, paganized and sensualized
though they may be. They always have been Greek
ideas. In the breaking-up of the Eastern world by
Alexander and the carrying of Hellenic culture into
the Orient even to furthest India, and the spread of
the Greek language through that half of the world (St.
Jerome said in his day, with the exception of the province of Galatia, settled by Gauls, Greek was the speech
of all Asia Minor) aided by the learning of Alexandria,
Pergamon and other centers of Greek culture, it was
in this way that Greek became the language of the
civilized world both east and west, and the world was
thus prepared to receive the Greek gospels and made

ready for the planting of Christianity. The Greek woman and the Greek language were the first missionaries of the faith. Greek continued to be the cultivated and sacred language of Christianity, and "for many ages Christianity itself was propagated under Hellenic forms."

In the first trip to Greece which I made when a young man, not long after leaving college, everything in the way of travel had to be done on foot or on horseback. It might literally be said that outside of Athens, there were only bridle-paths and not a road to speak of. Some one has said that "the son of Nestor drove his two-horse chariot from sandy Pylos to Sparta, but that there was no carriage-road in modern Greece till the time of Otho;" and that was the time when I first visited Greece. Since that time there have been made some 2,500 miles of good roads, and no less than seven railway lines, and more are projected, among the principal of which are the railway from Athens to the Piraeus; the Piraeus and Peloponnesian railway embracing Nauplia, Argos, Patras, Pyrgon and Olympia; the Piraeus and Larissa road; the Athens and Laurion; the Messolonghi and Agrinion; the Athens and Thebes railway; and it should be considered that Greece is a hard country to make roads and railroads over, so that this is the more creditable. This rugged and ragged little peninsula, like a half-decayed oak-leaf showing its ribs, and pushing down towards Africa with the great stepping-stone of Crete, Zeus-cradling Crete, that belongs to Greece geographically and racially, consists of three natural divisions, the mainland, the Peloponnesos and the islands, and in all scarcely larger than West Virginia, though by sea there is open to it a free road to the fairest regions of three continents, as it lies in the bosom of them, and of modern as well as ancient civilizations, drawing its life from all. It has a population of but two and a half millions, and, owing to its desolations, it is, in a great measure, a wild uncultivated land, only recently opened to improvements.

These improvements have begun, and some of them are on a considerable scale of magnitude. The most noteworthy, is the canal cut boldly through the isthmus of Corinth, making a watercourse one hundred feet in width and twenty-six in depth, fitted for ocean steamers—a thin line of blue water straight as a ruler across the neck of the isthmus, uniting two seas. What Julius Caesar and Nero thought to do and did not do, an enterprising Greek company has done. For another branch of public improvements, there are the native Greek steamboat lines plying between the Piraeus and the Argolic Gulf, Syros, the Ionian Isles, the Corinthian Gulf, Akarnania, Ambrakia and Euboea. There are tramways and electric cars in Athens. Some of the antique stone bridges are still in use in the land, as the one over the Eurotas; but at most seasons you cross dry beds of rivers which in the winter are torrents. I crossed the dry bed of the Inachos in the Peloponnesos, in which, the same year, an English traveler was drowned. Greece is a well-watered country, intermittently so, requiring the most constant and systematic care in the way of irrigation, which care it returns in smiling plantations and orchards. Greece may be made a very garden of the Hesperides, but the nymphs of industry and skill must nurture the golden harvests.

On both visits I came into Greece by the way of

Corinth, landing at Patras; the first time starting from Trieste, and the second time from Brindisi. I crossed the Adriatic from the Italian shore in a stout but dirty Austrian steamer named 'The Helios.' A notice which was posted on the cabin-door ran thus : "It is prohibited to middle (*sic*) with the captain's command. Passengers having a right to be treated like persons of education will no doubt conform themselves to the rules of good society in respect of their fellow-travelers, and paying a due regard to the fair sex."

The mountains of upper Albania, some of them snow-capped in the month of May, and forming the last point of the Turkish dominion in Europe, came in sight, which were the home of the unconquered Albanians, or Arnauts, mixed Mohammedans and Christians, whose language bears traces both of the Greek and Latin, and who in their war-like lyrics sing, "We know how to live with honor, and to die without fear.

Coasting along the base of these snowy mountains, about opposite Cape Kepholi, one enters a channel between small islands, and coming out of the turmoil of the restless "Adria," the same as in St. Paul's time, passes into a quiet harbor with hills around it, and a citadel on a steep rock overhanging it, back of which an old town of irregular white stone houses clusters. You here touch the shore of Hellas. The sky and the sapphire water reveal it. A change has taken place from the familar Europe of the west, and you are among the lovely islands of the bright Ionian sea. The atmosphere has a peculiar clearness, and the waves are as blue as in a land made by the poets. There is no delusion in this. The earth is genuinely Hellenic earth as it once was.

After many changes of modern masters, Corfu, in 1864, became again a part of the Greek kingdom.

This is Scheria, the blest island of the Phæacians, that was ruled by the wise Alkinoös, and to this strand Odysseus was borne by the waves, and had his · meeting with the .maid Nausicaa, "high of heart." A short distance south of Corfu, at a point reached by a road skirting the lake of Kalliopoulo, is the ancient Hillian harbor, into which runs the brook Kressida, the spot where the hero, helped by white-armed Leukothea, was cast ashore. One sees also the small triangular isle, or rock, named Pontikonisi, on which is a bit of a chapel, which is the Phæacian galley that bore Odysseus, and turned to stone. Of course it is. A Mormon once said to me, pointing to a mountain at Salt Lake city, "that is the mountain on which the angel Gabriel stood when he directed the prophet Brigham—do you doubt it, there is the mountain?"

The people who came off from the city in swarms of boats, still, as in Homer's phrase, "excel at tossing the salt-water with the oar-blade." They came to trade as the people once did with the Phœnicians who scoured these seas in their biremes, and brought the arts of the East to Greece, as well as tin and metals from Britain. This harbor with the boats and small craft darting about in the glassy sapphire water, is a vivid picture, and you pardon the Corfiote sharks who are after the steamer and its passengers with the hunger of greed. The mountains rise behind the city to a considerable height. The old town of 25,000 inhabitants has marks of Venetian, French, and above all, English rule. There is nothing classic of importance left in it, but nature. A drive in the interior reveals the superb richness of vegetation,

NATIONAL MUSEUM, ATHENS

not indeed tropical, but, better still, Mediterranean, charmingly green valleys with venerable olive-groves, orange, lemon, fig and cherry trees, magnolias and aloes, in an ever-abounding luxuriance. Superb roses and other brilliant flowers adorned the suburban house-fronts here and there. Homer must have visited this richly-dowered spot when he sings : ''And there grow tall blossoming trees, pear trees and pome-granates, apple trees with bright fruit, sweet figs, and olives in their bloom. The fruit of these never perish, neither fail winter or summer, continuing the year round. Evermore the west wind blowing brings some fruits to birth and ripens others. Pear upon pear waxes and drops, apple on apple, fig on fig. Here is a vineyard whereof one part is withered by the scorch-ing heat, a sun-dried level spot, while on another part grapes are gathered in, and still another where men are treading the wine-press. In the foremost row are unripe grapes, and elsewhere are grapes growing black to the vintage.''

Ancient Kerkyra sided with Athens in the Pelopon-nesian war fatal to that city, and this reacted on its own decline of power and influence. The picturesque double-peaked rock of the fortress, is seen for some distance on the way south to the larger island of Kephallenia ; and as you sail on you pass the white Leucadian rock, and also Actium (Aktion) on the main shore. We are in Homer's own land, who drew from its realness and whose art was nature, so that it is not to be wondered at that Homer was the book of religion, wisdom, law and life, to the Greek, and that there is no better book now to travel with in Greece, than the Odyssey, a golden key to interpret its nature, poetry, art and life.

I reckoned that, owing to the delay caused by a

disturbance of the Adriatic from an earthquake higher up near the Austrian shore, we should pass Ithaca in the very early morning, so I hurried on deck before any of the other passengers ; but just as "clear-seen Ithaca" came in sight over the billowy sea, there stumbled up also on deck an old German professor of metaphysics, a tall, lean, hard-favored man, but smitten with the same desire to see Ithaca, the furthest Greek land of all from the leaguer of Troy. The rocky isle and the wind-tossed sea formed a Homeric picture. The water, at the cold dawn of a rather stormy day, was "the gray sea." In order to be a trifle friendly so early on a windy morning, I said to the professor, "Doubtless the earth-shaker is angry at the approach of us strangers to his sacred land."

"*Ach, mein theurer Herr,*" he answered, "Poseidon is not angry at all, but he is agitated with joy at our coming, Hellenes as we are, and Amphitrite is weaving wreaths of sea-anemones with which to crown our heads ;" and his "inextinguishable laughter" reverberated like the splitting of an oak-tree by a thunderbolt. We exchanged sentiments and had a good time as the vessel plunged and rose.

"*Sehen sie,*" said he, "young men nowadays have no poetry. They do not love Homer. They do not revel in his joyful world of poetry and light, as we did, *gnädiger Herr,* and do now, *mein Gott !* There is my son," pointing to a tall youth who had at that moment emerged from below, "he is a student of physics at my own university, but he cares only for things as they are, not for things that are past or to come, he is all fact, *paff,* he is a good fellow, but he has no poetry. He thinks but of science, not art."

I agreed with him that education was often one-sided, not all-around and comprehending the moral and æsthetic as well as analytic powers, was lacking in the elements of a broad culture, in fine not Greek, not aiming at the development of the whole being, the καλόν, the perfect, the prize so difficult to obtain that the Greeks said χαλεπόν τό καλόν—the beautiful is hard to win and hard to keep, and calls for the union of art with philosophy, in education.

There was one small red sail off the northernmost point of Ithaca battling with the wind, which might readily be taken for the sail of the carved-prowed and home-coming bark of Odysseus, and complete was the illusion, as one gave himself up to the power of the muse, who, Plato says, accompanies every poet and every poetic mood.

The rugged island itself has two main parts about equal in size, joined by a low narrow strip of land, on the further side of which, to the east, lies the Gulf of Molo, like a Norwegian fjord, and at the end of this is the small town of Vathy (Βαθύς, deep), called in official language "Ithaca," the principal place on the island. Near this along the narrow bay of Dexia, is laid by some, the old harbor of Phorkys, where the Phæacians landed sleeping Odysseus. Listen to Homer: " There is in the land of Ithaca a port called Phorkys, the old one of the sea, and thereby are two headlands of sheer cliff, which slope to the sea on the haven's side, and break the mighty wave that ill winds roll without, but within the decked ships ride unmoved when once they have come to the landing." Oddly enough near the Gulf of Molo there is a stalactite cavern, which corresponds with the cave of nymphs near which Odysseus was landed; and at the back of this cave is an old altar-stone, showing that it was once used as a place of worship.

On the southern end of the island is the high

3

plateau of Marathea, in Homer's phrase "with wide prospect," where were the pastures of the swine-herd Eumæos, and from which the loftier mountains of the mainland and the Peloponnesos may be seen— enchanted ground which soon melted away from our view in the foaming sea like other golden fables !

Ithaca, small as it is, now supports 12,000 inhabitants, and its wine which Homer praises, is still its chief product. Dr. Doerpfeld says that "The singer of the Odyssey had no mere general acquaintance with the island, but was absolutely familiar with its local features. He makes Athene to say 'Verily it it is rough and not fit for the driving of horses, yet it is not a very sorry isle, though narrow withal. For herein is corn past telling, and herein too, wine is found and the rain is on it evermore and the fresh dew, and it is good for feeding goats and feeding kine ; all manner of wood is here and watering places unfailing are herein.' " As Homer says, it is a land of vines and goats. Its sailors are the boldest in Greece. The sea is their outlook, reminding us of the frequent question in the Odyssey : " Whence came ye, for ye did not come here by land ?" and the other saying too is true, "there is no place for chariots." It seemed a small area for what was done upon it, the tall men it sent to Troy, the high-roofed palace, and the wide wastings of " the lordly wooers." But the kingdom of Odysseus extended also over the larger island of Kephallenia, called by Homer, Samos, and between the two islands lies the islet Daskalion, evidently the place where the suitors lay in wait to slay Telemachos on his return from Pylos and Sparta ; and it follows that as Telemachos had to sail in the strait between Kephallenia and Ithaca in order to reach his own city, this city must have been somewhere on the west coast of Ithaca ; and Schliemann, who visited Ithaca in 1868, fixed its site and that of the palace of Odysseus at Mt. Aetos, a conical hill on the neck of land connecting the two portions of the island. Here he found a small plateau surrounded by a Cyclopean wall and a lower terrace, and also the remains, as he thought, of some 190 Cyclopean houses.

To this theory Dr. Reisch objects, and thinks that though there was a Pelasgic citadel here, the city itself was at Polis, somewhat further to the north, where massive archaic remains are said to be, and which is a more favorable and open site for a city. Still there is, as yet, no determinate name or date to be assigned to these ruins.

The real gateway of Greece is the Gulf of Corinth. This forms a majestic portal to the whole land. After leaving Ithaca and sailing south you turn almost at right angles from the Ionian Sea, entering the mouth of the Corinthian Gulf, and soon coming into the bay of Patras, spread out like a magnificent vestibule between the frowning headlands of Akarnania on the north and Mt. Erymanthos on the south. Two mountains of pyramidal shape, Vavassova and Taphiassos, rise directly from the sea and stand like vast sentinels on the Ætolian coast, giving a sombre impression, and shadowing the sea as if Greece were not to be approached trivially and was " no land of lightsome mirth ;" and, indeed, if a storm spring up, as it is likely to do at any moment in all seasons, it is a formidable though most noble entrance to the beauties and glories of the land. When, however, the sun shines brightly, the scene of the sparkling expanse of the broad bay of Patras is a splendid one, with its dark-blue water foaming with whitecaps, and the purple mountains on the opposite shore growing rose-tinted in the sunset light, as the great wind-clouds pile up at the west from the direction of the open sea.

CHAPTER III.

DELPHI.

When I went the first time to Greece, Patras, where you land from the outlying steamer in a boat rowed by swarthy Greek sailors, was an insignificant place (though anciently one of the most important towns of the Achaian League) and had only a dozen or so slight wooden houses, but not without the invariable καφενεῖον, in front of which a few baggy-trousered Hellenes squatted, sipping coffee.

That night I slept on the floor of a bare unfurnished room, and at midnight the house was shaken by the violent knocks of a company of dragoons, who had brought in three ironed brigands captured on the mountains. In the early morning these poor fellows were taken away, and all that gloomy day raged a fearful storm with such thunder and lightning as one experiences in Greece, and which plays its part in Greek poetry, for the land is one great electric battery of mountain and sea to breed tempests.

Having taken at Patras a guide named Andreas (after the patron saint of the place), a huge fellow, who had travelled with Sir Stratford Canning, and claimed, when a boy, to have been pipe-bearer to Lord Byron, I went on to Vostizza, and from Vostizza crossed the Gulf of Corinth in a small sailing craft, and, in the evening, we anchored off the opposite coast of Ætolia.

A crimson light shone on the stern rocks of the coast, while the rest of the scene lay in the gloom of a gathering tempest. The deck, the sails and the sailors were tinged with this lurid light, which, however, died out, and thick clouds and darkness came over the sky. Big plashes of rain began to fall, and the little craft careened at the irregular blasts which swept by ; and we supposed that there would be a repetition of the wild storm of the previous day, although not being pagans we did not sacrifice a black lamb ; but my guide, I thought, lost something of the manly depth of his voice. While waiting in some suspense, suddenly one star shone out after another, until the sky was full of them ; and as I lay on deck that night, the stars seemed to be supernaturally large and bright, and around the top of Parnassos, "Mount of Song," they crowded and clustered like a diadem.

The next morning we sailed up the Bay of Salona. The mountains on either side of the bay, this being the month of September, were covered with a short brownish red heather, which contrasted finely with the deep blue of the sea.

On landing, I saw several camels, odd animals to find in Greece, and that were survivors or descendants of those brought into the country by the Egyptian army of Ibrahim Pasha. Here were horses to take myself and guide to Delphi. We rode on through the village of Crissa, now Chryso, one of the most ancient places in Greece, and stopped to drink at the old fountain. Then we passed through a succession of orange groves and vineyards, and commenced climbing the path that leads to Delphi, coming upon traces of the ancient road called "Schiste" where two ways met, on which Œdipus encountered his father's chariot; and here one gets a view over the whole fertile Crissæan plain that sweeps downward toward the sea. Going on we soon reached a point where the site of Delphi appeared, which, at that time, was covered by the village of Kastri that the French have lately removed for purposes of exploration. Delphi lies 2130 feet above the sea in a hollow of the mountain running up to the base of Parnassos and presents a scene that from its romantic character might be called sublime, impressing one with a feeling of awe as something of extraordinary nature where you might expect extraordinary phenomena. Here issued a mephitic vapor that hypnotized the pythoness, though her mutterings, as in dreams, were sent forth to the world in polished apothegms, like arrows of destiny. Delphi forms an amphitheatre opening between Mt. Parnassos and Mt. Kirphis. The twin rocks of the " Phœdriadæ " (shining ones) separated by a narrow rift through which a strip of blue sky is seen, rise directly above ; and while looking at these tremendous rocks, two eagles, like those which Zeus caused to fly to opposite ends of the earth, were sailing slowly around the summits, the light glancing on their bronzed wings.

Between the two cliffs of the " Phœdriadæ," from a fissure in the rocks runs the Castalian spring, whose water, if no longer inspiring, is pure and cool. A bare-footed nymph came down from Kastri to draw water. A rock-hewn cistern in which the priestess may have once bathed exists, but time and earthquake have greatly changed the spot. I climbed into this cleft, its sides being worn as smooth as polished marble, to examine some niches made for statues or votive-offerings, and being alone at the time, it was troublesome business getting down again, and out of this gloomy earth-throat. In fact I had to take a flying 'shoot' over the rocks, which landed me in a rather confused state at the foot.

To the right of the spring are remains of the ancient "Helleniko," and there is a solid retaining-wall of polygonal work, and about eighty feet of the stylobate of the Stoa of the Athenians, built B. C. 460. The French Archæological Society at Athens have re-erected two columns of Pentelic marble belonging to this structure. An archaic relief of a four-horse chariot lies undisturbed. Delphi, we cannot doubt, has many such ruins yet uncovered. In walking about within a radius of a quarter of a mile, I saw half-buried fragments of sculpture, and one sarcophagus, especially, representing a reclining female figure of the best Greek sculpture. A number of inscriptions have been recently found on the east portion of this stoa wall, for the French have great aptitude for finding inscriptions, although some unimportant statues, dug up at Delphi, may be now seen at the rooms of the French School at Athens. It must be said that the French have settled the question that the carved metopes of the Treasury of the Sikyonians were formerly painted, proving the use of color on Greek carvings of the best period ; and a colossal statue also of Athens in *poroslithos* has just been found with traces of polychrome color.

In regard to the date of the old Doric temple of Apollo, at Delphi, which stood above the polygonal wall or terrace that I mentioned, M. Homolle of the French School, recently said in a paper on the rebuilding the temple, that "the foundations of the western face and the southwestern corner, show traces of an earthquake subsequent to the building of the Alcmæonidæ, in the sixth century. Many of the courses are constructed of pieces of moulding and fragments of a triglyph from the eastern front, which (as is known) was of marble. That side of the temple, therefore, must have been overthrown, and the debris utilized for the new building. None of the portions of architecture that have been discovered can be assigned to a date earlier than the fourth century. Consequently the temple must have been destroyed and rebuilt toward the end of the fifth, or the beginning of the fourth, century."*

This temple was once full of statues, and here stood the gold statue of Apollo, that may, possibly, have been the original of the Apollo Belvedere, since this is undoubtedly a copy in marble of a gold, silver or bronze statue, which fact is seen from the metallic folds of the cloak, and it might have held a bow as slayer of the Python ; but the original Delphic statue may have held an ægis, as defender of the shrine against the Gauls, such as is represented in the Stroganoff Apollo, which is of simple character, like a shrine-statue. There was also a statue of Artemis, which divinity, with Apollo, defended the temple against the Gauls; and this was probably of an archaic type, like that found at Torre del Greco, on which are traces of color and gilding.

The Nine Muses, constant companions of Apollo, god of Art, were carved on one of the pediments of the temple ; and there is known to have been a statue of Leto, and, without doubt, there was one of Dionysos, whose cult was intimately associated at Delphi with that of Apollo.

There was likewise a statue of Poseidon, who had an altar here, and there were bronze and marble effigies of other gods associated with Apollo, for Delphi was a centre of Greek religious art, to which the Greek world was accustomed to send its most sacred works.

* Am. Journal of Archæology.

In the city of Delphi stood a gymnasium, also a stadion for the Delphic games, and there was a theatre, at the east wall of which was the Leschi of the Knidians, where were the famous pictures of Polygnotos, of the "Sacking of Troy" and the "Descent of Odysseus into Hades." The sites of these buildings constitute the present field of exploration; and it may be said that as yet the results do not answer to the effort and cost of the undertaking, in which 70,000 cubic metres of earth have been removed and 100,000 dollars expended; but it should be remembered that Delphi was ransacked by the ancients themselves; the Phocidians plundered the sacred treasures; the Romans, especially the emperors Nero and Constantine, and after them the Byzantine emperors, carried off statues by hundreds to adorn their palaces and cities; and now but little more than the foundations and some of the solider parts of the temple, that have resisted time, have been brought to light. It is hard digging here, but highly stimulating, from the expectation of rich discoveries. The temple is found to have measured sixty by twenty-five metres, and was erected on an immense base approached by marble steps. A statue of Apollo older than the time of Pheidias, and sculptures of six warriors at the base of a monument erected by Gelon in memory of the victory of Himera, have been discovered, and this is about all, though the dimensions of the temple and of the city have been ascertained, with the exact positions and relations of several of the larger buildings; but I am convinced that much more of exceeding interest will be brought to light, for here was the religious heart of the Greek world. Here was the abode of the divine wisdom, of the word of prophecy issuing from nature.

Delphi was the centre of the Parnassian system of Hellenic nature-cult. Greek mythology was a form of the religion of nature that differed from other forms, inasmuch as it was modified by the beautiful Greek spirit. A writer on the religions of India notes the difference in the æsthetic aspect of nature-worship in India from that of Greece, and says that the first took on the form of mere decoration, but the last of true art ; and this is just. The Greek spirit moulded the Greek religion, which has been explained rationalistically, whereas it was neither a product of reasoning or of unreasoning, not a scientific fact or an astronomic symbol, neither was it a philosophy, nor, above all, a philology run mad, as Max Müller would have it, but simply poetry. It was the outcome of the genius of a healthy-minded people in their spring-time of bright fancies, as their interpretation of natural phenomena, accentuated as these are mountainous regions, and which correspond sympathetically to mental moods. It was the story of nature transmitted through the mythopœic faculty of an imaginative people. This imaginative interpretation of nature preceded Hellenic poetry and art, but ·it formed the material out of which Hellenic poetry and art sprang. It existed before Hesiod and Homer, and ages before the artistic period of Polygnotos, Pheidias and Praxiteles. Herodotus said "Homer and Hesiod named the gods and settled their genealogies for the Hellenes ;" but the gods, though more clearly delineated by poetic genius, lived in the apprehension of the people, as dim personalities corresponding to their own visions, thoughts, passions, fears, hopes and joys, before they moved and burned in the Iliad and Odyssey. They lived already when the people saw them in objects of nature, in cloud, mountain and sea, and in corresponding heights and depths of the soul. The sky, or cope of heaven, surrounding all, with its clouds, rain and lightnings, full of powerful influences for good and evil on the life of man, was, to the Greek, divine—αιθερος εκ διης—Dispiter—Dyaus—Deus—Zeus—all-encompassing Father.

Zeus, whose flowing hair is like the rain, was a thoroughly Greek personification, though prefigurings of Zeus (Dyaus) are seen in Indian poetry, as in a Vedic hymn to Earth, which has been thus translated:

> "In truth, oh broad extended Earth,
> Thou bear'st the render of the hills, (lightning)
> Thou who, O mighty mountainous one,
> Questionest created things with power,
> Thee praise, oh thou that wanderest far, (the sun)
> The hymns which light accompany.
> Thou too, O glorious one, dost send
> Like eager steeds the gushing rain.
> Thou mighty art who holdest up
> With strength on earth the forest trees
> When rain the rains that from thy clouds
> And Dyaus' far-gleaming lightning come."

Mt. Olympos, a higher mountain than Parnassos, and a great weather-breeder, was the place, indeed, where Zeus lived, but if Olympos was the home of the gods, Parnassos, a lower mountain (just as if these skyey influences had flowed down into human touch and expression), was the "Mount of Song." The sky was a god—Zeus; the sun too, or atmosphere golden with the sun's beams, was a god—Apollo—who came to Delphi from Delos and shot golden arrows of life and death. Apollo was, above all, the divinity of Greece. He was the embodiment not only of the outward brightness of the Greek atmosphere, but of the Greek mind, brilliant, joyous, terrible in its brightness. When the poets came, having the power of " the conscious adaptations of thought," Apollo—the sun—through the interpretation of these fine spirits, was the prophetic power of nature, the god of poetry, music and art.

In the same way the earth (Gaia), the vine (Diony-sos), the maternal principle of nature (Demeter), took their forms. The inborn sensitiveness of the Greek mind to beauty, the beauty of nature, made Greek art altogether to differ from Egyptian art which was symbolic, from Oriental and Indian art which was decorative, from Roman art which was monumental, and from every other artistic form ancient and modern. It was essential beauty. It was an accord with the inward and outward world. In his thought the Greek came into harmony with nature, and interpreted the elements as an order of divinities, each reigning over his own sphere, call it Zeus, Hermes, Aphrodite, Dionysos, Apollo.

Apollo, as the god of harmony, of music and art, is represented more formally in Greek art in the statue of Apollo Musagetes, who, in long robe and with laurel crown, advances with measured steps, as in a solemn dance, leading the chorus ; and it is inter-esting in this connection, while speaking of the Delphic Apollo and the poetic gods of Greek art, to note the discovery by the French exploring expedi-tion at Delphi, of the second Hymn to Apollo. This occurs in an inscription which was discovered on the Treasury of the Athenians. It is accompanied with the ancient musical notation and forms a fragment of forty-two lines. It was a thanksgiving hymn to Apollo to be performed by a chorus of Dionysos, musicians sent from Athens and called *hyperchermes*, since they chanted the words to the accompaniment of the lyre. Like the more ancient Homeric Hymn to Apollo, it closes with an invocation for the people of Delphi and Athens, showing the intimate relation of Delphi and Athens, which Hymn I give in another's translation :

"Come to the twin heights of beetling Parnassos that looks afar, and inspire my songs, Ye Muses who dwell in the snow-beaten crags of Helicon. Sing of the Python, God of golden hair, Phœbus with tuneful lyre, whom blessed Leto bore beside the famous water, grasping with her hands in labor-pangs the shoot of the gray-green olive tree. And the vault of heaven was glad and radiant with unclouded light ; the œther stilled the swift course of the wind to calm, while the deep sound of the furious billows sank to rest, and mighty Oceanus, who with his moist arms clasps the earth around.

"Then leaving the Cynthian island the god set foot on the glorious land of Attica, first dowered with Demeter's gift hard by the hill of Pallas ; and he was sped by melodies of the Lybian lotus, mingling its honey-sweet breath with varied notes of the lyre. Twice did the voice that dwells in the rock hail him with the cry of "Pœan," and he rejoiced because he laid up in his heart and understood the will of Zeus. Wherefore, from that time forth, our Attic folk, sons of the soil, call him "Pæan ;" and by that name he is invoked by the great sacred band of the servants of Dionysos, smit by the thyrsos, who dwell in the city of Cecrops.

"Advance, then, warder of the oracular tripod, to the summit of Parnassos, trod by the gods, dear to the Mœnads in their ecstacies. There once, garlanding thy golden locks with laurel boughs, thou wert dragging with thy sacred hand enormous blocks, the

foundations of thy temple, when thou did'st encounter
the monstrous daughter of Earth (the dragon
Python) abiding her onset, O deity of the gracious
eyes, thou did'st slay with thy arrows this child of
Earth, when the barbarian horde of Gauls, bent on
profaning thy rich shrine with plunder, perished in
the whirlwind of snow. Now O Phœbus, save and
guard the city founded by Pallas, and her famous
people, and thou, too, goddess of the bow, and mis-
tress of the Cretan hounds, and thou Leto, most
revered ! guard ye the dwellers of Delphi, their
children, their wives, and their homes free from woe.
Be favorable to the servants of Dionysos crowned with
the honors of the games !''

CHAPTER IV.

DELPHI AND MT. PARNASSOS.

Nature is full of a prophetic sense. We gain from nature a new uplifting life, an inspiration, rather than definite thoughts or formulated ideas. Nature is a revelation to the soul, a voice of the divine, and, with the Greeks, Apollo was the voice of nature, the word. In the Greek idea (to say this without profanation) Apollo was the word of God. He uttered the prophetic voice. His personation sprang from the highest region of the Greek mind, the ideal, the spiritual, the religious, and especially so as the god of art.

Some have thought that our admiration for Greek forms in sculpture, is solely the effect of our classical education, now that Greek religion has given place to a true religion. But the English scholar, John Sterling, maintained that "Greek sculpture was the expression of all that was worshipful or religious in the Greek mind as partaking of one universal humanity, and which, in so far as it was true, makes it venerable to all time and to all men, and since the highest achievement of art is to combine purest feelings with purest forms, and if this be done, we need not be fastidious about the medium, or deemed profane for honoring a head of Zeus."

Sterling's thought is generous toward Greek art; and we may believe that Pheidias' religious soul speaks to us in his works, and leads through them into a pure region of thought. Greek sculpture sought truth, and what is the true but the divine? It sought beauty, as does genuine art even the most realistic, that to be art can never lose out of it the ideal, the artist's thought, his conception of what is true, in order to be art at all.   Art strives to free us from all imperfection and deformity, material and moral.

This search of art for beauty, has been condemned as unworthy, and even immoral ; and so erroneous a conception as this is not confined to the ignorant and illiterate.   In a sermon I lately heard from a college professor, through the whole discourse was drawn a contrast between Duty and Beauty, as if one were good and the other evil.   But what is more beautiful than duty ?   Every quality that enters into and makes beauty—truth, reason, order, right, perfection—enters into and makes duty.   Duty and Beauty are one, not variant, and a broader generalization comprehends them both.   Beauty, in Greek thought, was another word for perfection, material and mental.   The Greek idea of beauty was predominantly intellectual.   The line of beauty was a line of strength.   The Greeks felt that the beautiful and the true were one ; and this lies at the base of the best Greek philosophy.   Socrates said that "Whatever is beautiful is for the same reason good, when suited to the purpose for which it was intended ;" and Plato goes deeper and seeks the beautiful beyond visible objects, finding it in the soul.   He said, "He who would proceed aright in this matter should begin with beautiful forms ; soon he will perceive that the beauty of one form is akin to the beauty of another ; and then, if beauty of form in general is his pursuit, how foolish would it be not to recognize that the beauty in every form is one and the same.   And, when he perceives this, he will become a lover of all

4

beautiful forms; and next he will consider that the
beauty of the mind is more honorable than the beauty
of all things outward. At length the vision will be
revealed to him of wondrous beauty which is everlasting, not growing and decaying or waxing and waning
. . . .   but beauty absolute, simple, everlasting,
without diminution and without increase. Thus one
learns to use the beauties of earth as steps along
which he mounts upwards, going from fair forms to
fair practices, and from fair practices to fair notions,
until from fair notions he arrives at the notion of
true beauty, and at last knows what the essence
of beauty is—so that if a man have eyes to see true
beauty, he becomes the friend of God, and immortal.''
Beauty, as Plato saw it, was divine, and it was this
divine beauty that his soul thirsted for. Paul came
to Athens four centuries too late for Plato. And is
not this a broader theory of beauty than the one
commented upon? Does it not come nearer the conception of the beauty of goodness, of holiness, as it
shines in the gracious face of Christ? It is not a
question of art without religion, but a question of
religion without art, or religion opposed to art. Art
has its place and rights. Art claims nothing more
than what fairly belongs to it. Art, in itself, is no more
moral than literature, or science. There is false art,
and there is false literature, and there is false science,
and there is false religion. I would go further and
say that art, or the science of the beautiful, represents a function of mind. It represents, more especially, the function of the imagination, the play and
action of the aesthetic faculty, which has the power of
reproducing in visible forms the images and forms
implanted in the mind. It is the "form-sense."
Carlyle perceived this when he wrote: "Not our

Logical Mensurative Faculty but our Imagination is king over us. I might say Priest and Prophet to lead us heavenward, or Magician and Wizard to lead us hellward." Why ignore art's heavenward prophetic office and drive it to be a minister of evil, when it was meant to be a minister of good? Our duty is to keep our ideals of art high and pure.

In the melodies of Haydn's "Creation" springing from nature, the soul is borne upward on wings of pure emotion; but music of another sort breathes strains appealing wholly to the senses, and to the lowest sense, and it may do this simply in sounds not words; and much of modern music is of this sensuous character, as well, indeed, as modern art. Art is good or bad according to its spirit. Art is moral or immoral, not in itself, but in the disposition of the artist and his audience. Yet art is not true art, let it be music, picture, sculpture, speech, poetry, book, that is intrinsically immoral; which truth might be demonstrated if it were necessary. Duty is an act of the will, but sensibility lies at the bottom of the will, and gives it its impulse. Love is the spring of duty. Duty is heroic, and the heroic both in morality and art, is beautiful. It is a question of perspective. A true analysis seeks not the contrast, but the identity, of Duty and Beauty; so that a deep-thinking Greek could say "Beauty is the splendor of truth." I, for my part, hold that Duty comes first, first always; and that Duty is a higher thing, or quality, than Beauty. To rescue a child from evil surroundings and train it up for the good of humanity and God's pure service, were infinitely more beautiful, than the loveliest statue Greek artist ever made or dreamed of. In this acknowledgment of the eternal superiority of duty, it is still a Greek poet who said: "No painter, no, by

the gods, nor sculptor, can place in form, such beauty
as has truth.''

As a practical lesson, he who desires to obtain true
culture must work on Greek lines; and if we catch
the spirit in which the best Greek worked, we catch
the spirit of true culture.   The Greek sought symmetry of body and mind, real harmony of the nature, a
result that was beautiful as a work of art, and not
knowledge merely, which may only cover the un-
wrought lump, but culture which penetrates all,
mellows and refines through and through, reaching
the soul and building it up in manliness (ανδρεια).

The old Greek had enormous faults, and this was
owing to his lack of Christian truth, but his system
of education, of culture, was thoroughly philosophic.
It was not only broad but it went deep.   The perfection he sought entered into everything he was and
did, into the spirit of everything, so that all he
touched was ennobled, from a coin or a bit of pottery
to a statue or heroic act; and this, indeed, is seen in
Greek literature as well, but, above all, in Greek art,
in which the Hellenic genius fully expressed itself,
expressed itself in the exercise of a joyous freedom,
since art springs from the emotions, from love, which
is the real joy and freedom of the mind ; and the best
way, therefore, to study Greek literature is to be permeated by the spirit there is in it, to study it in connection with Greek art, to study it as Greek art, not
as separated from that aesthetic culture which constitutes and embodies its very life.

Art, in the lowest sense of it, as a mere matter of
taste, is not unimportant to the man of education ;
for if bad taste be not a mortal sin, it nevertheless
implies a moral quality that as yet remains barbarized,
unannealed, unrefined, and untouched by the hand of
thorough culture.

At the house, or cabin, where I lodged at Delphi (the village of Kastri as it then was), on the edge of evening, an old *militarre*, an Epirote government-soldier, came to call on me, or presented himself in abrupt military fashion. He was a picturesque person with bronzed face, glowing eyes, enormous gray moustache, a quantity of pistols and daggers in his girdle, blue leggings fitting close and spreading over the feet, and leathern-laced sandals. He opened fire at once, and tried to dissuade me from going up Parnassos, because a band of brigands but a day or two before had been defeated by government troops, and were scattered over the mountains on their way to the Turkish frontier. Concluding to go, four men were detailed as an escort, the old officer to act as their chief. At 4 o'clock the next morning, we started on horseback up the craggy path from Delphi, accompanied by the soldiers clad in sheepskin coats with the wool outside, and carrying long old-fashioned carbines, looking like brigands, as perhaps they were on occasion. The path from Delphi that the ancient Greeks used to go to the Parnassian highlands, or the first great terrace of·the mountain, was an almost sheer precipice of a thousand feet, and was conducted by zigzag steps cut in the rock; but the path we went, though steep, was more circuitous. It was dark to begin with, and as we proceeded we met a furious tempest, a circumstance frequent among the hills, and the way was black as night illuminated only by flashes of lightning, but at length we reached some stone hovels called "The Huts," where we dried our clothes and took breakfast, and as the storm passed away, there was one of the most magnificent days I remember, a Greek day, when the air is so pure and clear that the most distant objects seem close at hand.

We had come up to the higher land above Delphi almost in darkness, and now, resuming the journey from ''The Huts,'' we set forth on the morning of this fine day to cross the plateau towards the summits of Parnassos. This is an irregular and broken region of hill and plain of considerable extent, and one might call it, in truth, the highlands of Greece, though it has some cultivation but is principally pasture-land, with here and there a village, such as the little town of Aràkhova, which lay to the east of our path; Aràkhova is a very old place, hanging like a bird's nest over the gorge of the Pleistus, and which was once celebrated for the beauty of its women, whence called καλγυναικα, and this reputation it retains. We met some of these Aràkhova people, men and women, and on this table land, this mountain territory, or circle of Delphi, constituting the rocky center and citadel of Greece, there is now to be found, if anywhere, a remnant of the old Hellenic stock. Races hold together in the mountains better than in the plains. They seem to be as hard to disintegrate as the mountains. The people themselves believe this, and boast of their pure blood. In the fine forms and graceful carriage of these Parnassian mountaineers, a handsome race, differing from the people of the towns, you can easily believe that you see the descendants of the ancient Greeks. Not so very far away, indeed, to the east of these mountains of Phocis, are those of Bœotia, and near the base of Mt. Kithœron lie Leuktra and Platœa, and it was from Platœa that the band of a thousand hardy men rushed down to help the Athenians at Marathon.

The very names of places in this Parnassian region, as I have remarked, are ten Hellenic to one Slavonic or foreign. The women of the villages, it is said, are seen to special advantage on festas, in their dances and processions, still half pagan in character, when they wear white garments ornamented with red and blue trimmings, their heads garlanded with flowers. They are great lovers of flowers, and exhibit much taste in costume and embroidery. These women may be the sisters and wives of patriots or of brigands ; for the men have traits of a free, bold race, good and bad, hospitable but fiery in temper, courteous and kind but capable of violent, even treacherous acts, in fact with a substratum of strong manhood. They are not merchants and traders as in the towns, but soldiers, turning their hands to horse-pasturing, vine-dressing, shepherding and foraying.

Continuing the journey more directly now to the westward, we came opposite the cave of Korykium, for a long time lost sight of and was a haunt of robbers, but was discovered comparatively recently ; and which was the old grot of Pan, spoken of by Pausanias. The *militaire* and myself, by a little climbing, came to its mouth, with an entrance like a black-browed arch. Within as it were its vestibule, hang large white stalactites relieved against the dark interior. The walls are encrusted with shining stones, and the ceiling spangled with these, though now blackened by torches. There are altar-heaps of stones, and curious chambers whose entrances are nearly stopped up, but into which one can manage to crawl. Going further into the cave the old chief fired his carbine, whose report echoed through the distant reaches of the cavern, as if it were of considerable extent.

This was formerly the scene of those Dionysiac rites, in which the frenzied revels of bacchantes and mœnads (whose clothed forms do not lose dignity in

Greek sculpture) took place, with the shrill cry of
" Io ! Io ! Dionysos !"—another phase of the Delphic
worship of nature, when, as if the new wine of
spring-time had overflowed the bounds of reason,
its votaries, delirious with the joy of life, tore in
pieces the best-loved object, animal or human—even
the gentle Orpheus.

The only evidence that now remains of these mad
classic days is a half illegible inscription, on the rock
at the right of the entrance, to the god Pan and the
nymphs.

From this cave, almost in the words of the Odyssey,
" so soon as early dawn shone forth, the rosy-fingered
* * * we fared up the steep hill of wood-clad Parnassos, and quickly came to the windy hollows," or
to the higher valley of Levadi, the four soldiers running alongside, with heads erect and streaming black
hair, in their shaggy capotes under the hot sun, as
fast as the horses could go, for there seemed to be no
tiring out of these men, superb specimens physically.

Passing swiftly over a sparsely cultivated stretch of
plain, the still distant top of Parnassos came in view,
a long straight-ridged mountain with a hollow like
a Turkish saddle, and then a slightly higher peak
like the horn of the saddle, giving the bi-formed or
twin-peaked aspect ascribed to it by the poets. It is
a mountain 8068 feet high, and snow lay on the
highest point, Mt. Lyakoura, as it is now called.

After some hours more of riding we dismounted
near the base of the summit, for a little halt before
going higher. I could not persuade or bribe Andreas
and the soldiers to go with me any further ; so the
chief and myself set out and accomplished the climb
in about two hours from the halting-place. It was
tough work; the small sharp limestone rocks cutting
the feet and affording only a loose footing.

To go back a step, at first we walked through some
sylvan scenery with large pine trees, which trees were
anciently consecrated to Pan ; and with green turf and
running brooks and mossy rocks, a region for sheep
and goats, and where at any turn in the fitful shadows
goat-footed Pan, or a pointed-eared faun, might be
seen playing on his pipe in the light and shade, a
piece of rough Arcadia, which, however, soon changed
its aspect, growing savage with dead trees, broken in
two and ghostly white as if cropped by an avalanche,
until all vegetation ceased, and we came out on the
bare, white, sweltering peak of the mountain, which
was so hot that my companion's red face grew to be
the color of mahogany. He was constantly peering
around the rocks to discover brigands, and this was a
time when there were brigands in Greece, but there
were none to trouble us, and all was as still as the
blue sky into which we climbed higher and higher,
until, at length, we stood on the top, and looked off
suddenly the other side toward the north, in one
tremendous precipice, sweeping down as by a single
bound thousands of feet into the Lokrian valley.

I never saw a much grander sight, though there
are profounder precipices in Switzerland. The wide
horizon under a cloudless sky showed mountain and
valley sleeping in the clear sunshine. To the north
lay the plains of Thessaly, and the summits of Olympos, Pindus and Pelion, with Thermopylae, or rather
the interval in the mountains where it was ; and,
somewhere over these heights, the Spartans had to
march to go to Thermopylae. To the northeast was
the island of Euboea, with the glittering line of the
separating strait ; to the southeast were the plain and
peninsula of Attica, and the Ægean sea beyond ; to
the south rolled out the billowy mountains of the

Peloponnesos, even to Mt. Taygetos, and the Gulf of
Corinth, a strip of deepest blue between ; to the southwest the Ionian sea, with some of the larger islands,
Kephallenia and Ithaca, dimly seen ; directly below
were the dark-wooded ridges of Helicon and Kithæron,
and the mountains of Phocis and Bœotia.

Greece, in fact, was stretched out at our feet,
mountain, island and sea ; and it was marvelous to
see how rough and wrinkled a land it was, a compact
Switzerland with few open plains, and with deep
valleys separated from each other by their rocky walls
and sea bays, a land of sharp separations and divisions, a land of small states but of individual development, progress and freedom.

There stood once, ages before, on the summit here,
an altar or shrine dedicated to Zeus ; but we could
not linger long, as a hard journey back to Delphi lay
before us.

On our descent we found the rest of the party
encamped in a pine grove, engaged in roasting a sheep
whole, spitting it on a pole like a western barbacue.
On a bed of branches at the foot of a pine tree, I
closed my eyes on Parnassos and slept the sleep of the
weary, until a cry was made that dinner was ready.
With daggers used as knives my companions carved
up the meat, and the best cut was presented to me on
a plate of green boughs, and was washed down with
an unpalatable draught of *resinato*. This Homeric
feast was in sight of the white mountain seen through
the trees, and soaring into the blue of the unclouded
heavens.

Walking away a little distance from the encamp-
ment, I was suddenly attacked by two large wolf-
dogs, and being unprepared for such an onslaught,
did, as was done in a similar scene in the Odyssey,

plied the dogs with stones, until the shepherds, roused by the barking, rushed in and beat off the beasts with their long staves. The passage in the Odyssey is this :

"And of a sudden the baying dogs saw Odysseus and they ran at him barking, but Odysseus in his wariness sat him down, and let the staff fall from his hand. There by his own homestead would he have suffered foul hurt, but the swineherd with quick feet hasted after them, and sped through the outer door and let the skin fall from his hand. And the hounds he chid and drave them this way and that, with a shower of stones."

This is the best way to meet these fierce shepherd dogs—with a shower of stones if they happen to be handy. The road was so steep in places on our return to Delphi, that in the growing darkness we had to dismount and pick our way down.

CHAPTER V.

MARATHON.

The next day after climbing Parnassos, I re-embarked on the little Greek vessel, and sailed up the Gulf of Corinth before a brisk westerly gale, and this was the time when the young Greek sailor sang his Klephtic songs. I will speak of the scenery of the Gulf of Corinth at another time, but I believe that the old Greeks loved nature rather as pure nature, than as what we call scenery, or landscape, and they more truly recognized and entered into the universal spirit of nature, esteeming it as a divine and life-originating power, which they felt, rather than a nature to be studied in its detail with critical eye like a picture; and yet the scenery of Greece must have sensibly affected the Greek æsthetic sense and given it delight, for it is truly a noble scenery, and this is the right word to use. Greece is not a lovely land like Italy, but a noble land. The mountains, though not of Alpine height, have a certain sculpturesque beauty of outline, and while often entirely stony and bare of verdure, take exquisite colors of pink, saffron and purple, as the day with its changing lights goes on. The atmosphere is of such crystalline purity that it has the effect, as has been said, of bringing distant objects near. This clearness of the Greek atmosphere has ever been noticed, so that "the amethystine hills" of Greece is no mere poetic phrase; but I may be allowed to slide into a poetic vein as I recall one particular sunset, seen when approaching Athens somewhere in the

neighborhood of Eleusis, though I cannot hope at all
to describe its colors, which were of the richest and
rarest kinds. Deep purple, yellow or saffron, sea-
green or beryl, were blended together, with great
crimson bars streaming upwards in broad rays, as if
Apollo's chariot had descended flashing from the sky,
and leaving its brilliant track behind the black hills
of sacred Eleusis. These broad streams of red light
were curiously distinct from one another, and yet they
were not dazzlingly gorgeous colors as in our American sunsets, but were mistily and softly shaded with
deeper tints of the same ; and after the richer colors
had died out, the outlines of the hills were luminously
rimmed as by a halo of chromatic light that lingered
long over them. Sometimes the photographs of Greek
scenery show this distinctness in the outline of the
hills, proving the marvelous clearness of the air.
Emanuel Deutsch, the scholarly Jew, who died too
young for the sake of literature and art, and whose
mind was imbued with the atmosphere of the Orient,
when speaking of some Arabian poetry, says : "There
arises out of this region of the Hamasa a freshness,
glory, and bloom of desert song, such as out of
Homer's epics rise the glowing spring-time of humanity, and the deep blue heavens of Hellas."—this
phrase, "the deep blue heavens of Hellas" describes
the sky and transparent atmosphere of Greece as well
as words can do this.

Marathon is a place and thought, which, if not
directly the source, became one of the chief springs, of
Greek heroic art ; and the special divinity that was
invoked by the Athenians when they started for the
field of Marathon, was Athene Promachos (Van of
Battle), shield and protector of the Athenian state.
At the period of the Persian wars, Attic art was highly

archaic in form, and the bronze statuette of Athene Promachos, in full armor, with ægis, spear and helm, that stands in the national museum at Athens, is an illustration of the fighting divinity to whom the Athenians looked for help on that morning of the battle, strong, yet without beauty. Pheidias, more than half a century later, transformed this rude conception of the war-goddess, into the majestic form which stood on the Acropolis, the glitter of whose golden spear-head could be seen by the Greek mariner coming in from the Ægean; and this might stand as a kind of symbol, or heroic type, in art, of Marathon itself.

I have been twice to the field of Marathon, the first time before there was a road to it, only a bridle-path, and the second time by a good carriage-road, such as there now is. On the first visit I met none but shepherds and their big dogs, in a ride to and fro, with halts, of some twelve hours.

At the present time, one leaves Athens in a carriage with four horses (if he choose to do it rapidly) by the Kephissia road, keeping Mt. Hymettos to the right, and then passing over the spur of Mt. Pentelikon, covered with pine trees and olive groves, and delightfully green with vineyards and cornfields. The pine trees were pitifully "blazed " in order to procure resin for the Greek wine. The road grows soon somewhat wilder and lonelier, and at a place called Pikermi, where the way crosses a torrent-bed, is the scene of the capture by brigands in 1870, of the four luckless Europeans, Herbert, Viner, Lloyd, and Count de Boyle ; and a rare place it is, you would say, for an ambush. It was a fearful tragedy, but one cannot help thinking that if better tactics had been employed by the military, at the time of the seizure of the brigands, the lives of those unfortunate people might have been saved. Brigandage in Greece, as in Spain, Italy and other countries, comes from the weakness of the government, which is unable to give proper protection to all in its borders, and this, combined with the sparseness of population in certain regions, makes it easy for banditti to escape. As the proverb is, "wild lands make wild men." War too, in such countries takes on the form of brigandage, and can hardly be distinguished from it, lawless acts and lawless men having in some sort the sympathy of the people themselves, and are sometimes aided and shielded by them.

The descent into the plain of Marathon from the village of Vrana, follows very much the course that the Athenians took on their way to the battle-field. It opens a superb view of the sea beyond, the opposite shores of Eubœa and the lonely plain itself—a "fan-shaped" amphitheatre six miles in length and three in breadth, encircled on three sides by gray mountains that run out into the sea at their northern extremity, making a curved arm that forms the bay of Marathon. At present the plain, though treeless, has a more cultivated aspect than when I first saw it, with its wheat fields and vineyards, and here and there a farm-house. On the earlier visit there was no object on the plain but the little tumulus in the middle of it, near the sea, which was raised over the graves of the one hundred and ninety-two Athenians slain on the 12th of August 490 B. C. Dr. Schliemann dug into this mound, making an ugly gash which rain has made worse, endangering the hill itself, and he discovered nothing important; and in the earlier diggings only a few bones and some arrows and lance heads and broken pottery had been found. These are

now in the National Museum. From the top of the
tumulus, overgrown with weeds and shrubs, one can
get a good idea of the lay of the land, the encircling
line of mountains, the pass of Rhamnus through
which the Athenians rushed down, and the morasses
that stretched between the sea and plain, leaving a
small strip of dry land, the larger morass being to
the north and the smaller to the south, which swamps,
in fact, were the decisive factors of the battle.

The Persian galleys sailing into the bay of Marathon were drawn up to the western beach, and the
men were disembarked and encamped on this narrow
strip of shore lying between the sea and the morass,
but on which there was not room enough for the
deploying of cavalry, the chief arm of the Persians.
Then came the marsh and beyond this the plain.
The small Athenian force descended from the mountain and across the plain at the moment the enemy
were employed in the process of disembarking and
forming, and in order to meet the assault of the
Athenians, the Persians were forced to cross the inter-
vening marsh leaving it in their rear, so that when they
were hastily rearranging themselves and being drawn
up on the plain, the Athenians were upon them, and
they were borne back by the resistless attack of the
Greek hoplites, until they became hopelessly entangled
in the swampy ground at the edge of which the Greeks
fought at an advantage, and pushed their enemy on
deeper to defeat and ruin. It was the battle of the
marshes. The strategy of the Greeks took prompt
advantage of the moment when the enemy was em-
barrassed by their treacherous footing, and before
they could form their cavalry on firm ground.

The picture of the battle of Marathon by Polygnotus,
in the Pœkile of the Acropolis, described by Pausa-

nias, supplements the brief account that Herodotus wrote of the battle, and explains the important part which the marshes played in the whole affair. Pausanias, centuries afterwards, in describing this picture, says, "Here is seen how the barbarians pushed one another into the swamp, and here the greatest slaughter took place." Art, in the picture of Polygnotos, became the oldest historic record of the battle of Marathon. In fact there were two battles, the decisive one at the swamp, and the other later on at the ships, on the embarkation of the Persians, in which the Greeks were repulsed, though they managed to capture seven out of the six hundred vessels; and thus by superior skill and bravery, ten thousand defeated ten times their number, and gained the day over what was then held to be the strongest fighting power in the world. Looking from the summit of the mound towards the west, over the whole plain, one can easily conceive how, towards evening, when victory began to declare for the Greeks, the fierce rays of the setting sun on that August day, dazzled the eyes of the Persians. In the conformation of the plain, it seems physically and poetically adapted to the event. Nothing could be more so. Nothing could be more striking. Nothing could add to its natural beauty and solemnity. It was an amphitheatre formed by nature where civilization encountered barbarism, or a lower order of Oriental civilization. It was intelligent force and heroic bravery, quality not quantity, the inspiration of freedom, that won; and to prove how small was the land which was rescued, and where these heroic scenes occurred, I heard at Marathon the sound of cannon fired at the Piræus, the port of Athens.

In the month of May when I was there, fields of

5

golden wheat seamed with red anemones and tall blue
flowers, such as grow in our New England wheat-
fields, closed up all around the sorós, presenting a
peaceful agricultural scene where such stern conflict
had raged.

To show how the heroic and the common sometimes come together, there was a party of tourists
who had driven to the field in a four-horse chariot ;
and their very important little courier bustled about
to spread the feast with bottles and dishes in royal
picnic fashion. There was absolutely no manifestation of the artistic, the contemplative, or even the
curious, in this company, but only of the gustatory.
Refreshed at length, they started off with much crack-
ing of whip, and doubtless made better time back to
Athens, than did the soldiers of Miltiades, when they
rushed home after the fight to save the city from the
revengeful swoop of the Persians.

CHAPTER VI.

TEMPLES AND EXPLORATIONS IN ATTICA.

Another excursion outside of Athens in Attica, was to Sunion, to see the temple that lingers there with some semblance still of perfect form. In going by rail to Sunion (Cape Colonna—Kolonnais) the road to Marathon as far as Chalandri, is run over. At Leipsi, the site of the ancient deme of Pœania, the train passes through the birthplace of Demosthenes, and one sees where were those paternal acres about whose possession in the courts, he brought himself, when a young man, into notice, and to which allusion has been made.

At Laurion are the antique silver-mines, in which may still be found some 2,000 ancient shafts, and these mines are to-day worked, or worked over, with considerable profit. At Laurion one takes carriage for a three hours drive or less to Sunion. The wind blew, as it can in Greece, lashing the waves which ran up in three or four lines of breakers on the coast, like wild horses with white manes, but as I walked up the little hill of two hundred feet on which the temple stands, the wind went down, although the sea still tossed and raged, making a grand sight of the Ægean and its islands fringed with foam.

Sunion is a very lonesome spot, entirely uninhabited with the exception of one small house where the temple-keeper lives, and is at the extreme point of the peninsula of Attica, and the temple stands like a

solitary watch-tower looking out on the broad sea.
You associate it entirely with the Hellenic past. The
edifice was dedicated to Poseidon and Athene, and an
ancient fortified wall once rimmed the edge of the hill
that forms the platform on which it stands, a Doric
peripteral hexastyle reared on a stereobate of three
steps. Eleven columns, sixteen-fluted, carved of
gray-whitish marble, are standing, or tottering, the
drums of most of them being started out of place,
which gives them a frail look, and the edges of the
flutings are much worn, but in spite of wind and
weather, these thin shafts have stood more than
twenty-three centuries, a beacon to the home-coming
Greek, golden in the sunshine and white in the moonlight, and sung by poets who loved Greece, in the
ancient and modern days. They have suffered greatly
from earthquakes, with which Greece is almost annu-
ally visited, and which, as scientists say, run sympathetically out from centers of seismic disturbance in
Crete, Cyprus and Asia Minor.

Another excursion from Athens, nearer the city,
was to the bustling port of the Piræus. The carriage
road to the Piræus is more satisfying for its views, and
makes a pleasant drive, but the short railway, opened
in 1869, is the oldest, I believe, in Greece. It goes
around the base of the low mountain, or hill, of Æga-
leos, where a portion of the Long Walls once joined
the walls extending inward from the port. A station
on this road is Phaleron, summer resort of modern
Athenians, and where one has in full view the islands
of Ægina and Salamis. Even down to the close of
the War of Independence, the name of Piræus had
been lost ; but now a city of upwards of 30,000 inhabitants, the largest in Greece next to Athens, with
extensive docks and regular streets and squares, has

sprung up, a center of commercial activity that would have delighted the eyes of the practical Themistokles. But the Piræus was a well-built, fortified city in the time of Perikles, and this brought down upon it the destructive hostility of Sparta. Kantharos, the naval harbor, snug and safe, where the war-ships of Greece and other nations lie, is the same as that in which the great Athenian triremes which sailed to Samos and Syracuse, some to victory and some to defeat, were moored. Here, now, come in the bigger ocean steamers from the Adriatic and the Mediterranean. The smaller harbors of Zea and Munychia near by, show tokens of antique sea-walls and fortifications. Modern villas scattered along the shore towards Phaleron, front the sea, where the sunsets are splendid among such waters and islands, though a trifle melancholy.

I saw here a tall old Mohammedan saying his prayers, at the back of his domed pavilion, or kiosk, by the sea-shore, turning himself as he bowed reverently toward Mecca, doubtless a religious man in his way, who had chosen to remain behind in the land his fathers once ground under heel, and reminding one of Greece's recent struggles. The Turk, let me say, has his good qualities, and before he becomes an official, or has power entrusted to him, is commonly an honest and respectable man, but he is not fit to govern others, above all, Christians, as the history of modern Greece has lamentably shown. The Ottoman government is the blind instrument of Islamism, the everlasting foe of Christianity, while the Moslem High Priest, with his junta of priests, at Constantinople, rules all—Sultan, state and army—decreeing the massacre of the Armenian nation, plotting the reconquest of Europe and Asia, and thoroughly believing, as in the days of Omar, in the inherent force of the Koran to

subdue the world. England and America, where are
ye, in your dream of material wealth and power?
Better little Greece that was ready to perish rather
than to yield its free intelligence and civilization to
the tide of Oriental barbarism !

From the Piræus one may go readily to the island
of Ægina, which forms a dark hilly mass, stretching
south into the Saronic Gulf towards the Ægean, and
lying, as it does, almost opposite the extreme point of
Attica. Ægina, home of the Æacides, and rival of
Athens for centuries in maritime enterprise and the
bravery of its people, played a considerable part in
Greek history, and at the battle of Salamis, one of
her. thirty war-ships took the first prize for valor ;
until Athens, jealous of her commercial and naval
fame, razed her chief city and expelled her inhabitants
from the island, which then became united to Athens.
But it was a land of heroes, above all, of athletes,
whose victories exceeded in number those of any other
province, and some of them sung by Pindar.   On the
entablature of the temple, now known to be a temple
of Athene (a Doric peripteral hexastyle), were carved
the figures which, perhaps, best exemplify Homer.
It takes a day and half from Athens to see Ægina
satisfactorily.   There is almost daily a steamer from
the Piræus to the island, and from the landing-place
on the island, in about two hours and a half, one can
go on horseback by a rough road to the ruins of the
temple, which stands on an isolated hill overlooking
the sea.

Not much of art now remains on this Greek soil excepting the temple itself, of which twenty columns
are standing.   The sculptures that adorned the pediments (now in Munich) are of Parian marble, most wonderful in a technical point of view, and once colored,

BAS-RELIEF OF MANTINEA

representing contests of the Eginetans and Trojans. It is the Iliad in a nutshell. The figures are not quite life-size, and were carved shortly before the battle of Marathon, so that they give us the conception of the hero in Greek art ; and, as having been naturally taken from life, they doubtless caught inspiration from the period of those who fought at Marathon. They are, as well-known, slightly archaic, preceding as they do the Pheidian sculptures of the Parthenon, and also those of the Theseion. In the faces the nose is sharp-pointed, and there is the inane smile, the masque of life, which, however, was a first effort to represent feeling in marble ; but the forms are symmetric, and though of light poise they have an expression of force—terrible fighters are they of the athletic type ! It is power without beauty, yet with a beautiful moderation, and with a freshness of motive, so that, in spite of their monotony they form lively and vigorous groups ; and with such beginnings as these, there is no knowing to what excellence Æginetan art might have reached, had it not been crushed at the outset by the envious hand of Athens. In these figures is seen the somewhat rigid bronze type of sculpture, in which Ægina excelled.

One might combine an excursion to the smaller island of Salamis, with that to Ægina, and this would bring us nearer to Eleusis.

The road directly to Eleusis is almost identical with the ancient "Sacred Way," and is a little more than twelve miles long. It begins at the "Street of Tombs," which was continued with its lines of funereal steles and monuments, nearly all the way to Eleusis ; and at this spot was the commencement of the way on which went the procession of "mystæ" (candidates for initiation) to the temple, where were set forth the mysteries.

A little further on from the Dipylon Gate, one passes over the Cephissus (when I saw it a ditch of a few yards wide), and at the bridge was the first halting place of the procession. At this place a singular phase of the ceremonial, and of Greek religion, was exhibited. The god Dionysos, who had a shrine at Athens, had been adopted into the circle of the Eleusinian Under-World gods, as god of the vine, and in the spring-time, the time of the new wine, Dionysos was thought to have journeyed from his Athenian home to visit his fellow divinities at Eleusis ; and here at this little bridge of Cephissus, the last link, as it were, to Athens and life, came the first halt of the Eleusinian procession ; and at this spot the Dionysiac spirit of wild license was let loose, aggravated by keen Athenian wit, so that the sober procession was turned into a dancing, shouting, thyrsos-swinging, ribald mob, but this delirium lasted only a short time, symbolizing mad life, the tumultuous freedom of earthly life before entering on the silent and solemn mysteries of the future. We do not know exactly what it did mean, but in its wildest license it had a symbolic significance.

Following the "Sacred Way" beyond the hill of St. Elias, at the left of the road, stands the old convent of Daphni, belonging to the 13th century, A. D., and now much fallen into decay ; and here originally stood a temple of Apollo. This Byzantine convent, built on the ruins of the classic temple, is worth a visit to see the mosaics, especially those of " Christus Pantokrator " in the dome, and of the " Anastasis," which last has been skillfully taken down and restored under the direction of the Archæological Society of Athens. The curious and skillful work of mosaic renewal, and of other architectural renovation, was going on when I was there ; and he who omits Greece in his study of Byzantine and Oriental art, that was the outgrowth of the Byzantine period, makes a mistake, for Greece is full of these ecclesiastical buildings, betokening the spread of that great Greek empire which once ruled over the eastern world.

Passing Daphni, we go on to what was the site of a temple of Aphrodite, on the right, which was another halting place of the procession ; and here you catch the first glimpse of the beautiful curve of the bay of Eleusis, shut in like a still lake by low hills, and at this spot there are some remains of the ancient "Sacred Way" ; and here, too, Eleusis, on the side of a narrow ridge, comes in sight, with the square Frankish tower, and the small stone museum, above on the hill ; and you reach Eleusis by skirting around the bay.

Eleusis, when I saw it the first time, consisted of scattered ruins that had been only partially excavated, and that seemed to occupy the yards of some miserable hovels, and consisted of fragments of pillars, large rectangular marble blocks half covered with dirt and rubbish, and two or three colossal broken statues. This was all that told of the spot whose mysteries, as Plutarch said, "had in them something of a soul divine." But this has been changed. The first to do anything in the way of excavations at Eleusis, was the "London Dilettante Society," early in the century, and its discoveries, not extensive, are set forth in Lenormant's work "*Grande Grece.*" Then came the more effective work of the Archæological Society of Greece, that cleared up the site of the temple, and is still digging there. The discoveries do not quite come up to expectation, but are important. While I was there in 1895, the workmen were making a deep cut excavation, and were finding every day and hour something valuable, carrying up from the pits basket loads of dirt and débris. It was a busy scene, this laying bare of the face of antiquity as if opening a tomb.

The remains of the Propylæa built by Hadrian, or a small temple *in antis*, are preceded by marble steps now exposed, and then come two parallel walls about thirty feet apart, with a transverse entrance-way, and bits of ornamental architrave belonging to this strew the ground ; for though much has been cleaned up, there are but a few ruins standing above ground.

By another low flight of marble steps one reaches the broad platform laid bare with its broken bases of columns, where was once the Hall of Initiation.

To speak a little in detail of what stood here, and of what now remains of this shrine, kept sacred by the Greeks for eight hundred years, and whose secrets were not revealed by any of the myriads who took share in them, Eleusis is situated on a rocky promontory dividing the Thriasian from the Karian meadows, and at the south and east of it stretches the bay of Eleusis, with the island of Salamis and the low mount Acamas. In or on the face of this hill, that was the Acropolis of old Eleusis, are evidences of the buildings of many ages and periods. There are Cyclopean walls which show that this was a sacred spot in prehistoric time, perhaps a cavern opening, as was thought, into the under-world, in front of which Demeter sat weeping by the spring, after the long search for her daughter ; as in the Homeric Hymn to Demeter :

" A terrible grief took possession of Demeter, and she forsook the assembly of the gods and abode among men for a long time veiling her beauty under a worn countenance, so that none who looked upon her knew her, until she came to the house of Celeus, who was then King of Eleusis; and in her sorrow she sat down at the wayside by the virgin's well, where the people of Eleusis come to draw water, under the shadow of an olive-tree; but the gods are hard for men to recognize."

A shrine was afterwards built by Peisistratos, an edifice whose foundations and fifty-six square bases of columns have been uncovered, which shrine, or temple, was destroyed by the Persians. Then succeeded the Hall of Kimon, of the same frontage but twice as deep as the Hall of Peisistratos, and lastly, was reared the enlarged and more stately Doric structure made by Perikles, or by the architect Iktinos who built the Parthenon.

Iktinos constructed this edifice by cutting further into the rock, so that he could get a portico to the north corresponding to the southern portico of the temple, which, when completed, must have resembled the Parthenon, and yet differed from it, for the Greek artist worked by instinct, and adapted his building to its site, his statue to its place, and this gave the aesthetic character to the Greek temple which was in entire harmony with its purpose and scenery, so different from modern buildings in or out of cities.

The hall built by Iktinos had two entrances in front, and twenty-five columns supporting the roof, and it is thought that though divided below into two parts, it had an undivided upper chamber, which was the Great Hall of Initiation (Teleterion), where the mysteries were celebrated. Heaps of broken pillar-bases are found on the platform, and confused remains of many periods of architecture, and finally of the Roman epoch; for the emperor Hadrian, reviver of classicism, erected here a Doric entrance-way called the Greater Propylæa, and there was also an inner smaller Propylæa. Roman remains and sculptures, highly carved, but not of the best style, are those chiefly now seen ; and around this precinct ran a wall. There are also remains of smaller buildings, such as the house of the Ephoros and Panagia chapel, where was the Virgin's well. There was also a sanctuary of Pluto, and a small temple or cella of Plutus, fitly god of the under-world, in which gold is found ; and there was, originally, somewhere, a temple of Demeter, which is now difficult or impossible to locate ; and ruins of a temple of Artemis lie beyond the Greater Propylæa. The mystic temple or Hall of Initiation (ὁ Μυστικὸς Σεκός), stood upon the terrace that was smoothed or cut partially from the living rock, where you now see the hollow into which the temple was partially set, and at the back of which, stone steps went down as into Hades. The sites of Greek temples are chosen with exquisite taste, and one is impressed with the view from the cleared platform that overlooks the slope to the seashore and the blue waters of the bay of Eleusis, the bare mountainous isle of Salamis in front, the opposite rock-promontory of *Keratopyrgos* on the mainland, which, tradition says, is the place where Xerxes sat on his golden throne, the glorious straits themselves to the left, the passage of which seems closed to the eye and where the battle of Salamis was fought, in which three hundred Greek contended against a thousand Persian wargalleys, as described by Eschylos who was there, and whose birthplace was at Eleusis. One sees also the curve of the coast-line trending towards Megara

"And the noise was heard that day
From Salamis to Megara "

a scene now silent, and painted, as it were, on the airy page of the mind, so that the very nature seems to belong to the heroic past, for Salamis was the counterpart on the sea, of Marathon on the land.

Demeter, the goddess "with yellow hair like the ripe corn," has been called the Madonna of Greek art, the lady of sorrows. There is a statue of Demeter in the British museum of very strong character, with "worn face" as in the Hymn. Demeter, great divinity of Eleusis, was the mother-principle of nature, of the revival or continuity of life, extending to the realm of the spiritual and symbolizing the resurrection—assuredly the most interesting of Greek myths, playing a powerful part in art, and showing that Greek art was not altogether taken up with Aphrodites and Eroses, but had a profoundly religious element.

What were the Eleusinian mysteries ? We do not know, but we know they were of deep import to the Greek mind. The five Eleusinian, or under-world divinities, Demeter and her lost and found daughter Persephone (ταιν θεαῖν), Aidoneus-Pluto, Iacchos, Dionysus and Rhea-Kybele, were added to by the semi-mortal Triptolemos. Demeter and Persephone, mother and daughter, says a writer to whom I owe suggestions here, were "regarded as one," and both together represented this life of sorrow but peace, of love with sadness, of death with life, since the Eleusinian mysteries entered into human life and its sublime problems.

Classic authors, among them Cicero, concur in declaring that the unrevealed mysteries of Eleusis pointed to a higher truth, and taught a lesson of virtue as well as of nature and of the changing seasons, leaving a mystic but sweet hope in regard to the soul, announcing that life and death were essentially the same, and that death was but the entrance to life. They probably perpetuated, refined and enlarged the Egyptian mysteries as set forth in the "Book of the Dead," and looked to the truth of monotheism ; for after that the "mystæ," or candidates for initiation, had been purified by ablutions, fastings and sacrifices, and had come to the "Home that welcomed the mystæ," and there had gone through the solemn ceremonies of initiation, they were ever after, Cicero says, more virtuous and happy men, and had a moral change wrought in them.

There is a small stone museum containing sculptures, some of good art and some crude, but mostly illustrations of Eleusinian rites and of the forms of Demeter, Triptolemos and other divinities of the lower world. The large relief sculpture of the three divinities found in the temple of Triptolemos near by, is now one of the treasures of the National Museum at Athens.

CHAPTER VII.

ATHENS MODERN AND ANCIENT.

The Odyssey remains still our guide to Athens, for it is Athene that leaves the distant shore to fly, swift as light, to the dear home and city of Pallas-Athene, "wide-streeted Athens."

Athens is so brilliant a spot on the world's map, and the map of mind, that one may hesitate to speak of it ; and can anything new be said of "the violet-crowned" city, whose history is the history, in some sort, of all modern art, learning and civilization ? I can talk of it only from a limited personal point of view, as a basis for discussing briefly some features of Greek art.

At my first going there, barring antiquities, Athens was a mediocre and half-oriental town, of some 25,000 inhabitants, and (contrary to Homer) with dirty and narrow streets, a few open places, the great white cube of a palace, then new, and a few other public buildings ; but at the last visit, Athens had grown into a brilliant city, of considerably more than 100,000 inhabitants, containing fine squares, broad well-paved streets, handsome hotels and private houses built of a light colored stone in the German style, like Munich, with electric lights and tram-ways, and having the glitter and show of a court-life, with military officers well-mounted and in natty uniforms, military music, new highly decorated Byzantine churches, solidly built museums and scientific institutions, and carrying the air of a gay modern capital.

When the sun shines at midday your eyes are
blinded by the reflection from the white pavements
and houses, and filled with an impalpable dust,
though none excepting American and English people
go about at that hour; but towards evening, when
the light is less dazzling, as one drives through the
long business street of Hermes, and the still longer
one of Æolus, cutting it at right angles, and crosses
the wide squares of the " Place de la Constitution "
and the new " Place de la Concorde," and traverses
the fashionable Stadion and University Avenues,
lined with the residences of Government officials,
foreign ambassadors and wealthy Greeks—the finest
being the white marble palace of Madame Schliemann
—you are struck with the order and handsomeness
of the city, although the Ilissus and Cephissus are
ditches, and "gray-eyed Athene" has withdrawn
her ægis and her mighty form has faded into air.

Modern Athens has mostly left the site of the old
city, that ran up on the west and south to the foot of
the Acropolis, and has extended itself on the plain
towards the east and north, street beyond street, section beyond section, the whole rimmed in by the
mountains of Parnes and Pentelikon in the further
distance.   Hymettos is nearer at hand to the southeast, while the curious horn of Lykabettos, on which
no classic association seems to rest, and the crag of
the Acropolis, from which the city has nearly withdrawn itself, and left it isolated, now, as in ancient
times, form the salient features of the scene.

One of the streets near the Acropolis has the name of
Byron (οδὸς βὸρωνος) ; and there are also other memories of the poet in and about the city, such as the
monument of Lysikrates, which (a tradition only) he
is said to have occupied for a short time as a studio,

and his portrait hangs in one of the rooms of the
palace. Byron, great poet as he was, most eccentric
of his eccentric countrymen, brought but the dregs
of a life to Greece, in which he was not permitted
even to find ''a soldier's grave''; yet the motive
that brought him should not be lightly spoken of as
a stage act, for it was the purpose of a high manhood.
He freely sacrificed his property and life for Greece.
From the time he landed on her shores, he worked
hard to bring about union among the factions in the
Greek army, and he was but thirty-six when he died,
his end hastened by ignorant medical treatment; and
there was time enough left for him to have risen from
the slough of earthly living to show the features of
his muse, like a winged Greek Victory, recording
heroic deeds on a shield. A faint heroic light only
from Hellas is shed around his name, or reflected
from this last noble flare-up of the lamp of his
genius, soon to go out in darkness. While not harmonious or strongly original, and essentially unclassic,
his Greek poetry has a fire and soul in it, and will
live with that of Sophocles and Alcæus, in Greece
itself.

One very interesting place in Athens, recalling the
heroic past, and brought into notice by active work
going on there in connection with the recent Olympic
games, is the Stadion, the scene of the ancient Panathenaic games. Following the main street leading to
the east, to the outskirts of the city, past the Zap-
peion and the public garden (παράδεισος) and crossing
the Stadion Bridge with a feeble stream of water
under it, one comes to a natural hollow, or bay, in
the hill side, where was the Stadion, that was originally surrounded by a wall, fragments of which
remain, and its sloping sides were filled in with

6

marble seats accommodating fifty thousand spectators.
The length of the running course was six hundred
and seventy feet and its breadth one hundred.   This,
when the restoration is complete, will be rebuilt at
an expenditure of a million drachmas, and it will
accommodate one hundred thousand spectators. ''The
remodeling of the Stadion is done by the architect
Ernst Tsiller, on the basis of the excavations made in
1873.   At the point where are preserved traces of the
ancient wall will be erected a wall made in the
Pelasgic manner.   At the two highest points of this
wall are to be built two four-columned stoas of belvedere form, surrounded by figures of wrestlers.   The
arena will be divided for the race-course by a long
lattice of marble.   Here will come a broad passage-
way and then the benches.   At their highest point, as
in ancient times, will be a passage-way, and stair-
ways will run across throughout the whole length.
The square in front of the Stadion (a modern feature)
is intended to include the leveling of the ground and
abolishment of existing houses, a long stoa with
double Ionic prostyle, two fountains with reservoirs,
statues and a prostyle for carrying standards and
trophies.''*

To see and talk with, as I did, a tall young Eng-
lishman, a student of the English school, who was
vigorously training to take part in the contention,
would have awakened any one's classic enthusiasm,
although you might be disposed to ask if training
under the fierce sun of Greece, would be as successful for an Anglo-Saxon born in foggy Britain, or in
our own changeable climate, as it would be for that
child of the sun, the Greek ephebos.

The result of this contest was highly honorable to

* American Journal of Archæology.

American athletes, who, I believe, beat the record of ancient diskoboloi ; but I rejoiced that the race to and from Marathon was won by a Greek. Perhaps an inspiration from the messenger of Marathon, winged his feet.

I would say that April, when these sports were held, is the month of all others in which it is most agreeable to visit Greece.*

Of the four hills in the city, viz: the Acropolis, the Areopagos, the Pnyx and the Museion, the Areopagos is the only one on which the light of Christian tradition fell, and even this is uncertain ; for it is held by some scholars that the hill of the Agora, occupying the space between the Theseion and the market-gate, which was the heart of Athenian popular life, was the place where the apostle made his speech recorded in the 17th chapter of the Acts of the Apostles. The "market-place" has been laid bare by the Greek Archæological Society. It lies immediately at the side of the "Tower of the Winds ;" and this whole precinct was originally consecrated to Ares—a "Mars' Hill." I ought to add that there is a difference of opinion in regard to the "Theseion ;" the latest view being, in connection with researches as to the situation of the Stoa Basileios, that it is identical with the temple of Hephaistos.

* In more extended travel for archæologic research, Col. Leake says : "If the traveler were to confine himself to the season which is both safe and agreeable, his objects would never be attained ; there is no alternative therefore but to travel during a part of the winter, which can hardly be said to conclude, even in the plains of Greece, before the vernal equinox. The portion of the year which I have found, after some experience, to be the best, is from the middle of February to the middle of June, and from the middle of October to December."

The hill of the Areopagos is a rugged natural rock
with sloping sides, flat on top, and only precipitous
to the northeast, with fifteen steps cut in the rock, and
probably in ancient times faced with marble.   This
rock, as is well known, was a spot of awful sanctity ;
but it has also long been associated, rightly or wrongly,
with the name of the apostle whose heart touched all
humanity, Athenian humanity as well ; else why did
he come to Athens?   Why did he live and speak
here ?   He was no bigot or iconoclast.   He knew the
power of Athens.   He recognized it as a world-centre
of intellectual influence.   He felt the genius of the
place and of its works of art.   He mildly rebuked the
abuse of Hellenic religious sentiment, but magnani-
mously and gladly recognized its reality.   He pro-
claimed to Athenians the *unknown* God, to whom they
had already erected an altar.   He acknowledged the
light of culture which the Greek mind had shed, and
quoted its literature with   approval.   His metaphor
of the eternal temple not made with hands, shows
us that the shadow of the Parthenon had fallen on
his imagination, and his strenuous illustration of the
foot-race, indicates that he might himself have gone
along with the crowd out of the city to the stadion,
to witness the athletic games ; and, indeed, the
relations of art to early Christianity, and to all
Christianity, is a great subject by itself.   The holy
martyrs died for the faith.   The first believers de-
nied and scorned the idolatry seen in the statues.
They are to be forever honored and praised by us,
who feel ourselves unworthy of this high consecration.   But art, as well as literature, is to be purged
and reformed by a purer spirit.   The forms which
spring from nature, and which have their birth in
the mind that contains the ideas in their conceptual

mould, are intended to ennoble us. The colors painted everywhere by the delicate brush of nature, are meant to warm us to purer passions, and to be used for simple and sacred purposes ; meanwhile a change is rapidly going on in the modern world, by which Art is coming to take its right place in human life, and the long unnatural divorce between religion and art, is beginning to be viewed in its true light.

The ' Theseion ' is the one completely preserved Greek temple.   It stands in its almost perfect integrity for the admiration or criticism of modern eyes.   Technically, it is a Doric peripteral hexastyle, faultlessly proportioned, the columns having a less entasis than those of the Parthenon, and leaning slightly inward ; and though of noble form, balanced and sturdy, it has less grace than the Parthenon, and appeals less powerfully to the sense of beauty, the better preserved though it be.   The relief-sculptures on the east front represent the labors of Herakles, and are thought by critics to have antedated those of Pheidias, and are in lower relief.   The only new truth about this edifice is, as I have said, that it is held by some to have been originally not a temple of Theseus, but of Ares, and that this ground was the precinct of Ares, in which the market-place stood.   When I first went to Athens this temple was a museum of antiquities, and the only museum in the city, and in fact in Greece.   The "Market-place" lying between the Market-Gate of Hadrian and the "Tower of the Winds," is now recognized as the Roman market-place, in contradistinction to the older Greek Agora, to the east of the Theseion.   It was excavated by the Archæological Society in 1891, and is a paved area somewhat sunk by time and its accumulations, surrounded by colonnades, and with four Doric columns supporting an

architrave still standing, and bearing an inscription
that Julius and Augustus Cæsar contributed to its
erection ; and this may have been the once busy scene
in which the apostle, in Roman time, borne there by
an excited crowd, stood and spoke to the Athenian
people.   Why should we consider his coming there to
proclaim the true God, moved, as he was, by love, to
have been an act of hostility to the Greek, or contempt
of Greek thought and works ?

The "Tower of the Winds," or, more correctly,
Horologion of Andronikos Khyrrestes, an octagonal
structure and a quaint one even for Athens, was built
as late as the last century before the Christian era,
and is in a good state of preservation ; but the relief-
sculptures on the frieze, facing different points of the
compass, and representing the winds, are not of much
artistic merit.   The north-east wind, a disagreeable
one in Athens, as well as Boston and New Haven, is
portrayed by an old man named Kaekías, who shakes
hail-stones out of a shield.   The tower gives the name
of Æolus to the longest street in the city, which com-
mences at this Tower of Æolus, and is one of the most
characteristic thoroughfares of the modern city, always
filled with a crowd of motley-clad people from town
and country, buying and selling, gesticulating and
screaming, in the little shops and booths ; it is the
Athens of to-day, and of the everyday homely life of
the people.

On the side of the hill of Philòppapos, are three
holes or small chambers cut in the side of a rock,
popularly believed to be the prison where Socrates
was confined previous to his death, and this is not
impossible, for there may have been once a structure
built in front of these rock chambers ; and if this were
the place where the conversation recorded in the

THEMIS FOUND AT RHAMNUS

"Phædo" occurred, it is almost a sacred place, even if we do not join in Erasmus's petition, "Holy Socrates, pray for us !"

The hill of the Pnyx, at present left stranded by the city, as this district is, is of a more undoubted authenticity, a flat, low, gray hill, or rock, lying in the very eye of the Acropolis ; and on its platform, four hundred feet long and two hundred and twelve wide, supported by a Pelasgic wall, was the ancient bema, and on this spot the "fierce democracie" held its noisy political assemblies, for freedom is noisy not silent. A higher bema facing towards the sea was just above it, and what a view of land and water was spread out before the speaker ! He could address under the open sky the whole voting Athenian republic. Nothing very marked, a lot of gray old rocks these, you say, but whence comes the light that springs from and surrounds them, the more you look at them ?

A small Greek structure, well-known but charming, might be noticed before we come to the theatre of Dionysos, and on the way to it, upon the street leading to the west from the arch of Hadrian—the monument of Lysikrates. Similar monuments were dedicated to victors in the contests of the Dionysiac games, but this is the oldest structure of the Corinthian order, known as now standing, and is of the elegant style of that ornamental order, the roof budding into a flower consisting of a single block of marble. The monument has been carefully protected by an iron fence put up by the French. The dainty frieze represents the grotesque punishment of the Tyrrhenian pirates by Dionysos, turning them into dolphins, the subject of a Homeric hymn ; and the inscription records that "Lysikrates was choragos when the choir of the phyle Akamantis won the

prize.'' If this little monument shows the Greek
beginning, the magnificent Olympieion, or temple of
Olympian Zeus, shows the Roman flowering, of the
Corinthian order, which might be called a Roman
order, suiting the luxurious tastes of Rome, though
she almost spoiled it by combining it with the Ionic.
Rome, by the use of the Corinthian order and the
development of the arch, succeeded in evolving an
imposing architecture, of which St. Peter's is the
culmination ; but the root of Roman architecture
was Greek, as it was also Greek in this temple
founded by Peisistratus B.C. 530, and completed by
Hadrian 130 A.D. Whenever the two styles come
together, as they do in Athens, we get a better conception of the ideas to which they gave form, the
Roman a grandiose, and sometimes grand, expression
of power, the Greek a harmonious expression of
reason. The one is vast, the other moderate. The
one is matter, the other mind. And I say this with
due respect to Roman art which is noteworthy, as
it is seen especially in the Pantheon, and Hadrian's
mausoleum, and which is the art of imperial law, and
in this it was original, but as art pure and simple, it
was secondary not original. The Christian basilica,
after all, was the finest outcome of Roman art, after
it met and assimilated into itself a Christian element,
which gave it productive originality and whose influence is felt in mediæval art. There is absolutely
nothing new in modern architecture, not even a new
capital, like the Lombard or Gothic, which does not
draw its form from a thought that is developed from
Greek original sources.

The Olympieion was a large temple to stand on
Greek soil, a superb anachronism on the banks of the
little Ilissus. One fallen gigantic column stretches

along the ground broken in regular pieces, as if it were laid down with the greatest care by a storm in 1852.

The bed of the Ilissus lies just below, and near by is the head-source of the ancient Athenian water-supply, the spring of Kallirohē, retaining the old name, past which runs the road to the cemetery, where, under a costly monument, Heinrich Schliemann is buried.

Excavations in this quarter were begun by Schliemann, and are carried on by Dr. Doerpfeld, exposing the ruins, or foundations, of a number of houses Greek and Roman, as of a thickly settled quarter of the city. Hereabouts was the Enneakrounos, the ancient building with nine water-openings, connected with the system of aqueduct supply, and some leaden pipes belonging to this have been found. The Greeks in their time were scientists as well as artists, as the engineering works to drain the Copaic lake, the military fortifications of strongholds, and the mechanical construction of temples and other buildings, testify. At these diggings one sees the mosaic pavement of a house which has been exposed, but nothing rich ; in fact, domestic Greek architecture was not remarkable. The houses were small with unwindowed walls to the street, and the interiors, we may surmise, were not as they were in Pompeii, highly ornamented, for the Greek, as Burke says, was ''a public creature'' who seemed to exist for the sake of the state, and he needed no costly house for himself, when he had the best the city could give as his own.

For the first time I saw the exposed remains of the Theatre of Dionysos, which, on a previous visit, were not uncovered, although the site of the theatre was then known. The Greek Archæological Society,

succeeding to the work of Ludwig Ross, Beulé and
Curtius, has done great things in Athens, and in
Greece, as from year to year reported in its quarterly
publication (Εφμμερις αρχαωλογικη), a mine of informa-
tion, but its soul and hand is M. Kabbadias, ephor of
the antiquities, a plain, modest little man, who has
not only the brains but the working capacity which
his countrymen seem to lack. The still later explorations of Dr. Doerpfeld have brought to light the
most ancient portion of the structure under the
Roman foundations.

The theatre of Dionysos has an elevated site at the
foot of the Acropolis, commanding a view of the city
of Athens, the harbor, the sea, the plain of Attica, the
seat of the court that tried Orestes, and the hill of
Kolonos. The present ruins mingle Roman relics
of the time of Hadrian, and later, with those of two
older Greek sanctuaries of Dionysos, the earlier dating
back to the time of the Persian wars. The cliff below the Kimonian walls was hewed perpendicularly
smooth and then faced with masonry ; and the theatre
was partially cut out of the rock in two terraces, the
upper terrace having a long wall with arches, still
there, and the lower made into an amphitheatre
(*cavea*) comprising a radius of one hundred and fifty
feet, the seats accommodating thirty thousand spectators, arranged in concentric tiers and divided into
thirteen wedges, or corridors. The lower rows of
seats remain, the foremost of them being of Pentelic
marble, as well as the chair of the chief priest of
Dionysos, that has an inscription, and is ornamented
with a relief of satyrs carrying bunches of grapes.
The priests, and sometimes the priestesses, occupied
the front rows. The marble seats are rectangular and
handsome in form, doubtless cushioned when occu-

pied by the more luxurious. The Dionysiac altar constituted the central point. That part of the orchestra which was situated outside of the cavity of seats, and which stretched on each side of the boundary wall, was the δρομος, four hundred feet long, and at the two ends of it were the side-entrances. The freize, or decorated supporting-wall of the proscenium, with its sculptured figures and large central kneeling satyr belonging to the cult of Dionysos, still presents a highly ornamental feature ; but while so many fine statues of divinities and of poets that adorn this place are gone, these ruder carvings are all that remain of a splendid theatre which, if not the birthplace, was the home, of Greek dramatic art. One can even now make out the three divisions of the stage, orchestra and auditorium, the parti-colored pavement, the spot where stood the altar to Dionysos, and the Dionysiac wall of the proscenium. Originally the stage was situated in that portion of the orchestra which was opposite the amphitheatre and on a level with the seats, and was divided into two parts, the first of them, or the front (λογεῖον) from which the actors spoke, being a narrow parallelogram projecting into the orchestra ; and all this could be distinctly read when the theatre was first partially uncovered in 1862 by the architect Strack, with the help of an ancient bronze coin on which a design of the building was stamped, and which is now in the British Museum.* You wonder at the simplicity of plan so well fitted to its uses for seating, seeing and hearing, so open, light and beautiful, and so strikingly contrasted, in these respects, with the closed-in, heavy style of the theatre of Herodes Atticus, the wealthy patron of Athens in Roman days,

* Monuments of Athens.

which edifice from the outside is conspicuous with its
heavy arched terraces, at the base of the Acropolis
It was originally surrounded by walls and arches, and
lies at the other extremity of the same face of the
Acropolis as the theatre of Dionysos, and its interior
resembles, in a general way, that of the Dionysiac
theatre, only it had a roof of cedar wood. Its seats
were hewn out of the rock and covered with Pentelic
marble ; and one can climb from within at the back
of the theatre, by steep steps, to the top of the
Acropolis.

This Herodean amphitheatre, comparatively recently excavated, has the heavy and gloomy look, like a
cavern, characteristic of Roman architecture, whereas,
on the contrary, the Dionysiac theatre was exposed
to the air and sky, and the clouds that sailed over it,
as if it were free to the immortal gods, with whom
the Greek tragedies had so much to do. These
dramas that treated of life, fate, and the spiritual
conflict of good and evil, expansive in theme, were
performed to much better advantage under the cope
of the sky, than in closed walls ; to better advantage,
one might say, than Shakspeare's dramas, treating
also of character and destiny, were enacted on the
pent-house stage of the Globe Theatre in London.
Neither in England nor in this country, could the
open-air Greek theatre be used, but for safety, com-
fort and the influences of nature, in such a climate
as Greece, how superior these edifices to modern
theatres ! It was nature, not gilding, nor upholstery,
nor artificial stage-scenery, that gave them their
charm, and their healthy inspiration ; and something
was left to the imagination, both of the poet and his
audience.

CHAPTER VIII.

THE ACROPOLIS.

The Acropolis is the central point of Athens and Greece. Early made the foundation for works of art, it is wonderfully fitted by nature for the part it has played, and even with its crowning works fallen into decay it is an impressive object seen from all directions. When one comes in from the Piræus and the sea, or when he goes out into the plain of Attica, and the country, this is the grand feature of the scene, at morning, noon and night, in the sunshine and under the moonlight—the white crag-base of the whiter Parthenon, as if it had been carved into a vast architectural pedestal, or an altar of the old gods.

From the east when below on the plain, one may get a good idea of the shape of the rock, forming a compact eminence of crystalline limestone, with rugged chasms and seams, a spur of the hills running south from Mt. Pentelikon, about two hundred feet high and a natural citadel from most ancient days, as is found in the remains of old walls and fortifications. In prehistoric times its uneven top was leveled off, and the natural steepness of the sides was made more steep.* In the remotest antiquity a Pelasgic town was built on this commanding hill. On the north side near the Erectheion, the heavy foundation-walls of a palace have been discovered, corresponding to similar palatial edifices at Mycenæ, Tiryns and Troy. Archæology has brought to light, all over Greece, a

* American Journal of Archæology.

prehistoric strong people, who, warlike and dominant, were builders of great walls, and possessed a rude artistic genius.   To this period belongs the narrow staircase cut in the living rock, such as one finds at Tiryns, that leads to the plain below.   Here was the tomb of Kekrops, the earth-born father of Athens (Kekropia), and here was the Kekropion, at the southwest corner of the Erechtheion.   On this eagle's nest was the egg of the city.   The wall of polygonal stones is chiefly found on the east and south sides, coeval with Cyclopean wall-remains in the Peloponnesos, and which follows the natural line and curve of the rock, with a heavy outwork on the west, for the nine gates anciently forming the entrance to the citadel.

The steep walls that the Persians scaled were the walls of the Pisistratidæ, who made their royal stronghold here, the Persians directing their attack from the northern and more undefended side.   They burned the temples that stood on the rock, the old temple of Athene, the Herakleion and the Hekatompedon.   Themistokles rebuilt the defensive wall and planned the reconstruction of the chief sanctuary, and Kimon and Perikles carried out the plan of reconstruction with still greater magnificence.   Kimon filled in and extended the dimensions of the Acropolis, hiding the Pelasgic wall and going outside of it, increasing the area one-fifth, and making a broad platform for the temple superstructures.

From the hill of the museum, you see the west front and southern line of the Parthenon, and have a side-view of the Propylæa.   The row of heavy arches to be here observed are remains of the Theatre of Herodes Atticus and the Portico or Stoa of Eumenes ; and the modern carriage-road runs by these, turning sharply to the left and ascending the hill to the Beulé gate, which is the present entrance to the Acropolis.

The Beulé Gate, named from the French architect who discovered or uncovered it, in 1862, was not laid open when I first saw Athens, and I went up the Acropolis by a rougher pathway near by. The Beulé Gate is but five and a half feet wide, and is said to be exactly in the axis of the Propylæa, but there is reason to think (contrary to Beulé's own opinion) that it is not the original entrance to the Acropolis, and only dates back to the time of Nikias, while the marble staircase above it, built irregularly of ancient fragments, belongs to a period as late as the first half of the first century A.D. Yet it cannot but be said, that as the rock is precipitous, there must have been originally a steep flight of steps to the summit, so steep that chariots could not have gone up by it, even those of the Panathenaic procession. There might have been, indeed, what now appears to be a narrow road-track between the two flights of steps, but this could have accommodated only mules and cattle for sacrifice; and all was taken into the walls of the fortifications, in later Roman or mediæval times.

The tower-like inharmonious pedestal in front to the left, is the pedestal of Agrippa, so-called, on which stood a statue of Marcus Vipsanius Agrippa.

To the right, standing high, is the lovely little square Ionic temple of Nike Athene, Nike Apteros ; and at the turn of the hill, to the left, you see the beginnings of the long northern wall of the Acropolis, and the place where are the ancient caverns of Pan and Aglauros, that may be reached from the outside. The walls on the north were once called "The Long Rocks," as here the length of the rock is greatest, and can be seen in its whole length from the plain.

There is a rude picture of the Acropolis stamped
on an ancient coin, showing the Propylæa, the Parthenon and the colossal statue of Athene Promachos ;
and the antique gateway and stairs represented on
the coin, are apparently on a much larger scale than
the Beulé Gate.

The projecting wing above the staircase on the left,
is the Pinakotheka, or Pœkile, where were those
votive pictures by Polygnotos, painted on marble
panels, one of them representing the battle of Marathon, and whose description by Pausanias centuries
after, adds so much to our knowledge of that event.

The western or outer front of the Portico of the
Propylæa, is composed of the row of Doric columns
whose flutings are almost as sharp-edged as when
they were cut, though most of the capitals are gone.
The Propylæa is certainly next to the Parthenon in
noble simplicity and grandeur, so that its ruins lure
you from the larger structure to linger under its
shadows ; and since it stands at an angle to the Parthenon, it is a monument by itself, like an overture
to some great work of harmony.

The eastern or inner front of the Propylæa, looking across the plateau of the Acropolis, is a favorite
place to sketch the Parthenon ; taking in the most of
it, from under these white columns, through which a
glimpse of the sky and the distant plain and mountains of Attica are seen, a fairy picture from this
height. Within are the rows of discrowned Ionic
columns (the Doric and Ionic commingling) fragments of whose capitals lie tumbled about ; the upper ceiling was in square coffers which have fallen ;
and both the western and eastern fronts of the gateway were probably closed at times by massive bronze
doors, the whole making a noble approach to the
greater glories of the Acropolis.

The form of the actual summit of the Acropolis is lanceolate, or better, leaf-shaped ; and passing through the Propylæa, one is brought into immediate sight of the majestic, scarred, west front of the Parthenon, standing a little distance to the right. When I saw it the first time, before and around it, covering the whole top of the rock, were scattered a thousand fragments of white Pentelican marble, sparkling as sugar. On the building, one has his attention drawn to two battered marble figures of the pediment, the only ones that remain, and for that reason they have a pathetic look. They lean against each other, and are supposed to represent Asklepios and Hygeia, the male figure partially reclining, while the other, beside him, has her arm about his neck. They cling faithfully to the building and to each other.

The west front, seen from the Propylæa, gives you the long northern side of the Parthenon, and perhaps this is the most satisfactory view, taking in a great part of the edifice at a glance. The archæologist has been busy, and while his is a careful hand to which we owe a great deal, caring tenderly for every fragment and orienting every stone, the old-time picturesqueness has been somewhat marred, and the impression of endless riches of marble fragments, carved capitals, broken pillars and sculptured pieces of marble, glistening in the sun, is diminished, and there is a spick-and-span appearance, as if the housekeeper's broom had set all to rights and left it in pimlico order. This besom has swept away the ugly mediæval tower that once disfigured the Acropolis. Near the Parthenon itself, some places which have been dug out are left open and are neatly stoned around, where the excavators went down to the rock, so that you can see the original surface beneath.

7

The old stairway by the Erectheion which led down
and out at the foot of the Acropolis, is also left open,
making a large cavity or well, but the way has been
barred further down for fear of accident.

It is now much nicer and easier getting about on
the cleared, natural rock-face, and you can study
the whole less confusedly, and a great deal of accurate
work, helpful to the comprehension of Greek art, has
been done, but the pristine charm is lost forever, and
this seems to be hardly made up by the excellent
arrangement of things ; and neither does one feel that
he can, himself, find anything new, or make a discovery of his own.   The field has been too thoroughly
cleaned.*   Archæology is a noble growing science.
In Greece it has wrought absolute wonders, and on
the coast of Asia Minor it has made the splendid discovery of the Alexander-sarcophagus, so-called, at
Sidon, richly combining all antique arts.   Archæology is a helpful and, in some respects, indispensable,
handmaid, of the lovely queen, Art ; but archæology
cannot, any more than science, take the queen's place,
or walk in her celestial robes, shedding about her
steps that sweetness, light and grace that blesses the
earth like the spring-time.   Archæology is learned,
but art is inspired.   Archæology treats of the old,
but art is ever new and young.   Archæology is confined within its own severe limits of scholarly research,
but art is free as the infinite imagination.   The explorations conducted by the childlike faith of Schliemann, and the almost infallible scientific sagacity of

---

* This observation has, perhaps, been disproved by the discovery of the inscription on the east pediment of the Parthenon,
by a member of the American School of Archæology at Athens,
and certainly Mr. Eugene P. Andrews' brilliant originality in
the manner of making it was only equalled by his patient skill.

Doerpfeld, down among the buried stones and walls of Troy, derive all their interest from Homer's poetic art.

The American school of Archæology at Athens, nestling under the shadow of Mt. Lykabettos, has done work which the learned world appreciates, and though not so long established as the French school, has not been excelled by that, or by the German and English schools, in the value of its researches at Argos, Eretria, Assos, and other points within and outside of Hellas. There should be a more generous support at home, of a school representing so many of our best educational institutions. When one becomes better acquainted with this school, and sees the genuine classic enthusiasm among its students, it makes him wish to be young, to take pickaxe and spade, and, with Pausanias in his pocket, to go a-digging. Perhaps he might solve some important historic or architectural problem, or strike upon some sculpture that would hold the world ravished by its beauty.

The Parthenon is an example of pure Doric. Its beauty, notwithstanding the variety of the decorative sculpture that once enriched its walls, is mainly in its constructive lines. It is perfect in the harmony of its proportions. Its unbased columns rise directly from the stylobate, yet with a swell slightly diminishing at the top where they meet their capitals, and with sharp flutings producing in the rich sunlight lovely light and shadow, modifying the bold simplicity of the round. The edifice has an air of eternal repose, or duration, that its ruined state does not disturb; for if its lines were extended upward from the four corners of the sides of the parallelogram far enough, they would meet at a point above, the structure, in fact, being a truncated pyramid, the mathematical form of greatest strength. This strength is combined with grace. These delicately curved lines of the foundation, aesthetically conceived, and imperceptible without closest examination, spring from a rhythmical instead of a straight line, which was discovered through incredibly delicate measurements by the English architect Penrose; and this, together with the slightly increased entasis of the corner pillars, to correct the diminished look from their standing against the sky as background, and subtle touches guided by no rule but by the spiritual eye, gives this building an organic unity, as if it were filled with a glorious harmony, so that even in its broken state the eye reconstructs the perfect edifice. It lives in idea more than in reality. It is a form of mind more than of matter. And yet to think that but two centuries ago, this temple was in as perfectly complete a condition as the Theseion, the main columns standing, the sculptures of the pediments in place, the metopes and architecture preserved, and only some little injury done to the pronaos and its pillars from turning it into a Christian church!

In the year 1687 came the bomb from the batteries of Morosini alighting in a gunpowder magazine of the Turks within the temple, and the heart of it was blown out, the eastern end nearly overthrown, the middle of it made a mass of ruins.

Of the sculptures that softened its Doric sternness and wrought it into the most elegant as well as majestic of buildings, the central group on the west front was Poseidon with his chariot drawn by hippocampi, a representation of the salt-spring that rose from the stroke of his trident, the ocean and accessory figures, Athene with her olive tree as she contested with Poseidon for the soil of Attica; and these

HEAD OF BEARDED YOUNG MAN

figures perished and "went up in dust," it was said, when they fell from the clumsy hands of Venetian sailors who were lowering them. What sculptures still exist from other parts of the building constitute the Elgin marbles in the British Museum, where they may be studied by scholars though they no longer shine in their proper place, under the clear sky of Greece, and are but white ghosts of the past seen in the fogs of London.

The length of this temple (not a large one) is two hundred and thirty-eight feet, the breadth one hundred and one, and the height of the top of the pediments sixty-six feet; and it consists, or rather consisted, of a simple cell surrounded by eight columns on either front and seventeen on either side, counting the corner columns twice. It was engirdled by forty-six columns, making the glorious peristyle of the tetragon under whose shadow walked Perikles, Iktinos and the great men of that epoch of the revival of Greek art, which splendid period lasted but a short fifty years!

Perikles, a man of both culture and energy, is a fit example to prove that these qualities are not incompatible with each other, and that culture enhances power, for if ever there was a man of cultivated taste it was Perikles, and if ever there was a man of affairs, it was Perikles. He was the soul of that magnificent renascence of Hellenic intellect after the upheaval of the Persian wars, in which those perfect works of art, literature and philosphy were created.

It was at the time of the Peace Congress of 447 B. C., convoked by Perikles after the death of Kimon, that the Parthenon was commenced, or rather planned. All the Hellenes everywhere were asked to form a national congress at Athens to deliberate con-

cerning the shrines cast down by the barbarians, and
concerning other matters pertaining to the welfare of
Greece.   This was a time when by the skillful states-
manship of Perikles, there was secured the hegemony
of Greece to Athens, and the application of the common treasures of Delos to the building of temples on
the Acropolis.   "In 445 B. C." says Furtwaengler,
"the Parthenon was in full swing."   This statement
may be true, but the beginnings of the work met
with very serious obstacles, and especially with determined opposition from the party of Thucydides,
yet in spite of difficulties, this temple and that of
Eleusis, Pan-Hellenic works, were pushed forward by
Perikles and the Athenians, under the plausible, perhaps real, motive, of common religious zeal.   In a
wonderfully short time the edifice was reared to the
virgin divinity, as by an impulse of Athenian will
and genius.   If it be an axiom of architecture that a
building should express the purpose for which it was
designed, no building is truer to this than the Parthenon.   It is not a palace, nor a civic structure, nor
a church, like a Christian or Mohammedan church,
fitted for holding audiences for worship and instruction, but it is a shrine for the agalma of a Greek god.
Athene moved into it, so to speak, from her old temple.   This was the new home of the virgin goddess,
and when it was new, how resplendent it must have
been ! The ivory and gold statue of the " Parthenos,"
the virgin, with a Nike in her hand, was wrought by
Pheidias to occupy the front middle space of the cella.
The house was hers.   She here was enthroned.   She
was the guardian power of Athens.   She comprehended the spirit of the Athenian state, its wisdom,
wit, culture, ruling force.   All sculpture on pediment
and frieze had relation to the virgin power, as did the

splendid ceremonials connected with her worship. The delivery of the peplos, embroidered by free Athenian maidens for her statue, the Panathenaic procession to her shrine, her nativity, her contest with Poseidon, her triumph, were carved on the walls. Her treasures and furniture were stored in the opisthodomos. Other gods, such as Zeus, Demeter, Hermes, Apollo, Aphrodite, Ares, grouped in sculptures, were her guests, symbolizing the union of immortals to guard the Athenian state. The temple and its architecture expressed this unity, the perfection of Athenian art, government, intelligence and power. It strikes one as a perfect whole, to which nothing could be added. I had carried away with me on my first visit a strong impression of the symmetry and beauty of the Parthenon, but on the second visit I received an impression of its power. The columns are grand as well as beautiful. It is a massive structure especially as seen from the Propylæa, standing full against the sky. It has the richness of coloring of the old painter, time. Pentelic marble takes on many shades and tints. The building is white at a distance in the morning, whiter by moonlight, but at sunset it is crimson, and near by you see its weather-stains of orange and brownish purple making up for the loss of original color which it undoubtedly had ; but under a frowning sky it is black and menacing. Athene shakes her mighty war-spear. When you catch sight of the ethereal blue of the sky of Hellas, as seen between the mass of the building and a corner column that juts out boldly, you perceive the effect the architect wished to produce in perching the temple on this height, and sending its white, pillared wedge into the clear sky up above every other object ; and the hill itself of the Acropolis is full of such rarely colored pictures.

Seated one evening a little further down on the northwestern edge of the Acropolis wall, I watched the light of sunset passing over Mt. Pentelikon and Mt. Parnes, on whose bare summits lingered a broad yellow tinge, while a warmer rose-red glow spread itself over the sea and the straits of Salamis and Ægina ; and on the northwest lay the bay of Eleusis, and the cliffs of Megara even to the rock of Acrocorinth, with the loftier mountains piled up misty in the distance beyond, that belong to the Helicon and Parnassian range, while directly beneath was Athens, the fair city, stretching out into the level plain of Attica.

Before speaking of the present state of the Parthenon, I would say a word of a discovery that exemplifies Dr. Doerpfeld's theory in respect to the history of this temple, one of the most interesting discoveries of modern archæology, viz : the finding of the foundations of the " old temple " of Athene destroyed by the Persians.

Doerpfeld maintains that the " Parthenon " is not the only temple, but that there have been four temples of Athene on the Acropolis, viz : the temple of Athene which was the first smaller Erectheion ; the " old temple " of Athene which was destroyed by the Persians ; the first Parthenon of Kimon ; and the Parthenon of Perikles that now exists. The Erectheion is supposed to occupy the site of a more ancient Erectheion. The " old temple " of Athene destroyed by the Persians was a Hecatompedon with double " cells " dedicated to Athene and Erectheus, whose foundations overlapped the present Erectheion at one corner ; uncouth archaic capitals of this rugged temple have been dug out of the Acropolis walls, and have still some coloring. This probably was the εκατομπεδος

of the Iliad, a name derived from this building when
it was a hundred feet long, but was applied afterwards to the longer Periklean Parthenon in token of
its size, proportions and beauty.   This ''old temple ''
existed until 480, at the end of the Persian war.   All
these were temples of Athene, or of Athens and
Erectheus.

The first Parthenon, called by that name, was built
in the time of Themistokles and Kimon, on the site
of the present Parthenon (Doerpfeld has demonstrated
this) after the demolition of the "old temple," and
its foundations lie under the Periklean building,
having almost the same dimensions with the present
Parthenon.   Doerpfeld supposes that it had the same
number of columns on the short sides, and two more
on the long sides.   It was, in fact, a longer building,
but its cella was narrower.   It was of Poros stone
instead of marble, and was never finished in marble,
on account of the political downfall of Themistokles.

We see thus that the Parthenon, old as it is, was
not the first temple of Athene on the Acropolis ; but
that it was the consummation, the perfection, of four
temples, a flower from an old stem but surpassing all
that went before.

The east front was the real entrance, facing which
sat the goddess in the interior, awaiting the salutation of worshipers, and she was here under the softly
shaded light, a snowy-skinned, peaceful and beneficent goddess, the mild patroness of the olive-tree,
agriculture, government, letters and art.

The carvings on the east were symbols of the
beginning of Athenian life, and of the birth of
Athene, with her image as central figure ; and next
to her sat Zeus, from whose head—wisdom from
power—at the blow of Hæphaistos, she sprang ; while

Nike, or Iris, flew to spread the glad news to immortals and men.

The three "Fates," the mighty Sisters, half rising to receive the message, are figures of a large heroic life, and of the gigantic mould of elder time, yet are noble and beautiful figures, headless and armless though now they be. The hundred-pleated raiments covering but not concealing these Titanic forms, are as delicate, as if the linen had been woven on royal looms for some Egyptian queen.

Fragments of these Pheidian carvings, with the exception of the head of Iris, are in the British Museum, and the only sculptures clinging to the eastern pediment are the heads of two horses of the chariot of Helios, and a head of the horse of the chariot of Selene, sinking into the sea at the approach of day. The head of the horse of the moon's chariot, at the northern extremity of the pediment, lingers there like the ghost of a horse struggling for life, but going down in the waves with the heroic past of Hellas.

The Panathenaic procession, with the ship bearing the peplos, approached the east front to enter the temple, and the sacrifices must have taken place upon altars on the outside ; probably only priests and magistrates entered the temple.

To discuss the sculptures that ornamented and vivified the Parthenon, is not my object, since most of these are now on foreign and not on Greek soil ; but these brought Ionic beauty to the Doric temple, and softened its stern character with touches lovely and enchanting.

The sculptures may be looked upon as forming a threefold cycle : 1. Those of the two ends that illustrated Olympian scenes and personages, the divine history, the birth and triumphs of Athene.   2. Those of the metopes that ran around the architrave, the contests of Athenian civilization against barbarism. 3. Those that surrounded the inner frieze of the cella that brought to mind the real cult of the Athenian people.   On the east pediment, as example of the first Olympian sculpture, there is the masterpiece of Pheidias called by the different names of Theseus, Herakles, Olympos, which is now in the British museum—a young immortal reclining on a lion's skin, characterized by the large, square, heroic style, the perfection of nature with something beyond nature, or the conception of a god resting on the summit of Olympos. There is careless ease in the attitude that is not commonplace but that of power.   There is no show of power as in Michael Angelo's convulsed giants, but the simple repose of it.   The Parthenon is the monument of Pheidias.   Pheidias was sculptor of gods, as Praxiteles was sculptor of men beautiful as gods. There is ideal greatness in one, and human loveliness in the other ; but Pheidias stands at the head.   The periods of Greek sculpture may be classed into five : the Archaic, the Perfected or Naturalistic and Pheidian, the Beautiful or Praxitelian, the Decadent or Alexandrine, and the Græco-Roman ; but all look on or back to Pheidias.   His was the mind that organized a whole system, a cycle of sculpture.   There is proof from classic authors, that Pheidias had the entire superintendence of these art-works, and some of the sculptures were, without doubt, by his hand, since there is a marked difference in the execution of them.

The sculptures of Pheidias were not wholly, but mainly, architectonic, combined with architecture as an organic part of it, and did not stand isolated with-

out reference to the plan and significance of the whole;
yet in all he did, he was first to draw freely from
nature, to grasp the deep principles of beauty in
nature, to seek perfection. He took nature first from
the Greek forms seen in the palæstra, but combined
with these an act of his own thought, and he thus
created the ideal, the more complete conception of
beauty, differing from the sensuous and characٔer-
ized by an immortal grace; so that Plutarch said :
" (Perik., 5:13) μορφή δ'ἀμμητα ἔργα καί χαρῖτι—his works
had a form of inimitable grace and seem endowed
with perpetual freshness which preserves them untouched by time." To illustrate this "inimitable
grace," there was, especially, the Lemnian Athene,
famous in antiquity, and which the critical Lucian
thought to be the best worth seeing of Pheidias's
works. We are not sure that this now exists in
original or copy; but it once stood on the Acropolis
near by the Propylæa. There are two fine statues of
Athene at Dresden, a head of Athene at Bologna
which is very beautiful, and another which is called
the "Hope Athene," in which critics see the possibility of finding the Lemnian type. The "Hope
Athene" at Deep Dene, Surrey, England, is thought
by Furtwaengler to be purely Pheidian, as it is one
of peculiar beauty. The forehead slightly raised in
the middle is delicately modelled, and the eyebrows
are curved as in the Lemnian. The thin eyelids, the
narrow finely cut nose forming an angle with the
forehead, the beauty of the mouth and the exquisite
proportions of the oval face, bear the Pheidian type,
which is refined, a shade hard and loftily spiritual as
in the Amazon, and, above all, in the Aphrodite
Urania. But Pheidias's master-touch is found everywhere in the Elgin marbles; and if an art-student

could have the Elgin marbles before him, and could sit for hours and days, pencil in hand, to copy them faithfully, to come at their spirit and life, to enter into the feeling of the artist, to compare them with the sculpture that was before and after them, to compare them with contemporary works of literature, to discover their faults as well as beauties, their failure to reach the perfect as well as their success, and to let them speak with full tone to him as expressions of nature and mind, he would come in touch with the creations of that same Greek mind in literature as well as art; and it would be seen what a deep influence these works would have on his own nature and culture.

The second class of Pheidian sculptures, those of the metopes, were next in size and importance to the carvings on the pediments. The metope was originally but a hollow space; it was then a block of stone to fill the space, and was of no use constructively and might have remained a blank, had not Greek genius made use of it for decoration, for carvings that interrupted at intervals the plainness of horizontal lines and surfaces. The Parthenon metopes contained, for the most part, sculptures of contests of Greeks and centaurs, struggles of civilization with brute forces, and this had a ready interpretation to the Greek in his own history. There were contests of Greeks with Amazons. The "Amazon," mythic fighter of a legendary world, may have had a shrewd onlook to the "new woman," who was to give man a hard tussle; or to the rivalry of the sexes for power in intellectual things resolving itself into the great truth that genius has no sex, or the still profounder truth of Christianity, that the soul has no sex. These sculptures were cut in high relief, catching the light and shade, and producing lovely effects.

Then there were the relief-sculptures, smaller than life-size, that ran around the frieze of the inner cella, and, to my mind, they were the noblest of all. They are supposed to be representations of the Panathenaic procession that every four years bore the peplos of Athene to the Parthenon, culminating on the east side, where the gods were gathered, as in the fine relief-group of Zeus, Demeter and Aphrodite.

The processions of horsemen are peculiarly life-full and spirited. There is, however, no exaggeration, but the moderation of truth and nature. It is perfect beauty, and, at the same time, perfect reality. There is truth which bespeaks highest genius, wondrous fire in the horses and calm grace in the riders, "witching the world with noble horsemanship." In the sacrificial part of the procession, the form of a young man leading a restive heifer for sacrifice, exhibits a restraint without anger, and a repose in action. These figures are taken from nature, and that was the secret of the freshness of Greek sculpture. It glistened with the morning dew of perpetual youth. "This frieze exhibits the festival of Panatheneia; but not properly the feast and procession, nor as some think the preparation for it, but the artist freely chose them with an eye to artistic effect. They are episodes of the reality; some pictures from the procession, others genre-pieces from the preparations; in part quite common subjects, men such as he saw and lived with, noble horses with their youthful riders, beasts for the sacrifice, stubborn bulls and patient rams." In a word, I believe that the sculptures of the frieze manifest to us the form and spirit of the Athenian democracy—old age, young manhood, maidenhood, childhood, the tillers of the soil, artificers, warriors, scholars, magisitrates, priests, all ranks and conditions of the people who climbed the hill of the Acropolis, bringing their glad offerings. Greek art struck into Greek humaniłty. The artist was the interpreter of life, Hellenic liːfe, proud, gay and poetic ; and all true art, from the ttime of Niccola Pisano to the present, springs from this Pheidian conception, drawn freshly from nature, thıought and love.

CHAPTER IX.

THE ACROPOLIS MUSEUM.

The Erectheion, if not the greatest work, is a veritable gem of the Acropolis. It once consisted of three parts separated by cross-walls, viz: a large portico or cella of Athene-Polias to the east, and to the west two shrines, one of Kekrops and another of Poseidon-Erectheus, Athene thus sharing her sanctuary with the other Chthonian gods, especially the mystic founder-hero Erectheus; and the building also covered several objects such as the sacred olive-tree and the salt spring, that were connected with the cult of Athene.

The Erectheion is a decidedly irregular, and, as it were, not Greek building, differing from other temples, and adapted by Greek genius to its diverse purposes. It was, originally, not a large but an elegant structure, the vestibules on the east, north and south, each beautiful in itself, and the main oblong of sixty-five feet raised on a basement of three steps ten feet high. The east portico is a prostyle with six Ionic columns, one other having been carried off by that raider of temples, Lord Elgin. Athens received a large infusion of Ionic blood, which is shown in the luxurious and feminine grace of this Ionic temple, that stands side by side with the masculine Doric of the other structures. Here is shown the highest richness of the Ionic capital. The Erectheion capital, has a neck of delicately beaded mouldings with a frieze of palmettes, above which the egg-and-tongue moulding supports the cushion, decorated with exquisite flutings and beadings, and the spiral of the volutes is a double spiral, ornamented once with enamel and gems, splendid examples of this ornate style. The perfectly proportioned doorway of the north portico, well preserved, with its egg and honeysuckle mouldings, has been copied more times, perhaps, than any other doorway. In walking about the enclosure of the Erectheion, one treads on rich fragments of Pentelic marble cut with intricate traceries running into each other in endless convolutions, and on fallen coffers with their corbels touched with gold. Parts of pillars and walls have lately been dug up virgin white as if just quarried. Around the Erectheion is the richest area of the Acropolis in this wealth of fragmentary ruins and ornamental carvings, heaped in careless confusion; and here and there are the diggings of 1884 and '90 which revealed foundation-walls of the "old temple," or Hekatompedon, that I spoke of, which encroached on the stylobate of the Erectheion.

The famous portico of Caryatids, on the south side, jutting out from the main edifice, is a unique inspiration, where six stone maidens instead of stone piers hold up a roof, and while exhibiting great beauty of artistic skill, was too unnatural, even painful, an idea, to be repeated. The figures are colossal, and it was called anciently simply " portico of the maidens," and handsome powerful maidens they are, with harmonious costumes and basket-like carvings on their heads. The second figure from the west is of terracotta, in imitation of the one carried off by Lord Elgin. There is a rather heavy architrave resting upon them, with a rectangular moulding decorated with dentils.

8

There has been controversy among archæologists in regard to the date of the Erectheion, but the view of Michælis prevails, that it belongs to the time of Nikias, or the period after the peace of Nikias, since there could not have been the thought of erecting temples during the previous war with Sparta. The "old temple" of Athene was demolished to make way for the new Erectheion, probably in the year 409 or 408 B.C. In 413 the porch of the Caryatids was well advanced.

Dr. Doerpfeld says that when the new glittering Parthenon arose in all its splendor, the old poros temples looked shabby, so that it was necessary to rear a new Erectheion to Athene-Polias, and call one the Parthenon and the other the Erectheion; but Mrs. Jane Harrison suggests that the Erectheion was built for a kind of depository, or house, of the statues and symbols of the old cults. This seems to me contrary to the fashion of the Greeks, who worshiped by and through these statues the powers they represented, and they had not learned the modern custom of making museums of art. But the explanation of the design of this elaborate edifice is obscure though so much has been written about it, yet the lines of the Odyssey would seem to be enough to prove its original complex occupancy: "Therewith grey-eyed Athene departed over the unharvested seas, and left pleasant Scheria, and came to Marathon, and widewayed Athens, and entered the good-house of Erectheus" (πυκινὸς δρόμος).

Thus Pelasgians, Persians, Romans, Goths, Byzantines, Slavs, Venetians, Turks, Franks and moderns swept over this stately rock in successive conquests, and, as one writer says, "not until the year 1833, when the new movement was established, did there come an end to the destruction of antiquities on the Acropolis ''; and this was the time when modern excavations, under the leadership of the architect Klenze, were begun, which were followed up by the French school at Athens, the Greek archæological Society, and the German, British and American Schools of archæology.

A step down from the east end of the Parthenon and quite near the outer wall of the rock, stands the low, small, inconspicuous stone museum of the Acropolis. I do not think it time lost to mention, not too minutely, some of its treasures, as well as those of the National Museum, which are invaluable in the history of art. This museum contains exclusively antiquities discovered on the Acropolis. It has a vestibule and ten rooms, exhibiting carvings, bronzes and statues, arranged chronologically. In the vestibule there is a lovely piece of architrave moulding from the Erectheion, the egg-and-tongue moulding above and the honeysuckle pattern below, proving that the Greeks drew out from nature these architectural conventions, and were satisfied with a few designs of plants and wild flowers, and having perfected these they did not change them for artificial fashions, nor seek novelties, but were content with the simple beauty of a few of nature's forms.

There is also in this vestibule an antique marble pedestal, sculptured with an exceedingly interesting, and, as far as I know, unique, representation of the virile Pyrrhic dance; also a relief-sculpture of a woman entering a chariot, showing much spirit of execution for such an antique work. There is, too, a relievo representing the civic relations of Athens and Samos, with two figures, of Athene and Hera,

symbolizing these cities, and a long inscription.
This is archaic but of considerable freedom of style.
The warlike figure and equipment of Athene bring
to mind lines of the Odyssey : " She bound beneath
her feet her lovely golden sandals, that wax not old,
and bear her alike over the wet sea and over the limit-
less land, swift as the breath of the wind.   And she
seized her powerful spear, shod with sharp bronze,
weighty, huge and strong, wherewith she quells the
ranks of heroes with whomsoever she is wroth, the
daughter of the mighty sire."

   In one corner of the vestibule is a gigantic stone
owl, immemorial emblem of Athens, a grey battered
bird of wisdom—wisdom and silence.   These first
rooms of the Museum are filled entirely with archaic
art, and in the "Room of the Bull," to the left, is a
group of two lions seizing a bull, and a group of
Herakles fighting with the Lernæan Hydra.   This
sculpture and the one of Herakles subduing the
Triton, show traces of green, yellow, and red color.
The scales of the snake are green.   These were from
pediments of the Herakleion which stood on the
Acropolis.   The hero, though grotesque, has a good
grip and is choking the scaly monster.   It was found
in 1882 to the southeast of the Parthenon.   Then
comes the Room of the " Triple-bodied Monster," or
Typhon, overcome by Zeus, with three human heads
and bodies.   In the fourth Room of Marbles and
Vases is the famous statue of the "calf-bearer"
(αἴθουσα μοσχωφὸρου) on a vase of poros stone, representing a youth carrying a calf to the altar on his
shoulders, interesting as primitive Greek type of
statues and paintings of Orpheus, in early Christian
art, only substituting a sheep, or lamb, for a calf.
An antique enthroned Athene with ægis, headless,

and there is no-knowing how old, is in this room, and the sculpture of an archaic priestess.

In the next long room comes that remarkable series of statues which were found ten years ago in the diggings of the Kimonian wall, piled in with other fragments of statues, drums of pillars and capitals, pedestals, architraves, or whatever came to hand at that time of stress, and these sculptures form the most curious and debatable objects of the museum. These " *Tanten*," as the Germans call them, are many in number, and of a certain uniformity. They are thought by some to be pre-Persian statues of Athene, by others to be priestesses of the goddess Athene who was enthroned in the "old temple"; but the problem is not solved, though terra-cotta statuettes of Athene more recently found and resembling these, would almost seem to decide the question in favor of the latter theory. They are interesting as a study of costume, and, in some respects, for their individual character and expression, for, notwithstanding their archaic inaneness there is variety in them ; and from abundant traces of color, they reveal the fact that the old Greeks colored their statues. They are in a good state of preservation, marking the period of Peisistratos as one of some artistic development.

While I was looking at these one day, Dr. Paul Wolters, a distinguished professor of the German School of Archæology at Athens, was giving a peripatetic lecture to a class of thirty or forty students, composed of many nationalities and of both sexes, showing how these Hellenic works draw students of all nations to them, as to a head-spring of Art.

In the Athene statues mentioned, the manner of dressing the hair in tresses falling over the back and breast, and the straight folds of the woolen garment, and other peculiarities, are noticeable, as they show the Greek style of costume before the Persian war, and also the multitude and splendor of the sculptures, antique as they were, that adorned the Acropolis at that time.   It was even then a centre of art.

In speaking more particularly of these sculptures, I take some hints from the official catalogue.   These figures are, for the most part, clad each in a chiton, and holding the border of a himation in the left hand. The hair is divided in the middle on the forehead, and, descending in curled locks, is bound in some cases over the head by a ribbon, or ornamental diadem.   The right hand is in advance of the body, and the figure holds sometimes an apple or a pome-granate.   The head is surmounted by a bronze nail, which perhaps served to support a kind of screen to protect the colors.   The physical type is like that of the figures found at Delos, that we shall see in the National Museum, but they are more graceful, and contain germs of a natural style to be developed. The polychromatic colors employed are green (the best preserved), red, blue, yellow and grey ; and on the borders of the chitons and himations, bands of meander pattern are painted, green and red, with palmettes and rosettes.   The hair has sometimes a red tinge, or yellow, distinctly seen.   The eyes were also painted, and, in some instances, are made of a crystalline metal.

One observes differences in the disposition of the robes, the forms, the expressions of face, which speak different periods of style, and of various places, such as Athens, Delos, Eleusis, and, also, perhaps, of attempts at actual portraits; yet only the caprice of the artist may, possibly, be seen in them, and they may refer to but one subject, the goddess Athene-Polias.

The statues are carved of Parian marble, and composed of many pieces for convenience of transporta-
tion, and are joined together by a curious method, not
of plugs or bolts, but of cement. They were found,
as I have said, heaped in pell-mell with broken columns, capitals, inscriptions, heads and feet of statues,
piled one on another, as used by order of Themistokles to make the new wall. They recall that extraordinary time, when the Persians, having burned the
temple, cast down the statues from their pedestals,
broke off their hands and heads, and then retreated,
like lions surprised in rending their prey ; and the
Athenians returning after the victory of Salamis,
hastily put the citadel in a state of defence, with
everything they could lay their hands on, with statues
that may have been objects of adoration but were
rendered valueless from desecration and mutilation.
Names of some of the artists of these statues are
found in inscriptions on them, but only one of them,
Antenor, is a name of after note.

These statues fill a void in the history of Greek
sculpture, which, before they were discovered, was a
blank, viz : the 6th century B. C., and though they
are not, all of them, in an artistic point of view, of
uniform merit, two or three exhibit progress in the
plastic art. They all, however, belong to the same
type or family. Statue 671 is a dignified figure, the
hair painted yellow, and the costume with woolen
garment beneath, is really not ungraceful. The
features are refined and piquant, and it is one of the
most pleasing of the series. Statue 672 has coarser
features, but the head-dress is the same as that of the
last named. No. 675 is a profile view, in which the
manner of head ornamentation is better seen and with
much color. No. 677 is a bust with hand holding an

apple, the hand well carved. It is probably not a work of Attic art, but came from another region. They are plump, well-appointed dames, accustomed to be idolized themselves, and of not extremely youthful age. No. 679 is quite archaic, in the style of the old Delos statues, but the face is rather good in spite of the idiotic smile. The patterns of the dress are variously colored. No. 680 has a costume with more elaborate tinted patterns, and the hair somewhat different in style from the rest. The character of the face, too, differs essentially from what has gone before. One of these statues (as the inscription on its base states) was carved by Antenor, which was the name of the artist who was ordered to make the commemorative sculpture-group of Harmodius and Aristogeiton, and this would seem to fix the period. The historic group of the tyrannicide was carried off in 480 B. C. to Persia by Xerxes, and was restored to Athens either by Alexander or Antiochus. A supposed copy belonging to a much later epoch, made by the sculptors Nesiotes and Critios, and without archaisms, is now in Naples.

The figure 682, holding an apple or pomegranate, is dwarfed and grotesque ; but No. 684 is a head of fineness and nobility, and one would hope that it was a portrait. It showed considerable development of artistic skill, and the costume resembles a soft colored Indian shawl. In the oval face and the quiet dignity of expression, who could not recognize a refined and noble woman? The statue No. 686 is much less interesting than the last, but of a similar type. These figures recall the luxurious Ionian element in Attic art, reminding also of the Neo-Ionian vase-paintings, in which the elaborateness of the Asiatic costume was revived, perhaps in the time of Perikles and Aspasia,

or later ; and we see an example of this in a picture
of Medea, with a most rich robing, on a vase-painting.

In the room of the Ephebos is the head of a young
man discovered in 1887 on the site of the museum,
and which is, as Dr. Wolters said in passing,
"*prachtvoll !*" In the treatment of the hair it resembles the Apollo from the temple of Zeus at Olympia.
Another head of a young man, in a more advanced
style of sculpture, though injured, shows manly
beauty. There is an interesting relief representing
Athene leaning on a spear and contemplating with
pensive expression a funereal stele, probably that of a
hero fallen in battle, and belongs to the middle of the
5th century B. C. It was found to the south of the
Parthenon in 1889. Its posture is natural, with right
hand resting on the hip. This sculpture is thought
to have furnished, in dress at least, a model for the
bronze statue of the Lemnian Athene, of which I
have spoken. The point of resemblance is in the
costume, which is the Doric peplos made of a simple
piece of woolen stuff fastened upon the shoulders
and falling over the neck, so that the upper portion of
the body is covered with a double piece of drapery.
On the right side it is open, but it is confined by the
girdle which is bound over the whole, so as to com-
press the diplöis. This Dorian costume was adopted
also in Attica and in Attic art, just after the Persian
wars, the dress before this, as we have seen in the
statues of the priestesses, having been the Ionian
chiton and himation. This Peloponnesian type
formed a precedent for Phidias, though in his Lem-
nia, and other sculptures, there was, of course, infinitely more naturalness and grace.

In the two rooms of the "Sculptures of the Parthenon," or those illustrating its history, are sculp-

tured metopes, mostly plaster copies ; but there are
originals, as, for example, the group of a centaur
carrying off a woman, and a marvelously interesting
fragment of the head of Iris, belonging to the great
group of gods that stood on the east front, which is
now in the British Museum.   This head of the messenger who announced the birth of Athene, alone of
all the groups, remains on the Greek soil, where, one
cannot help but thinking, all these sculptures, illustrating not only the art, but the religion and thought
of Greece, ought now to be.

There is also in this room a copy of the red chalk
drawings of Carrey made in 1674.   In room No. IX,
next to the last, are the unsurpassably lovely sculp-
ture-reliefs of the temple of Nike Apteros, and some
fragments of the frieze of the Erectheion.   The sculpture-piece from the balustrade of the Nike Apteros,
of Victory fastening her sandal, is justly renowned
for the inimitable lightness in the folds of the drapery.   The cutting is as clear and round as when first
made.   The grace, nature, exquisite elegance and
living bloom of this figure, have hardly a parallel in
art.

The group of the two Nikes conducting a bull to
sacrifice, and of the same perfect type, is also from
the balustrade of the temple.

CHAPTER X.

THE NATIONAL MUSEUM AT ATHENS.

That long one-storied building of the National Museum, where I spent days of study and felt that I never could exhaust its riches, is situated in a modern part of the city, on the street Patissia. This edifice was begun as far back as 1866, though in 1829, before the establishment of the Greek monarchy, and under the government of Capodistria, a museum of antiquities was formed at Ægina, and in 1834, under the reign of Otho, the greatest part of the marbles were transported to Athens and placed in the Theseion, others being piled about the Stoa of Hadrian, the Temple of the Winds, and on the Acropolis. In the course of years the National Archæological Society began to gather together all collections in a building called Βαρβάκειον, and then in the *Ecole des Beaux Arts* (πολυτεχνεῖον) in the street Patissia, near the present building. The National Museum (*Musée Nationale*, or *Musée Centrale*) was inaugurated in 1874, but at that epoch only one wing of the edifice, at the west, was constructed, and it was finished in 1889 at the state's cost. It was intended to receive all antiquities found in the kingdom outside of the Acropolis; the antiquities found on the Acropolis being placed in the Acropolis Museum, an annex to the National

The National Museum is the glory not only of Athens but of Greece. The sculptures, vases, bronzes and other objects have been arranged in historic sequence, under

the supervision of M. Kabbadias, who, as has been
said, is at the head of archæologic activity in Greece,
and of whose official catalogue I have made some use.
The plan of the museum is simple and superior to that
of any European collection. It is an education to
walk through its halls, and the antiquities are unsur-
passed in interest and value. There is nothing inferior
or commonplace. You enter the vestibule, and to
your right are a series of rooms, just opened, forming
the antiquarium for the reception of bronzes, terra-
cottas and vases. Exactly opposite the entrance is
the Hall of the Mycenæan Antiquities, wonderful and
unique. To the left of the vestibule are a series of
Halls of Greek sculpture: (1.) Room of Archaic
sculpture. (2.) Room of the Athene. (3.) Room of
Themis. (4.) Room of Poseidon. (5.) Room of the
Kosmetæ. (6.) Large Hall of the Sepulchre Reliefs.
(7.) Room of the Sepulchre Vases. (8.) Room of the
Votive Reliefs. (9.) Room of Miscellaneous objects.

There is also an Egyptian Hall, corresponding to
the Mycenæan, and small side-rooms of Byzantine and
Latin Art. This is a general description, and let us
look at it more in detail, although I can give but a
glance at the endless wealth of this collection of Greek
art on Greek soil.

The Mycenæan Room I shall leave until I come to
speak more particularly of Mycenæan art. Suffice it
to say that it is a hall of extraordinary richness,
colored dull red and yellow, decorated on wall, ceiling
and pavement, with pure Mycenæan patterns; and its
cases and shelves gleam with the golden treasures
of prehistoric art dug up by Schliemann at the citadel
of Mycenæ in 1876. There is not another such golden
room in the world—gold was the standard of those
old inhabitants of Hellas. The Sculpture-Rooms run

through all periods of Greek sculpture but are peculiarly rich in the early periods.

Greek art may be roughly divided into 1: the ante-Hellenic or prehistoric art, 2: Greek art, properly so called, and 3: Græco-Roman art. Of these the museum affords examples, but especially of the prehistoric epoch from the 1st Olympiad to the classic epoch, or from 776 to 175 B. C. In the first archaic room is the rudely carved Artemis, found at Delos by the French school, resembling one of those primitive ξόανα to which the Greeks attributed supernatural origin, and dating probably from the 7th century B. C., or at the beginning of anything like sculpture. It was dedicated to the goddess by Nikandra of Naxos. A Nike also from Delos is important in the history of art, as it seems to have been made by Archermos of Chios, one of the first artists ever known to have wrought in marble; it had wings originally, and though the wings are gone there is a vigorous upward movement in the legs; but this grotesque figure struggling to mount was the germ of the splendid Victory of Samothrake.

The celebrated stele called "Aristion" was made, as the inscription states, by Aristocles, and is a bas-relief portrait of a warrior in hoplites armor, less than life-size and with decided remains of color, sometimes called "The Warrior of Marathon," though probably it antedated the battle of Marathon. It is skillfully carved for the 6th century B. C. period, and the details of armor are distinctly given. The simper is less pronounced and the character of the face firmer in the original, than in copies.

The archaic head of a youthful athlete was found in the ruins of a wall at Athens near the Dipylon. It is the figure of a beardless youth who holds a large discus which makes a background for the head, a sign of incipient artistic invention. His head-dress is that of the old elaborate Attic style, but the exaggerated features and smirking face show that Hellenic sculpture had not dawned ; yet it is wonderful to see these fragments of statues renowned in early art, collected here together where they naturally should be, and leading the army of sculpture like battered warriors. In the Athene room, so called, is the Lenormant statuette of Athene, one and a half feet high, which was discovered at Athens, and which is considered to be in some respects (base, shield, etc.) a more faithful though ruder copy than the Varvakeion statue, of the chryselephantine Athene of the Parthenon.

In the same room is the Varvakeion statue, found in 1879, which exhibits, doubtless, many of the details of the great statue of Pheidias, though it is an execrably rude copy only three and a half feet high. It resembles those plaster casts of statues such as an Italian vender would hawk about the streets.

There is also the grand relief found at Eleusis, one of the most classically interesting of all the older sculptures, representing Demeter and Persephone, and standing between them the boy Triptolemos, and it probably belongs to the 5th century B. C. As a specimen of religious art, it is compared to Italian religious works of Duccio and Giotto, before Raphael's time.

In the room of the Hermes, we come to the good period of Greek art, in the 5th and 4th centuries B.C. The Hermes, which gives the name to this hall, is a beautiful work found at Andros. Its manly, earnest expression, may, nay must, have been that of a portrait. The form and attitude resemble those of the Hermes of Praxiteles, and doubtless it belongs to the same school. It is, perhaps, the finest statue in the National Museum, and reminds one of the Hermes of the Vatican, with a variation in details, and one of these sculptures must have been a replica of the other, though I have not seen this noticed.

In the room of the Hermes, is the head of Hera, recently discovered in the Heræum at Argos by the American Archæological School, and there are also sculptures that were found in the sanctuary of Asklepios, at Epidauros, but I will defer a mention of these until we come to the description of those places.

There are three marble slabs of no great size but of very noble bas-relief sculpture, which were brought to light at Mantinea, in the excavations directed by the French School. These are of marvelous beauty and character. Pausanias recounts that in the temple of Latona and her children at Mantinea, he saw a group of Latona, Artemis and Apollo, carved by Praxiteles; the pedestal, he adds, was adorned with a bas-relief carving representing a muse, and Marsyas playing the flute. The sculptures are, doubtless, a portion of those referred to by Pausanias, as executed by Praxiteles, or by an artist of his school. This gives them an extraordinary interest. They delineate the musical contest between Apollo and Marsyas. Two of the slabs represent the Muses, who are the companions of Apollo, and who figure as arbiters in the strife. The Muses hold musical instruments, such as the lute and harp. They are majestic figures, grouped harmoniously though apart from each other, of noble bearing, and, to my mind, the finest relief-

sculptures that exist, as regards free, artistic touch
and simplicity of genius. The Muses are gracefully
but simply clad with chiton and outer garment, and
their faces serious, as if judging in a strife of life and
death. The extreme figures are more bent and pliant
than the middle one, breaking the monotony of the
grouping. Two of the Muses hold harps, the one on
the right a harp of antique shape ; and they have a
sympathetic relationship to the middle figure, and
seem to be turning to her. The lines, or plies, of
their garments, mark a difference in the material, and
the perfect pose of the forms is indicated by the
swaying lines of the costumes.

One of the slabs represents the contest itself, Apollo
seated, holding a harp, Marsyas playing on the
double lute, and between them a Phrygian slave who
holds a knife prepared to slay and flay the van-
quished. Marsyas, in his agitated and violent attitude, contrasts with the calm of Apollo, whose mind
seems to be filled with the vibrations of his own
harmonies. If such contests artistic, intellectual, or
athletic, nowadays, took place under the same conditions, they would die out, or their umpires would
have to be directed by infallible inspiration ; for we
ought not to think that the Muses, though companions of Apollo, were governed by favoritism.

I know of no better representation in ancient art
of the magnificent Greek harp (phorminx) than that
which is held by Apollo.

There is also in this Hall of Hermes a lovely
frieze, belonging to the 4th century B.C. representing Tritons, Nereids, and Eroses moving rhythmi-
cally on the waves, a delicate and delicious play of
Greek fancy, found near Thermopylæ, and, in joyous character so different from the stern genius of

the spot. There are other fragments of the best period in this hall,

"infinite riches in a narrow room."

We come to the Room of Themis, representing the Alexandrine and Græco-Roman periods. It is named after the colossal statue of Themis, which stands at the head of the small hall. This was found at Rhamnus in Attica, which brings to mind associations of Marathon, but the statue belongs to the commencement of the 3d century B.C.

There is no nobler representation of Justice, in art, and though, unfortunately, its hands, and what they contained of symbolic nature, are gone, the wide breast, firm pose of the figure, and strong yet placid expression of the face, are of exceeding power and beauty. Two floating graceful figures of "dancing girls," found at Athens, are in this room.

The statue of Poseidon, that gives its name to the Poseidon Room, was discovered in the island of Melos, and has a rough energy without much technical finish, the powerful arms and turn of the body being remarkable for a sculpture of the Alexandrine period. In the same room is the torso of a fighting warrior, recently found at Delos, in the diggings of the French School there, and is supposed to be a copy of a work by Lysippos, or it has the style of that artist who had so great a knowledge of anatomy, this fragment resembling the Borghese gladiator of the Louvre.

There is a fragmentary head of a young man, bearded, and peculiar in racial type, which is not Greek though found in the Dionysiac Theatre at Athens, the form and expression of whose face, the treatment of the hair and beard, and other points,

9

recalling the features of Christ. In it there is a mingling of strength, sweetness and melancholy, and there is a mystery about it not yet explained.

The head of a young man, probably a portrait, of marked individuality, and blunt natural honesty of expression, though not of classic features, is also noticeable ; but there are not, in this collection, such grand portrait sculptures, as are to be seen in the Louvre, or as the magnificent bust of Julius Cæsar, in the Naples Museum.

We have now come to the Halls which contain the funerary monuments, or steles, that form one of the most interesting parts of the Museum.

But let me speak of the "Street of Tombs" in Athens, outside of the " Dipylon," Dipylon meaning the ancient two-fold western gate of Athens, which was excavated, or what remains of it, in 1870. The road separates into two, one of which traversed the outer Ceramicus, and formed the Sacred Way, and the other led to the Academeia, and on either side of this were the graves of celebrated men, such men as Perikles, Chabrias and Phormion, some of them marked by simple pillars, others by large sarcophagi, others by steles with sculptures, as in the streets of tombs at Rome and Pompeii, outside the walls ; and here most of the tombstones in the Museum were found, but some of the monuments remain *in statu*, and the excavations are still going on to the north-west of the Acropolis on the road to the Piræus. You see there a conspicuous monument surmounted by a bull, and one by a Molossian hound, such as accompanied the Greeks at Marathon, and there is also a small stele representing a scene of leave-taking. At this locality stands, as found in 1871, the well-known monument of Dexileos in the best style of art.

It is a soldier's monument, or one of a youthful warrior who fell in the Peloponnesian War before Corinth. The bas-relief is a group of two persons, one of whom (Dexileos) is on horseback, who forces his antagonist to the ground; the composition is full of action, and it is remarkable that this delicately carved relief should have been so well preserved. In this Street of Tombs, is the sculptured tombstone of the wealthy dame Hegesa, daughter of Proxenos, representing a lady at her toilet attended by a female slave; indeed, all this ground in the direction of the railway station, is strewn with sarcophagi, cippi, broken vases and steles, among which is the beautiful monument with a sculpture-relief of a girl with a pitcher, "the pitcher broken at the well," and of another seated female figure.

I will mention some of the monuments, or the best of them, collected in the walls of the Museum itself. First comes the Hall of funerary vases. One of them, of superb size and form, stands in the centre of the room, belonging to the classic epoch of the 4th century B.C.; for whatever the Greeks touched they made elegant, be it a cup, a vase, a human figure, a column, a building, and it becomes pure form, the perfect form that delights, meagre as is the decoration, few and simple as the lines may be.

In looking at these funerary monuments, we are touched by their gentle religious sentiment, calm in the expression of sadness, and with no violence done to the emotions, following the Greek motto "nothing overmuch"; for the sorrow is shown in a natural way, as if there had been no sudden wrench, and as if the happy existence of to-day went on, only a thought ennobled by death's mystery. They are shrines of domestic affection, family groups where

the ordinary life proceeds, the different members of
the family grasping hands to bid adieu, as if they were
to meet again happily on the morrow.   Members of
the same family are represented in their common
avocations, the matron with her children and servants,
the old man absorbed in thoughts of the past, the
child with its bird, the musician playing on his lute,
the hunter at his rough sport, the warrior brandish-
ing his spear, the maiden looking over her jewel-box,
the young man and his dog, the mother bidding fare-
well to son and husband, the daughter to mother.
These are as pleasant as in life, probably portraits,
and it is hard to determine which figure in them represents the departed, there being a controversy among
critics on this point, but the weight of proof is in
favor of the sitting figure, as that of the deceased
person, thus occupying the place of honor and devotion.

One stele is inscribed with the name of "Miltiades,"
and whether it has a reference to the leader at
Marathon I do not know ; but another of these steles
contains a portrait of Plato as a young man, taking
leave of his father Epicharis, who has died.

One stele, from the name inscribed upon it is called
Polyxene, and portrays a sitting figure of the mother
who has died, embracing her little son who leans on
her knees, and holds an apple in his hand, and is full
of tender sorrow, not at all artificial, but real.   The
monument which, in my judgment, is the most beautiful in the collection, and was found also at Athens,
represents a family group, mother, son, daughter and
smaller children.   The life expressed in them is wonderful.   It is, here, the Athenian mother who has died,
the noble seated form apparently swayed by a powerful emotion of love, that makes her more alive, and

FUNERARY RELIEF OF ATHENIAN MOTHER

even more joyful, than her living children, whose faces denote grief. Indeed, a few of the monuments, though these are exceptional in Greek art, express poignant grief; but art seems to have acted as a viaticum of love and consolation, a mild angel to smooth the roughness of separation, touching the features of death with a rare beauty ; and how strange it is that a faith, with so faint a light shining on the unknown, could have evolved so calm a sentiment regarding the utter extinction of this life, which to the Greek was so joyful ; showing that there was depth of sweetness in the Greek nature that death could not touch ! We should remember that a nation which produced a Plato, could not have been a nation of atheists.

I might give more examples of this lovely department of Greek art, which can be seen at its best in the National Museum at Athens, but will speak of only one more composition carved on a sarcophagus found at Patras, representing the hunting of the Calydonian boar, which, though faint in its lines and of low relief, is very vigorous. It belongs to the later Græco-Roman period, and shows signs of decadence.

In the first hall to the right of the vestibule as you enter (the hall of the bronzes and terra-cottas) there are three archaic bronzes that have been brought from another collection ; and the first of these is the Athene Promachos, valuable from the fact that it is an effigy preceding by centuries the colossal bronze Athene Promachos by Pheidias, and may have entered into his conception as an archaic type of the divinity of Athens, with shield and spear, and which I have remarked upon. There is another ancient bronze Athene ; and an archaic head of a bearded man of foreign type found at Olympia, probably the bruised head of an athlete.

In the same room with the bronzes, and the two
succeeding rooms, are the delightful collections of
terra-cottas, conveyed from the *Ecole Polytechnique*,
gathered from all parts of Greece, although Tanagra,
in Bœotia, was the chief centre where they were
found. The most antique of these little figures are
divinities, and, as a general rule, divinities of the
Lower World, such as Demeter and Persephone, and
were of the nature of *ex votos* deposited in the tombs
with vases and funerary objects. These statuettes
were made either by hand or by mould, but moulded
figures were retouched by hand, and then baked in
an oven, and painted and gilded. The most beautiful
of these were, certainly, those of Tanagra, found in
a vast number of graves, dating from the 4th and 3d
centuries B. C. They have the freedom and nature
of every-day life, as seen in market-place and home,
the city and country, citizens, traders, farmers, vine-
dressers, singers, fighters, and fine ladies. In later
stages, the design of these seems to have changed,
and they appear to have been buried for the sole
solace of the deceased, to give them glimpses of the
life they had lost. The religious idea was merged
in the human, and yet these statues were usually
broken before they were thrown into the tombs ; but
here they are, as moving in life, dancers with a spirit
of grace on their flying steps like a zephyr's breath,
the queenly repose of seated forms, and those walking
under the queer-pointed hats and parasols with measured steps, the glint of beauty on them still, the
coloring enough to lend them brightness, the sweet
nobility of some of the faces, evident types of
Greeks found in country and hill towns, with now
and then a coarse figure and a broad caricature.
These tiny figures have also been found in Tegea,

Cyprus, and Myrina in Asia Minor, in Locris, Athens, Eleusis, Chalkis, Megara and Crete ; brought to light mostly by peasants who drove a brisk trade with them, so that they were irretrievably scattered, until the government took charge of the excavations ; all showing that the art created by this rapid work, and which gives us true pictures of old Greek life, was by no means confined to one locality, as Tanagra in Bœotia, but was spread wherever the Greek artist was found, and proves that he was capable of producing realistic as well as idealistic art—in fine, impressionism in sculpture.

Passing from these rooms of the Terra-Cottas, we come into the Great Halls of the painted Vases, a vast collection, and a subject which such writers as Furtwaengler, Leschke and Collingnon have spent immense labor in elucidating. There are here gathered vases of most primitive styles, from the Troad, the islands of the Archipelago and Mycenæ, Thera, Amargos, Melos. The bulk of the collection found by Dr. Schliemann at the Troad, went to Berlin, but there are still some precious specimens given by Madame Schliemann. The oldest of them were modelled by hand, though the potter's wheel was early used, but at first they had neither color nor figures, and only lines made by pressure of the fingers, or some pointed tool in the wet clay.

The vases of Thera, have color and ornamentation, with a variety of bands, hatchings and checkered lines, and even attempts to imitate flowers. Among this pottery of Thera, or Santorin, are vessels made anterior to the geologic cataclysm which took place in the island before the 19th century B. C., by which they were for ages covered up. Specimens of these are collected in a room at the French School of Arch-

æology at Athens, where, one day, I was courteously
allowed to copy some of them. The vases of Amor-
gos, found at Syra, of equal antiquity, are decorated
in a bizarre fashion, but the most important of all
this prehistoric pottery, are the Mycenæan vases.
These are painted and glazed, and the ornamental
designs are applied to a yellow ground in straight
lines, wavy lines, and lines based on some rude copy-
ing of vegetable and aquatic life, especially sea-
plants, sponges, corals, octopuses and cuttlefish.

In its later development Mycenæan pottery attempted the representation of human forms; and
while the colors of the Thera and Archipelago pottery
are unpolished, the Mycenæan vases had a polish
apparently given by the rubbing of some hard substance.   This pottery has been found not only at
Mycenæ but in other parts of the Peloponnesos and
Greece, and at Rhodes, showing that at one time it
was widely diffused.

In the centre of the halls stand the huge *pithoi*,
each of them almost large enough to hide one of the
forty thieves in the Arabian story ; and one of the
largest came from Crete, and was given by the Crown
Prince Constantine to the museum.

Troad vases go back twenty centuries and are without much color, stone clay vessels of a single color
and greyish brown or black, for the sense of color had
not awaked.   They are without beauty, sometimes
hut-shaped ; but an idea of ornamentation is seen on
the vessels of the third and fourth cities, that makes
its appearance in incised points, zigzags and continuous lines, and in eyes like those of an owl.

The Mycenæ vases exhibit a slight advance in form,
line and color, and the paintings have more varied
effects, the brush being charged with a red tint and

the whole covered by a transparent glaze, the decoration having the wave of circular patterns, afterwards continued in Greek vases. The designs are lines combined and intersecting, with curves and spirals, imitations of insects, aquatic plants, shells, sea-products and dolphins. In the Santorin vases, is seen an attempt at flower decoration, and in more refinement of form.

The *advanced* examples of Mycenæan vases, ran into the archaic Greek, the lines of discrimination between the two being rather obscure, but it can be traced by the careful student; and it finally merged into what might be called, in a general term, geometric, but still varied with original animal forms. The pictures are produced by straight lines, awkward and attenuated like a child's drawing, as in large amphoræ on which are pictures of horses and chariots with the meander pattern above them. This childish art began to show greater truth in the portrayal of bird and animal forms, and there are, indeed, elegant vases of this type distributed in horizontal zones with birds, antelopes and plants, and with Oriental motives especially about the neck, lid and handles, and with the old schwastika pattern. Not only plants and animals, but human figures, and scenes of warlike character and costume, came to be attempted, as in a Homeric illustration of the suicide of Ajax, with the figures of Diomedes and Odysseus, from a vase of Coere; and a still quainter scene of pointed-nosed Athene presiding over a fight.

In the vases of Coere, contests of racers and boxers frequently occur, as on Panathenaic amphoræ, and if not graceful, a tremendous energy is displayed by the athletes.

In the transitional style, where the Greek motive

and the Greek hand are exhibited, the drawing grows
stronger. Wrestlers in the palæstra are well drawn,
and they form a very ancient illustration of the athletic
games, presided over by their directors and umpires.

The vases of Corinth are excessively old, and are
easily recognized by the porcelain which is clear and
fine, and by the figures of brown color and vivid red,
mostly those of divinities and warriors. The vases of
Bœotia are quite individual, though exclusively of
the geometric style, but the form, the tone, the ornamentation are entirely different from the geometric
style of vases found in Attica or other parts of Greece.
Their surfaces are divided into vertical bands, and in
the compartments are painted a flower, or a bird, or
a fish, but generally birds. The colors are strong but
the vase-forms are homely, like modern beer-jugs.

There were schools of artists who devoted themselves entirely to vase-painting ; and there is (not in
the museum) a very curious representation of a work-
shop, and a youth seated in a chair with a two-handled
cup on his knee, which he is painting, and near by a
low table on which are pots containing the paints and
varnish ; and there are other figures at work, while a
jar and a large drinking cup (κανθαρος) stand on the
ground, and Athene, patron of art, and a Victory,
hasten to crown the artist.

We come to the fine vases of the best period, as in
the Panathenaic amphoræ of Attica, of higher form
and style, elegant vases painted with combats of
horsemen and footmen, on the body of the vessel, and
flower-ornamented tops. There are specimens of two-
handled vases decorated in vertical lines, with rims
on which are animals, and bands of black ground with
human figures.

Then there are the noblest of all yet spoken of, the

vases with figures that match the paintings of Polygnotos or the statues of Pheidias ; and the pictures on
those vases of the best period, are frequently copies of
celebrated masters in painting, not isolated figures
but freely grouped, and of beautiful forms. The
marked individuality of youth and age, and of the
female and masculine forms, is finely discriminated.

In such drawings of the best period, or perhaps
slightly decadent, there is, for example, a vase representing the departure of Triptolemos, who, seated on
a wheel, looks for all the world as if he were going
to take part in a bicycle race ; and, on another vase,
there is a group of Hera and Hebe. The outlines in
these paintings are traced with a point, and followed
rapidly by the brush, and then the vase was covered
with a fine silicate glaze, and the faces of women
painted white, with a coat of white chalk. Sometimes the figures are colored deep brown and black
on a yellow ground, and by leaving out the black the
natural red of the pottery is left, as in the nude
forms of men. The outline of heads, especially, must
have been executed with a continuous sweep of the
brush, and so in drawing a leg or a limb. The
artist conveyed expression to the face simply by
profile, and to the form by contour. There was no
perspective, and the colors were flat not allowing
shading, though this was attempted in the later stages
of the art. The scene, for example, of the last night
of Troy, was copied from some celebrated painting, in
which one recognizes the slaying of Cassandra, and
Æneas with his son escaping from Troy.

But I would say a word of the loveliest vases in
the museum, the *lekythi*, or the funereal vases, with
polychrome ornamentation delicately laid upon a white
or cream-colored ground, generally delineated with

burial scenes, and executed with masterly touch and design. Their form is simple, limited and precise, but of exquisite elegance. The neck and foot of the vase are covered with black varnish, and the contrast of black and white is most pleasing. They are exclusively sepulchral vessels, with a religious symbolism, the paintings representing 1. a kind of funerary cult, as in the offering made to a stele, where a maiden holds a basket of flowers before a monument, 2. the exposition of the dead, 3. the deposition in the tomb, 4. the descent to Hades, with the boat of Charon and other scenery of the world of shades.

These white *lekythi* are the most beautiful products of the ceramic art, and belong exclusively to Attic art, although some of them have been found at Eretria. They are from a period in the 5th century to the middle of the 3d century B. C. The drawing on these is delicate yet free, with a pure almost severe outline to the figures; and these slight tints of pink and blue are laid on creamy white ground, and are lovely because moderate in tone, and touched so lightly.

There is a scene upon a funereal vase of the deposition of the dead, where Thanatos, angel of death, with wings (we get our winged angels from Greek art), is laying down the body of a young girl in the grave reverently and softly, the drawing simple and clear, done rapidly with firm hand and pointed stylus. There is also a scene of ceremonial toilette connected with the funerary cult. One noble picture, I remember, is that of a young warrior in full armor, offering his shield at the stele of a companion in arms, his form and face manly, and the action full of modest and earnest reverence. There is variety in these scenes and groups, but all is kept down by severe taste, and evidently the best artistic talent is made use of, so that Greek drawing shows as much skill, grace and aesthetic sentiment as Greek sculpture, or Greek architecture. Who can say that the Greeks did not know how to draw and paint ?

There is another scene of deposition in which two angels are engaged in depositing carefully and tenderly the body of a maiden in the tomb, while Hermes, the god who conducts spirits to the lower world, stands silently by as witness.

Some of these vases are of larger size, truly superb objects, and, to my eye, they are the most lovely products of Greek genius, pure and delicate exhalations of art, blending the highest perfection of form with the subtlest feeling ; and they show the Greeks to have been a refined people, who, though with a strong tendency to the sensuous, had thoughts of elevated purity and purified affection. This collection of *lekythi* would make any museum unique.

I cannot dwell longer on this field of Greek vase-art, in which there is every form, color and style, vases with red on black, and black on red ground, huge bowls, two-handled cups such as in the Odyssey were brought out at the feasts of Nestor at Pylos, and of Menelaos at Sparta by white-handed Helen ; pateras and great hydrias ; tall vessels and shallow, with ornamented rims ; scenes of war and peace ; Sappho reading her poems ; Achilles arming ; an old man teaching a youth music ; a scene of flower-crowned bride and bridegroom with happy faces and clasped hands, or rather the young man clasping the wrist of his partially veiled bride in a masterful way, and leading her along ; Thetis bearing the magnificent armor made by Hephaistos to her son ; victory riding on a swan ; domestic and toilet scenes ; bridal and funereal scenes; and all with the utmost tenderness in treating death and sorrow; some grotesque and coarse paintings, but not many of such as are found in debased Pompeiian art; in fact, the best life of the old Greeks, represented on these frail vessels which have, nevertheless, lasted for ages while generations of men and their solidest works have perished, and which constitute the oldest and one might say the most imperishable form of human art, certainly taking us back to a time before the seige of Troy.

There is one case of deep interest, containing some broken black vases from the field of Marathon, which were found in the soros, in 1891, mingled with a few bones and ashes, and fragments of later Attic pottery. In one of the halls is also a case with objects discovered at Cheronæa, in a tomb of Thebans who fell in that battle with Philip 338 B. C. The skeletons lie just as they were found, and on some heads are seen marks of the terrific blows of swords and lances; and we might imagine, in the clenched teeth, is expressed the death-resolve of men to die rather than yield.

I will speak further of the Mycenæan art to be seen in the National Museum, when treating of Mycenæ, which lies next in order to do.

In this great museum of artistic works on Greek soil, are also little side-rooms containing collections and fragments that have come in from later diggings, not yet arranged or even taken out of the straw hand-baskets in which they have been packed; and here is the work of our American scholars, as well as of others, to classify these findings from Argos, Eretria, Orchomenos, Crete and all parts of Greece. One of our scholars, a student of architecture, interested me very much in his architectural comments, for his mind seemed aglow by contact with this old Hellenic art, and he was full of enthusiasm in the work of dry analysis and combination. He showed me some bronzes connected with the drainage system of the Heræum at Argos ; also some Greek skulls that may have done this planning and thinking ; the indefatigable little Ephor Kabbadias (master spirit of the institution) the while flitting in and out of the rooms and directing all.

A thunder storm that I witnessed one morning when I happened to be standing under the portico in front of the National Museum, afforded fine effects of the hills about the city, and of the white Acropolis against the black sky, with the dazzling zigzags of golden lightning. Big hailstones rattled down as I drove home, making one feel that Zeus still ruled in his Greek land.

What a life was once lived in this city of Athene ! Just before the Peloponnesian war, Athens was an imperially powerful naval, commercial and political state, perhaps the most powerful then existing, but her life, above all, was the intellectual life of an intellectual people. And it was the common life of the Athenian demos, not nourished by king, priest or aristocracy, but glowing in the bosom of the whole community of the people ; and the artists were men of the people, true αριστοι ; they mingled in the public resorts, were seen in the market-place, voted and spoke in political meetings, and shared with the commonest their seats in the theatre, their games in the palæstra, their campaigns in war. The people criticised their works, rejoiced in them, and really formed the standard of artistic appeal. It was a bright, free, and, in some respects, beautiful public life, notwithstanding its black blots of sensuality and slavery. The public buildings were magnificent, but they alone had splendid façades and pillars, since private houses were unornamented on the exterior, with no windows on the first story, and but two stories high. There was no regular plan in the laying out of the streets, hardly no streets at all, and it was not until the time of Hippodamas of Miletus, who lived about the middle of the fifth century B. C., that there was any improvement in the houses and streets, and then only in the lower city near the Piræus. The streets were unpaved, and very muddy or dusty ; but the temples, stoas, agoras, theatres, gymnasia, shone in great beauty and splendor, and thither the people resorted not for amusement only, but for education, education limited in range in comparison with modern education, but, in some respects, more philosophic, reaching deeper, training the nature symmetrically, making intelligent and habile men, citizens ready for every public work, act and need. This, it seems to me, is of the greatest importance for young men to learn, since now-a-days they have so large a voice in the disposal and direction of their own education ; and might we not, too, draw from it the lesson, that the study of classical languages should not be abandoned, that this fatal error should not be made, for nothing can take their place in the finer culture of the mind ; and, already, I believe, a strong reaction is felt in this matter of the hasty exclusion of the classics from the university curriculum, while at the same time it is to be conceded that they should be taught in a living way, and in due relation and proportion to modern studies, so that the scientific fact and life of the present shall be blended with the wisdom and beauty of the past.

CHAPTER XI.

MYCENÆ AND MYCENÆAN ART.

Starting for Corinth from the Peloponnesian station at Athens, in a train running across the plain of Attica, after passing Eleusis one comes to Megara, a place of 6250 inhabitants, who, as another has said, "pride themselves not a little on their pure Greek descent in the midst of a surrounding Albanian population." Megara now occupies almost the site of the old city of Megara, climbing up two steep hills in masses of square yellow limestone houses. This ancient town, through which the highway from Northern Greece to the Peloponnesos once ran, while it was situated at some little distance from the sea, was a commercial centre at one time, almost rivaling Corinth. It won renown in the Persian wars, and afterwards successfully resisted the encroachments of Athens; and though not noted, like Athens, for its wit or intellectuality, it was the birthplace of Greek Comedy, and the home of one who has caused unnumbered sighs and groans of studious youth—Euclid.

Immediately beyond Megara, the train passes through rock-cuttings at the foot of the Geranion hills, a piece of bold engineering along the face of a precipitous cliff where legend places the Skironian rocks, down which the robber Skiron tumbled his victims; and one gets here a view of the blue expanse of the Saronic Gulf, with its glittering opalescent waters near the shore, and of the Peloponnesian mountains of Epidauros, hill shouldering hill in misty confusion. Soon we come in sight of the newly built sea-walls and lighthouses of the modern port of Isthmia, the eastern entrance of the Corinthian canal ; the old east port of Corinth, Cenchreæ, lay about three miles to the south of Isthmia. At the west end of the canal, there is building a port called Poseidonia, with two immense breakwaters, each eight hundred feet long extending into the Corinthian gulf. As the waters of the two seas are almost on a level, the labor and expense of locks were avoided. The Isthmian games were in honor of Isthmian-Poseidon, and were frequented largely by Athenians, since the games were of Ionic origin. They were held a little to the southwest of the eastern entrance of the canal, and the "Sanctuaries," so called, have been excavated by the French School, as well as portions of the Stadion and the temple of Poseidon. It was a fine breezy open plain between two murmuring seas, for the meeting of those vast assemblies which formed such an important part of the social and political life of the Greeks. The Athenians came sailing across the Saronic Gulf in a great decorated galley, and they were accorded a place of special honor in the Stadion, although Corinth had the regulation of the ceremonies, and gave, as the prize of victory, a garland of pine, showing that it was but a crown of valor and virtue.

New Corinth, a little business place of five thousand inhabitants, is quickly reached after leaving the bridge over the canal, and here opens a view of the Gulf of Corinth, narrow at this end of it almost as a river, but beautiful from its setting and coloring. Old Corinth lay inward some four miles to the west, near the foot of the Acro-Corinthus, which towers up

TEMPLE OF ELEUSIS

i

an isolated mass of grey rock, and more of a mountain than the Acropolis at Athens ; and when I went the first time to Greece I rode to the top of it, which it is worth while to do on account of the view, where one sees spread out before him, the site of old Corinth, a wide plain gently sloping to the margin of the sea. At the back, are the mountains of the Argolic Peloponnesus, that plunge abruptly into the Saronic Gulf; to the west, the Arcadian chain ; and immediately in front, is the blue Corinthian gulf, beyond which are the mountain ranges of Bœotia and Phocis, ending in the cliffs of Parnassos ; to the east, are the peninsula and plain of Attica, and the hills that lie in and near Athens, the white-pillared Acropolis on a clear day being distinctly visible though fifty miles distant. There are many springs of water on the Acro-Corinthus, some of which the Turks choked up (as a bright Greek boy told me, his eyes flashing with indignation), but on the southern side of the rock, a little way down, is the famous spring of Peirene, now a kind of well, or cistern, though the water is good and clear. This spring, every schoolboy knows, was made by a stroke of the hoof of the winged-horse Pegasos, symbol of Corinth on coins. It was so terribly hot, that I gladly minded the injunction to drink deep of the Pierian spring, that may have made me ever since a lover of anything Greek. Ruins of fortifications, and of Turkish and Christian houses, encumber the summit, which is of the circumference of some two miles, a commanding rock-citadel.

The old temple of Corinth is interesting from the fact, that it is almost the sole relic of the luxurious city which was once the commercial centre of all Greece ; and it is a singular fact that this rude old

Doric edifice, going back to the middle of the 7th century B.C., should be the only artistic exponent now standing of a metropolis where the splendid Corinthian order got its name.   It stands near the foot of the Acro-Corinthus, and on the site of the old city, which, beginning at the rock, extended its long walls down to the sea.   The temple is built of poros limestone, covered with a yellow stucco, and has massive monolithic columns tapering to the top, on which rests a heavy entablature, a portion of which remains; and of these columns seven are standing. The building consisted of two cells, perhaps belonging to two different cults; and one cannot but be impressed by its rough antique grandeur.

Corinth has just now become a new field of exploration by the American Archæological School at Athens, that happily secured this great privilege from the Greek government.   Deep digging is said to be necessary to find the Hellenic city.   Already the digging and the trenches that have been sunk have resulted in finding the principal theatre of the city; but while results of the utmost value are to be anticipated from excavations carried on by such energetic and skillful hands, the original Greek city was wiped out by the Romans, so that the completeness of its destruction was a by-word of antiquity. According to Pausanias the desolation was total and entire.*   But let us hope for rich results.   How magnificent must have been the art of a city drawing from all sources of a land like Greece at the fullness of her power, and which commanded the commerce of two continents, and was the strongest and longest opponent of Rome, its very might and splendor bring-

* Κόρινθον δὲ οἰκοῦσι κορινθίων οὐδεὶς ἔτι τῶν αρχάιων, ἔποικοι δὲ ἀποσταλέντες ὑπὸ 'Ρωμαίων.

ing down its own destruction ! Its spacious market-
place, the broad plateau between the Long Walls that
ran to the Lechæum and the Corinthian Gulf, and
the rock that rose above, were covered with marble and
golden temples, theatres, gymnasia and baths, and
also statues. On the top of the Acro-Corinthus stood
in the sunshine a temple containing statues of the
Sun and of Eros with a bow, and a famous statue of
Aphrodite. In the plain below were shrines of the
same power, which here was not the heavenly Urania
but earthly Pandemos ; also temples of Chthonian
Zeus, Apollo, Herakles, Fortune and Poseidon ; a
fountain with a bronze statue of Bellerophon striding
a winged Pegasos with water flowing from the hoof
of the horse ; and yet, notwithstanding all this, it is
to be doubted if there were in this superb city anything so beautiful as the Parthenon, and the works
of Pheidias ; for wealth cannot insure artistic genius
that comes from a spring deeper than Peirene, that of
faith and unconscious sublimity.

From Corinth I went on to Nemæa, this last time
by rail, but at the first visit I journeyed there on
horseback, by a path among the hills that was toil-
some in September heats, though part of the way lay
along the oleander-fringed stream of the Charadra ;
and most of the route was through the rocky vale of
Tretus. The little plain of Nemæa lies under the
hill of Mt. Aphesas, and in the centre of the small
plain are three grey shafts of the Doric temple of
Zeus, the rest a heap of ruins, with no life of any
kind where once were the silver poplar-groves that
surrounded this sanctuary of the whole Peloponnesos,
and where the Nemæan games were celebrated ;
though, at the present time, vineyards have been
planted, and a little village has sprung up at some
distance from the ruins.

Two of the worn columns, slender for this order, are those of the pronaos, the third belonging to the outer row of pillars. The temple was a hexastyle, sixty feet broad, not large but, as Col. Leake remarks, the Greeks studied place and site for effect and would not have set up a massive temple like the one at Corinth, in the small and narrow valley of Nemæa. Perhaps, too, the temple was of later date. It was lone grey Nemæa, when I first saw it, a place of absolute silence and desolation, where the charm of its melancholy solitariness took hold of the imagination; but the shriek of the steam-whistle now breaks the poetic charm.

The winding valley through which the modern railway runs northeast toward the plain of Argos, along the site of Mt. Aphesas, described in the Odyssey as "the deep-wooded hill," was the scene of some desperate fighting between the Greeks and Turks.

It seemed odd to me, who had been in former years a solitary traveler to these hills, among which lies Mycenæ, to stop at a railway station called Mycenæ, or Phicthia-Mycenæ, which is about half an hour's drive, or walk, from the citadel, and near which are three or four farm-houses; but when I was there before, there were no houses or signs of them, no human being, in fact it was a scene of savage loneliness; and then and there losing my guide, the big Andreas, while I was exploring the ruins, having spent more time in doing so than I was aware of, the night was fast coming on. I was about making my way alone to Argos, setting my face in that direction, or towards the sea, when, luckily, at the last moment, the guide was recovered, he having stupidly hid himself and the horses in the sunk entrance-way to the Treasury of Atreus; and after taking our dinner, and seeing the treasure-house, we rode in the evening shadows down the mountain into the plain ; but I was seized with an attack of malarial fever contracted from sleeping out-doors at Corinth, an unhealthy place from its heavy night dews, and was taken care of faithfully by the huge fellow, who, after two days got me somehow to Argos, and there, procuring an ancient chariot that might have been already old in the siege of Troy, we drove on to Nauplia, where a barber treated me in the Sangrado fashion, which, perhaps, under the circumstances, was the best. It was on my second visit that I explored Mycenæ more leisurely and carefully.

The situation of Mycenæ (Mykenai) is exactly described in Homeric words " μύχῳ Αργειος ἱπποβοτοιο, in the inmost recesses of horse-nourishing Argos." It lies like an eagle's nest between craggy ridges of Mt. Elias (Hagios Elias), whence it commands the upper part of the Argolic plain, and also the pass by which roads, still traceable, led to Cleonæ and Corinth, through which passed the traffic between the eastern and western seas, an important commercial and strategic point from earliest time. It is a rugged spot amid overhanging mountains, and the Acropolis occupies a rocky eminence nine hundred and twelve feet high, that juts out, spur-like, from Mt. Elias back of it, and on either side are two ravines, in fact an isolated precipitous rock, though the north side is connected by a narrow ridge with the mountain, and below this, once lay the city of Mycenæ, spreading over the slope of the hill.

Behind the citadel, is the fountain, or brook, of Perseia, mentioned by Pausanias, and still running, from which led an aqueduct into the fortress.

The citadel was of a triangular shape surrounded by massive walls, now remaining, though ruined, and built of Cyclopean masonry with immense stones, not, however, entirely uncut or undressed, as at Tiryns, but hewn in polygonal shapes, and, in some spots, leveled and square, showing advance over elder Tiryns.

On the front running down from the northwest angle, is a lane leading to the principal entrance, which is the well-known Lion Gate ; but before speaking of it, I would notice the most perfectly preserved of those subterranean chambers, of which there are four more, this being variously named " The Treasury of Atreus," " The Treasury of Menelaos," and " The Tomb of Agamemnon," and is situated half way down the eastern side of the hill. Its plan consisted of an entrance-passage (δρομος) a hundred and fifteen feet long and twenty wide, a vaulted apartment, and a small square chamber adjoining. The work is of "the same massive ashlar masonry used for the angles and gates of the citadel." The door, seventeen feet high, is framed by a moulding of three bands of sawn stone. Close by the door, when I was first there, stood two alabaster half-columns, growing larger to the top, with zigzag lozenge figures, or *guilloches*, and also a capital of Oriental style, carved with lancet-shaped leaves, now in the British Museum.

The entrance-way has since been dug out, and carefully fenced in by the Greek Archæological Society. These "beehive" structures are called φουρνοι, ovens. The interior makes a domical room, or conical vault, fifty feet in height and in diameter, which is formed by horizontal courses of stone projecting each beyond the other in a false vault, laid in shelves and the angles smoothed, growing narrower at the top, closed by a single slab. The walls of the apartment are polished, and the room has an imposing unity. Holes in the stones, and a few clinging bronze nails, have been thought to prove, that there was a metallic casing to the vault such as we read, in the Odyssey, of the palace of Alkinös, where the words "resplendent" and "sparkling" are used; but Doerpfeld thinks that these nails were to hold bronze ornaments attached to the walls, as in the "Treasury of Minyas" at Orchomenos.

In the middle of the smaller square chamber, there is a circular depression cut in the rock-floor, now thought to have been the place of a tomb, so that this structure, as well as the "Treasury of Clytemnestra" near by, excavated in 1876 by Madame Schliemann, was a tomb, not a treasure-house. This inner room was the grave, opened only for burial, and the larger apartment was for the cult of the dead. Schuhardt says, and reasonably, that no prince would have trusted his treasures outside the walls of the citadel. To give some little idea of its original rude magnificence, it was coated with variegated marbles and metallic affixes, and the triangle above the door, ten feet long, was closed by slabs of red porphyry, ornamented with running patterns and spirals. The alabaster columns, with carved cornice and architrave, the polished masonry, the variegated marbles and enormous lintel, made of a monolith projecting beyond the doorway, show curious skill in the art of masonry and decorative architecture. These "beehives" give a strange impression of age, and have been traced outside of Greece to Phrygia and Lydia, and to conical forms of Phrygian houses made for the habitation of the living.

But let us ascend the Acropolis, to see what are

named the "Shaft-graves" within the temenos of the citadel, where Dr. Schliemann, in 1876, made his startling discoveries, unearthing, as he thought, Homeric heroes. The graves are on the way leading to the upper citadel, and form a circular place enclosed by upright marble slabs ; and there is a retaining-wall of Cyclopean masonry above it, which divides the upper and lower parts of the Acropolis, and on the lower terrace is this enclosure, which was covered by a thick deposit of earth heaped upon it either designedly or by the accumulation of time. Schliemann dug a trench in this earth one hundred and thirteen feet square, and sank shafts, and, as fortune would have it, the excavation was made over the very circle of the graves, whose diameter is about eighty-seven feet.

In his "Mycenæ," Schliemann affirms that this was the Mycenæan *agora*, and that the marble slabs formed seats for magistrates, some of them having a slope inward. This view has been abandoned, and the Acropolis proved to be a fortified royal house, without any market-place. The tombs, five in all, on the west part of the enclosure, were hewn in the natural rock, and covered by earth levelled to the east, where the rock rose higher, and in these graves, thirty feet down, were found the bones of fifteen persons, with a great quantity of gold objects and ornaments ; and a sixth grave has more recently been discovered to the south (by the Greek Archæological Society, whose diggings are going on), containing also bones and ornaments ; and a round Cyclopean altar over the fourth tomb, and some nine steles were excavated, and the theory now is, that this was a consecrated burial-place, in which the cult of the royal dead was celebrated. The bodies were found imbedded in a layer of river-pebbles, surrounded by a great wealth of ornaments and arms, covered with fine clay. The dead, or some of them, had been partially cremated, though the ashes might have been the ashes of sacrifice. There were signs of hurried burial, skeletons crushed as if done simultaneously, so that Schleimann thought this was evidence of the tragic fate and hasty burial of Agamemnon and his family, the riches deposited with them confirming this.

It is curious that Pausanias says that he saw in Mycenæ five graves of Agamemnon and his companions, and that these were inside the walls of the citadel, but later critics dissent from the theory of simultaneous burial, and believe that this was a royal burial-place, and that the graves were reopened for fresh interments. Doerpfeld holds that the crush and disorder in the tombs was owing to the collapse of the beams of the slate-roofing. In the third grave were found the greatest amount of treasures, and this has sometimes been supposed to contain the veritable body of the hero-king.

The passage in Pausanias on which Schliemann chiefly relied, is interesting as bearing on the question, and I take it from another's translation : "Some remains of the circuit-wall are still to be seen, and the gate with lions over it. These were built, they say, by the Cyclopes, who made the wall of Tiryns for Proitos. Among the ruins at Mycenæ is the fountain called Perseia, and some subterranean buildings belonging to Atreus and his children, where their treasures are kept. This is the tomb of Atreus, and of those whom Æginthos slew at the banquet on their return from Ilion with Agamemnon.   *   *   *
There is also the tomb of Agamemnon, and that of Eurymedon the charioteer, and the joint tomb of

Teladamos and Pelops, the twin children of Cassandra, whom Ægisthos slew with their parents while still babes, for Orestes gave her (Electra), in marriage to Pylades, and Klytemnestra and Ægisthos were buried a little way outside the wall, for they were not thought worthy to be within, where Agamemnon lay, and those who fell with him."

Pausanias declares that he saw five graves. It is, however, supposed to be quite impossible that the graves, or any external signs of them, could have been seen by Pausanias, so late as the age of the Antonines; and he is held to have used the eyes of others before him and borrowed from literary traditions; while some scholars, among them Doerpfeld, conjecture that what Pausanias saw were "the bee-hive-structures" outside the citadel, but which may have then been included within the city walls.

But whether Pausanias saw the five "shaft-graves" or not, may not these have been the graves of Agamemnon and his companions? On one of the steles is carved the bas-relief of a charioteer and a two-horse chariot, and another relief is that of a Homeric combat; and the splendid ornaments found in these tombs, are those which might have belonged to a rich and powerful ruler like Agamemnon; while the skeletons of the women were, Schliemann says, "literally laden with golden jewelry."

CHAPTER XII.

MYCENÆ AND MYCENÆAN ART.

Among other treasures discovered at Mycenæ, were two large golden diadems, and one of these, from the third grave, was bound on a head, leading to the supposition that this may have been the body of "the lord Agamemnon," though similar diadems were found in other graves, with gold bosses and ornaments of elaborate patterns. The round gold plates from grave IIId, containing designs of octopuses and marine creatures, like those on Mycenæan vases, and gold crosses made in the shape of laurel leaves, are now in the National Museum at Athens, where are numberless such objects of strange device, dazzling the eye with their opulent abundance. In fact the ornaments seen in that wonderful hall at Athens, illustrating the phrase in the Odyssey "Mycenæ rich in gold"—the pendants, brooches, necklaces, buttons, whorls, rings, carved ivories and balls of rock-crystal, show the exceeding wealth of this Mycenæan decorative art, and denoting a great if semi-barbaric civilization.

On the gold rings taken from grave IV, are intaglios of battle and hunting scenes, such as might readily have belonged to Homeric times, but the most remarkable of this goldsmith's work, above its metallic value, are the bronze weapons with inlaid patterns of gold and silver done with an exquisite art. One dagger-blade, decorated in its whole length with figures of running lions and hunters, is executed with amazing spirit and vigor.

The lion-hunt, executed in different tints of gold and silver, displays details of costume, weapons and forms, equaling and almost excelling modern intaglio art, the ground being a dark enamel that sets off the work. But of such work, the embossed gold cups from the Vapheio dome-tomb at Amyklæ, near Sparta, belonging to the Mycenæan style, are even more highly artistic, and may be mentioned with it, although they were not found at Mycenæ. But a similar gold cup adorned with running lions was dug up at Mycenæ. On the Vapheio cups are portrayed the capture of wild bulls, one of which has caught a man on his horns, and another bull is falling to the ground meshed in a net, and there is a landscape where bulls are pasturing. The men have long hair and waist-cloths, otherwise nude, and the scene calls to mind the bull painted on the wall at Tiryns. These scenes are executed in the style of what the Italians call *graffite ;* and Dr. Doerpfeld says of them : ''The cups are of pure gold, of riveted work, but with designs in *repoussé*, which for originality of design and delicacy of execution are unrivaled, except perhaps by the finest goldsmith's work of the Italian Renaissance.'' A modern Athenian goldsmith has exactly reproduced these cups in silver gilt, and has them for sale in Athens, where one can see and compare them with the originals in the Mycenæan room of the National Museum.

In grave Vth, two of the bodies of unusual size wore over their faces gold masks, and one of the faces was preserved under its mask, full-bearded. The features of the mask are well-formed, the nose straight, though the eyes are too close together for symmetry. I am inclined to think that these gold masks were prepared before the burial, and that they did not take the perfect impression of the faces, so that we cannot judge of the features with certainty.

The most solid find of all was an ox-head of silver with golden horns, in grave IVth, remarkably true to nature, especially the nose and mouth of the animal ; in the forehead is a gold rosette. It was probably a dedicatory offering, but one cannot help being reminded (at least it occurred to me) of the scene in the Odyssey where the heifer was brought for sacrifice at the house of Nestor : '' The smith came holding in his hands the instruments of his craft, anvil and hammer and well-made pincers, wherewith he wrought the gold. And the old Knight Nestor gave the gold, and the other fashioned it skillfully and gilded therewith the horns of the heifer that the goddess might be glad at the sight of the fair offering.''.

Madame Schliemann related to me, as she has done to others, that when this silver head was come upon, she and her husband were alone, and she wrapped the head in her shawl, so that it might not be seen by the workmen, being in a state of trepidation lest the whole body would be discovered, and that she could not hide this silver-mine in her shawl.

The Greek Archæological Society in 1886 undertook fresh excavations at Mycenæ and laid bare, on the summit of the citadel, the palace, having the same general ground-plan as the palaces of Troy and Tiryns ; but it seemed to me to be too confined a space for a palace, smaller than the palace at Tiryns ; yet it must have afforded rooms with magnificent views over the plain of Argos to the sea, like views from turrets of mediæval castles on lofty mountains in Germany and on the Rhine. There are, however, the main divisions of the Homeric palace, a hall with

two ante-rooms, a court yard, and several small apart-
ments surrounded by a wall, to reach the top of
which and of the citadel, by the ruined zigzag steps,
when they are swept by the wind, is a bit of a steep
climb.　A piece of the palace on the south has been
carried away by a landslide.

There are remains of painted decoration or wall-
fresco in the megaron, but not at all so important as
at Tiryns.　The crowning achievement of the Mycenæan period in building-art and in sculpture is the
Lion-Gate.

The famous Lion-Gate is, undoubtedly, of the same
period as the great walls.　The walls form just here
an equilateral triangle, and upon the side subtending
their eastern angle, lies the gate.　It is the principal
entrance to this robber castle (I was going to say
were I not rebuked by the shade of Homer), although
the street that goes through it is so narrow and so
steep, the cliff being precipitous here, that Schliemann thought, in spite of the supposed marks of
chariot-wheels, that no chariot, be it of Agamemnon
or any other, ever was driven up it.　Three kinds of
masonry seen at different parts of the walls—Cyclopean or uncut stones, rectangular as in the "beehive"
structure, and polygonal, or polygonal blocks fitted
closely,—are found also at the gate, immediately
north and south of it.　Skill in military fortification
is shown, so that a continuous narrow approach between wall and tower must have been traversed before
the gate was reached.　The gate (quite familiar now
by photography) is slightly pyramidal, narrower at
the top than the bottom, and has a breadth of nine
feet ten inches and a height of ten feet and four
inches.　In the colossal lintel are seen round holes
for the brazen gate to swing on.　The upper part of

the gate is the most noteworthy, bearing as it does a heroic sculpture, which is the oldest known sculpture-piece in Greece, perhaps in Europe. It is a slab of grey braccia limestone, ten feet high and twelve broad, filling the triangular opening above the gate, and the relief-sculpture carved upon it represents two lions rampant, with their fore-paws resting, heraldic-wise, on the pedestal of an altar column, which, like the columns at the treasury of Atreus, increases in thickness towards the top, and is crowned by a capital composed of a fillet, a cyma moulding, and a rather thick abacus.

A similar lion-guarded gate has recently been discovered by an English explorer in Phrygia; but the carving of these lions is more free than Phrygian or Assyrian sculpture, the anatomy and the muscular development being very natural, or at least, by no means conventionally accentuated, as in Oriental art. The heads are gone, and were probably of bronze, looking full-face to those approaching, and the loss of them is great in an artistic point of view.

If the gate did not belong to the heroic epoch of the brass-greaved Achaians, one cannot but think that it ought to have done so. But what is its date? Who reared these mighty walls and palaces for the glorification of kingly power?

Mycenæan art is now demonstrated to be the name of a wide-spread form of art, which has been found not only at Mycenæ, Tiryns, Amyklæ and the Peloponnesos, but at Sparta and Menidi, at Attica, Orcomenos in Bœotia, Cyprus and the Ægean islands, the coasts of Asia Minor, Troy, Phœnicia, and from its pyramidal type in architecture, even Egypt. Undoubtedly its centre was Argos, and its period at least some time before the Dorian invasion. Its decorations of animals and marine forms—the lion, bull, stag, dog, star-fish, octopus, dolphin—predominating over the human, go back to Oriental, even Egyptian types, as well as look forward to early types of Greek keramic art, in the dipylon pottery that is usually associated with the Homeric period. There is an Asiatic luxuriousness in these golden ornaments, inlaid arms, barbaric spirals and rosettes, polychrome wall-decorations, the use of bronze, the golden goblets, the amber, ivory and metal enameled work, reminding also of Egypt, and especially of the extraordinarily rich finds of Egyptian jewel-work recently made. It was not Greek art, but an art that had adorned the coast of Asia Minor, Cyprus and the Ægean islands, which was imported art, and yet art which had acquired a local character, a touch of real nature, to be seen in the lions of Mycenæ, the silver ox-head, and the dagger and ring intaglios, as if only a contact with Greek soil had inspired it with something of nature's secret.

In Mycenæan art there are three styles marking progress; the conventional, the linear, and the organic, the last looking even to a human interest. An æsthetic sense had assuredly been awakened, and a certain justness of representation in living objects, as in muscles of the lions at the gate. The lions have been thought to be the work of an artist formed in the Asiatic School, but of an art somewhat released from its rigidness, an art which grew to have more and more truth, freedom and cohesion of parts, till it really became Greek. It formed a kind of basis for Hellenic art.

Among the many theories advanced in regard to the date of Mycenæan art, the view of Collignon seems the most reasonable, that Mycenæan civilization was not an ephemeral but a permanent civilization, whose actual centre was in Greece, in the Peloponnesos, and that it was essentially ante-Dorian, and yet Achaian, representing mainly the Pelopid dynasty; and that the family of kings who ruled at Mycenæ, came originally to Greece from Asia, probably Phrygia, bringing with them the decorative arts of Asia. It was also the heroic age of Greek civilization, or the beginnings of it, not limited to the Argolic Achaians of Homer, but extending to the rest of Greece, to the Ægean isles and the shores of Asia Minor. The chronologic limits of the period are not easy to bound as it is purely prehistoric, but it might be placed in the time between the 15th or 14th centuries B.C. and the 12th century.

This civilization disappeared after the Dorian conquest in 1104, which cast down the Mycenæan dynasty, but passed away gradually, since in 800 B.C. the city of Amyklæ remained still Achaian; and Greek art, as in the Dipylon vases, temple architecture and sculpture, bore strong traces of Mycenæan art, and the period of transition to the 9th century was a long one, long enough to furnish material for the Homeric epics. Dr. Schliemann's theory that the Homeric heroes positively reigned and were buried at Mycenæ, may be, and does appear to be a little enthusiastic, but it has Mr. Gladstone's equally enthusiastic endorsement, whatever that is worth; and it has the affirmation of Edward Freeman, who affirmed that "the Pelopid dynasty at Mycenæ is an established fact."

I would say a single word in regard to the use of metal (χαλκος of Homer) in Mycenæan art, for weapons and the sheathing of rooms in tombs and palaces. No iron but only copper has thus far been discov-

ered at Hissarlik, in the oldest city, probably 3000
or 2500 B.C.; but the Mycenæan layer at the
burnt city of Troy (1500–1000 B.C.), representing the
Homeric Pergamos, contains bronze weapons and no
iron. There can be no doubt that the Phœnician
traders and metallurgists influenced the Greeks,
through their relations with the Ionians of Asia
Minor who were Greeks by descent, introducing the
rudimentary moulds of Greek art in metal-work and
sculpture ; and the Achaian Greeks, affiliated with
the Orientals, accepted them to a certain extent as
their teachers, though they soon went beyond them,
and broke their moulds ; and from this semi-Oriental
civilization in other relations and ways, in history,
customs and legends, Homer, or the author, or
authors, of the Homeric poems, himself of Hellenic
race and speech, drew freely.   He found the rough
material of his song in the Pelopid wars and Achaian
raids in Asia Minor, as Scott obtained his poetic
material in the Scotch border-wars, and Tennyson
his, from the cycle of the Arthurian legends; and
Homer, like Tennyson, clothed his heroes, "fleet-
footed Achilles," Menelaos, Odysseus, Helen, Priam,
Hector, with a Greek beauty and brilliancy, that the
lawless heavy-handed fighters on the plain of Troy,
and the chiefs of the craggy strongholds of Mycenæ,
Phthiotis and Ithaca, did not possess ; and thus
poetry, even the most splendid, is built up by the
creative power of the artistic imagination, from a few
rude facts and ruder lives of men.

Since Tiryns also belongs to the epoch of Mycenæan art, I will say something of this prehistoric
stronghold. The ruins of Tiryns form a very impressive pile of Cyclopean wall, not made of polygonal

stones cut and joined, but of great polygonal blocks unhewn, immense stones filled in with smaller; and no measuring line or stone-axe was raised upon it, and yet how enduring, as if giants of older time had reared it! Tiryns is older than anything out of Egypt, older than Mycenæ itself, lying nearer to the sea than Mycenæ, which is nine and a half miles further inward, while Tiryns is about a mile and a half from Nauplia, and the contrast of the busy modern town with the silent discrowned hill is striking.

Mycenæ and Tiryns sent a contingent to the battle of Platæa, but both of these towns were destroyed by the Argives. The rock on which the citadel of Tiryns stands is nine hundred and eighty feet long and three hundred and thirty broad, with massive walls running around it thirty feet thick, and the structure presents, perhaps, the most perfect plan of a Homeric royal stronghold, and, for this reason, has a place with Troy, in Greek literature.

Tiryns is a unique pile. At two points, its thick wall grows thicker, and holds within it unexplained chambers and covered passages which Dr. Schliemann cleared out. These are curious galleries with ogival vaultings connected with an internal system of fortification, or storage, and which are the first examples of the pointed arch. They are accidentally so, but it is odd to find in this incredibly antique ruin, the counterpart to the eye at least, of the cloistered walks of San Michele of Pavia, and of Gothic Canterbury and Norwich cathedrals, and the illusion of these pointed vaults is perfect.

The central part of the palace is the "megaron" for men, with its great hall (aule) containing the sacrificial altar with a pit beneath it, as at the palace of Ithaca described in the Odyssey. The "megaron"

was covered by a roof, portions of whose central supporting pillars exist, and within these pillars was an
open round fireplace, such as may be seen sometimes
in mediæval palaces, as late as Penshurst, Sir Philip
Sidney's home.   Here gathered the stalwart forms
that fashioned the Homeric bow and lance.   The
flooring was of hard cement, and one sees the remains
of the finer alabaster lining of the walls.   In an adjoining chamber is a bath-room, lately discovered, having
a polished limestone block floor, surely an evidence
of civilization, and proving that these old fighters
were not savages.   The traces of wall-painting and of
marine plant Mycenæan patterns, found at Tiryns,
have been transferred to the Mycenæan room in the
National Museum at Athens.   They are done *al fresco*
on wall plaster, the four colors of white, red, yellow
and blue being employed.   Rows of rosettes and
spirals with palmettes and other floral variegated designs, if rude, must have produced a bold effect ; they
are the oldest mural frescoes in Europe.   Those of
the Church della Carmine in Florence with the dawn-
ing light of the Renaissance upon them, those at the
Sistine chapel at Rome, the frescoes of San Gimignano,
the panel decorations of Pinturicchio in the library
of the Cathedral at Siena, all of them, as hundreds
more, are the children of these wall-decorations in the
Homeric palace of Tiryns.

The greatest effort of palatial painting at Tiryns, is
the famous running bull with a man on his back,
which is now in the National Museum.   The original
lacks a part of the body, and is painted yellow with
red spots.   There have been many conjectures as to
the meaning, and some have thought it was the picture
of an acrobat such as is mentioned in Homer, who
leaps on the back of running horses and animals ;

others that the bull is a river-god as seen on a Greek
coin of Sicily ; but the discovery of the Vapheio cups
with the great bulls, proves that this is a scene in
herding-life ; of the pursuit and subdual of a wild
bull by a hardy neatherd.   The costumes of the men
are similar.   A writer in the American Journal of
Archæology suggests that the herdsman represents a
man not leaping on the bull's back, but running on
the other side of him, the skill of the artist not being
able to indicate this, so he puts him on top in full
sight.   This is strengthened by Egyptian pictures, as
in a funny painting of a wine-press, where figures in
the air twist the press, and in a picture from a tomb
at Gizeh, where an oxherd, standing on the back of a
bull, is evidently meant to be a man running on the
further side.

Some broken pottery has been dug out at Tiryns.
The oldest Tirynthian vases are similar to the Hissarlik, with perforated projections through which a
string was passed to serve as a handle, and the clay is
of like reddish yellow.   The concentric circles and
herring-bone patterns are similar to Trojan terra cottas.
There are also found vases of the Mycenæan period,
jugs with a string-handle that are ornamented with
broad stripes, and the decoration to right and left of
a vertical center.   Figures of animals and birds occur,
and the paint used is lustrous and lasting ; and pieces
of vases have been found which are thought to represent the transitional period between the Mycenæan
and the Dipylon, in which human figures are sometimes introduced, as in a comical warlike scene of a
big-eyed horse, bird-headed men, and a spiral-tailed
dog, evidently a *chef d' œuvre*.   The would-be splendid
action of the warriors and their grasshopper legs and
inflated chests, as they draw back to hurl spears, is

laughable enough, but the men who could make mighty walls and attack them, and pull down bulls and lions, were weak in drawing. These figures are painted in brown on light yellow ground. In the picture, the space above the horse is artificially filled in with ornamentation, exactly in the style of Mycenæan pottery.

The ruins of a Byzantine church have been discovered in the court yard of the Tirynthian citadel, and, as I have said, these tokens of the former existence of a widespread Greek empire, are seen in every part of Greece.

I staid at Tiryns till the shadows of evening began to fall, succeeding the lurid sunset, sitting by the circular fireplace in the center of the hall of the palace ; and, in the ghostly gloaming and shadow, one could recall the scene of the Odyssey in the palace of Alkinoös : "therewith he (Odysseus) sat him down by the hearth in the ashes at the fire, and behold a dead silence fell on all. And at the last the ancient lord Echeneus spake among them, an elder of the Phæacians, excellent in speech and skilled in much wisdom of the old time. With good will he made harangue and spake among them : ' Alkinoös, this truly is not the more seemly way, nor is it fitting that the stranger should sit upon the ground in the ashes by the hearth, while these men refrain them, waiting thy word. Nay, come, bid the stranger arise, and set him on a chair inlaid with silver, that we may pour forth likewise wine before Zeus, whose joy is in the thunder, who attends on reverend suppliants.' "

CHAPTER XIII.

THE ARGOLIC HERÆON AND EPI-DAUROS.

An excursion to the Argive Heræon, may be made either from Mycenæ or Nauplia, and I went by the first of these routes; and this, perhaps, was well, as thereby one sees the two places together, or almost simultaneously, that anciently were closely related, the temple of Hera having been the shrine of the Pelopid race and the starting-point of the Iliad. When coming down from Mycenæ, you pass around the foot of Mt. Zara, then enter the upper corner of the Argolic plain, as into an amphitheatre enclosed by mountains. Towards the northeast rises the grey top of Hagios Elias, on the lower slope of which hangs Mycenæ, while to the south is Mt. Eubœa, on whose eastern spur lie the ruins of the Heræon.

A menacing cloud closed over this mountain of Eubœa,

> "The ragged rims of thunder brooding low
> With shadow-streaks of rain,"

that gave the scenery for a time a scowling look, but which rolled off and left the hills and plain sunny again, and a truly magnificent plain it is, opening to the sea. The Heræon, or temple of Hera, has a commanding site overlooking the whole plain of "horse-pasturing Argos," sacred earth of Hera.

Here was her chief shrine in Greece, now reached by a path diverging from the main road, if road it may be called, like a wagon track over a western prairie.

The remains of the Hera-temple stand on a terrace, with a massive retaining-wall, partly hewn out of the rock, on each side of which are two ravines that are torrents in the rainy season.   It is a lordly place for a temple.   The first temple of Hera, of unknown age, was destroyed by fire 423 B. C., and everything of this edifice as well as of the temple that succeeded it, was swept flat ; and until recent excavations, there was little left to be seen, although the site was known. Indeed, at my first visit I must have ridden over or near it, unconscious of its locality.

But here, as tradition is, at the awful shrine of Hera, the leaders of the expedition against Troy, from Pylos, Mycenæ, Argos, Sparta, assembled to swear allegiance to Agamemnon, and here opened the first scene of "the tale of Troy divine."

We owe what is now known of the second and more splendid temple, chiefly to the labors of the American School at Athens ; and thus we, in our young America, seem to have some share in these Homeric ruins, seat of Argive art even before the glory of Athens had arisen.

The Heræon is six miles or so from Argos, and once constituted its chief sanctuary, although it belonged originally to Mycenæ.   The upper terrace on which the older temple stood, is a level plateau more than fifty metres in length and the same in width. It is bounded by a wall of irregular stones of utmost antiquity, and there is a gradual slope from this to the new temple terrace of similar length.

In February, 1892, Dr. Waldstein, Mr. Fox and Mr. Brownson, commenced digging, and according to their report, sunk trenches, soon coming to the wall of the long stoa built of well-fitted stones. Here fragments of pottery of the most ancient kind, brown on yellow ground, were found. An iron strigil such as athletes use was turned up. They also came across a passage, or tunnel, and cisterns connected with the water-system of the temple.

On the uppermost terrace, or platform, of the old temple, many discoveries of metal and pottery were made—bronze objects, glass articles, and the relics of sun-dried brick walls of great age.

But when the broad courses of the foundation of the new temple were laid bare by cutting down the entire top of the stylobate, no portion of the superstructure was revealed ; yet the form and dimensions of the temple were revealed, and the capital of a twenty-channeled column was unearthed, which gave the dimensions of the columns of a peripteral hexastyle Doric temple, with twelve columns on the long side. The usual cella, pronaos and opisthodomos, were surely, but rather vaguely, marked. Some bases of columns only were found, and the red paint and lettering of the old stone-masons, were yet seen on the facings of the walls ; but the most valuable objects discovered were fragments of sculpture, of which the small head of Hera, now in the National Museum at Athens, is the most interesting.

The head of Hera, was found about a foot and a half below the ground, just west of the outer foundation wall ; the place was pointed out to me both on the spot, and afterwards on a plan, by the architect of the American School. This fragment has naturally been made much of by Dr. Waldstein, the discoverer of it, from the fact that here, at the principal seat of the Argive School of sculpture, stood the chryselephantine statue of Hera, by Polykleitos,

famous in antiquity ; and this fragment is not unrea-
sonably regarded as a head of Hera, or a supposable
type, at least, of the Hera of Polykleitos. It is of
Parian marble, and the face has a straight onlook, as
if it were a shrine-statue, earnest in character. The
full face shows symmetry in the two sides, and this is
seen in the even treatment of the hair, with the
parted locks on the forehead. There is, certainly, a
calm beauty about it, which is not hard but yet
slightly archaic, and that might have belonged to the
5th century School of Polykleitos. The large head
of Hera that is in the Naples Museum, is considered
by Brunn to be a still closer reflex of Polykleitos
than the Ludovisi Juno—a broader, simpler, somewhat
coarser and stronger Argive type, more bony and
powerful, less oval, with fuller under lip, and also of
a slightly archaic character.

Polykleitos stood at high-water mark of the Argive
School. He strove to retain nature, so that while he
did not rise so high as the Attic ideal, yet was true
to the perfection of nature. He was a younger contemporary of Pheidias, belonging to the last half of
the 5th century B.C., and studied at Sikyon, under
Ageladas, but made Argos his home. He was not
only great in gods but in athletes, as in the Dory-
phoros and Diadumenos. The first of these is of
round full proportions, but marks of archaism are to
be observed, as in the flat conventionalized abdomen,
and the large planes of flesh. The head has the
angular contour, as seen in the Hera. The Diadumenos, or athlete binding on his forehead a fillet of
victory, is a beautiful work, and the hair is arranged
in bunches as in the Hera. The Amazon which won
the prize over the Amazon of Pheidias, has the unmis-
takable Polykleitos head. It is not, therefore, strange,

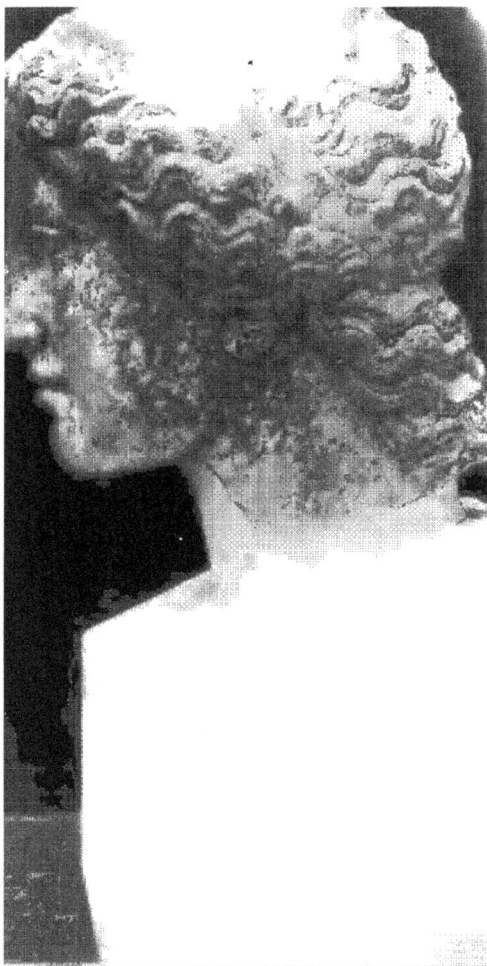

HERA HEAD FROM ARGOLIC HERAEON

that the head found in the Argive temple of Hera
should be thought to bear the stamp of Polykleitos,
if not to be by his very hands. Mr. Waldstein in
speaking of it says : " As to the question of how the
statue stood, I was first inclined to believe that it
must have stood alone on its base, probably immediately at the west end of the temple. The beautiful
delicate finish of the surface, made me doubt of its
being a pedimental figure. But since the metope was
found in which the surface is so well preserved, the
careful finish and elaboration of the surface in this
piece of architectural sculpture, makes me consider
it possible that the Hera stood in the pediment under
which it was found, and represented the goddess
standing immediately beside the central figure, or
figures, in the scene of the departure of Agamemnon,
and the Homeric heroes, for Troy."

The original head, now in the National Museum,
impressed me more than any plaster-cast of it, and
led me to believe in the possible truth of Mr. Waldstein's view. It is of vigorous character, and has a
touch of higher skill, so that it may possibly be the
only original Polykleitos that we have, though not
equal to the great sculptures. The marble is honey-
combed on the cheek and neck, and stained quite
yellow, and the tip of the nose was chipped by the
pickaxe. The hair is not too much worked up for
the best art. The modelling of the cheek, the nose
and the eye, has delicacy and purity. The curve
from the lower lip to the point of the chin is considered to be particularly lovely, and the chin is neither
heavy nor weak. The slightly parted lips, the full
lower lip, and the breadth of the face, are thought to
be characteristic of the Argive School, while the band
which binds the hair is characteristic of Hera, the

Hera of Polykleitos. But this was not the only
sculpture-fragment discovered. There is the torso of
a nude warrior from a metope of the second temple,
of fine marble, the head and legs missing. The
anatomical articulations of the chest and ribs are well
moulded, and the hand of the prostrate foe pressed on
the breast, is particularly good. The head of an
Amazon, a helmeted head with signs of color, an
architectural bit with elaborations of the lotos pattern, as well as other objects, have been dug up, and
the excavating is going on, and, indeed, the structure
on the southwest slope promises to be the richest yet
explored, and some fragments of carving of exceeding
interest have recently been found.

The still more interesting excursion to Epidauros,
may be made also in two ways from Athens, either
by steamer from the Piræus sailing by the islands of
the Saronic gulf along by Ægina, Poros and Hydra,
with fine views of the Peloponnesian mountains, or
by rail to Nauplia, and thence by carriage to Epidauros.

I went by the latter route to Nauplia, itself a gay
little half military town worth a visit, situated between
the two cliffs of Palamidi and Itsh-Kaleh, the last
jutting into the sea, and is strikingly picturesque
from situation, and from its old Venetian walls and
fortifications, that the modern inhabitants are pulling
down with that fever now in Greece to do away with
everything foreign, and to become purely Hellenic.

At the bit of a hotel on the Agora, I occupied a
room next to that of the Greek minister of war, who
had come down to Nauplia to inspect the garrison of
this important military post, which was formerly
held against the Turks when all other places in

Greece had submitted, and was the capital of the kingdom until this was removed to Athens. The war-minister was a small, dark, gilt-bedizened man, but looked as if he had no lack of energy and self-asser-tion, and he was said to be unpopular at the time on account of this last quality, that had been exerted in some way highly exasperating to public opinion.

Nauplia, anciently, was the seat of the worship of Poseidon, a divinity opposed (as different members of a quarrelsome family) to Hera, who had her shrine at Argos, which city finally took possession of Nauplia in the Messenian war ; and the road from Nauplia to Argos, about five miles distant, to the northwest, skirts the marshy shores of the Argolic bay, the ancient Lernæan marsh.

Argos—venerable name—is a town now of 9,600 inhabitants which, ever since it was ruled by "the princes of Pelops' line," has been an inhabited and im-portant place. It is the city of the plain, the "horse-feeding" Argolic plain, even now noted for its pastur-age, and its horses and cattle, and one of the most fertile corn-bearing spots in Greece, although a great part of it lies untilled. Argos was a power second only to Corinth in the Peloponnesos, and dominated all the region round about, but nothing now is left of the classic epoch, excepting a terrace of polygonal stones, and an amphitheatre hewn out of the rock, with tiers of seats divided into three sections by two corridors, and that could have once seated twenty thousand persons ; but there is a roughness about it which does not belong to the theatres of Athens and Epidauros. When I passed through Argos, the peo-ple, children especially, black-eyed little Argives, swarmed into the streets from the low stone houses, an out-of-door population such as you see in small

Italian towns. The sharp, refined look of the people
of Athens is not seen in the Greek country towns.
Overhanging Argos is its old Acropolis of Larisa,
crowned by a crumbling mediæval fortress, which
was defended by Ypsilantes against the Turks, and
this hill is a commanding feature from the plain, as
is indeed the whole dark cincture of the Artemision
and other mountains, running to the south and west
like an encircling wall.

The road east from Nauplia to Epidauros, which is
now our destination, across the upper part of the
neck of the Argolic peninsula, soon after it leaves
Nauplia, begins to go through barren valleys and
hills that are exactly described in the phrase of
Homer "rugged Lakedæmon cleft with glens." I
have, indeed, rarely seen a more blank and desolate
region without a human habitation, though now and
then a shepherd and his family with their pattering
flocks of sheep and goats are encountered, the people
stalking on without a word of greeting. They look
as if it was a hard matter to live, and to get together
the means of living, and that they could waste no
time in trivialties of intercourse with strangers.
They do not seem to be good-natured, or kindly,
though this may be a harsh judgment ; and they form
in this respect a contrast to the mountaineers of the
Austrian Tyrol, who are a religious folk and bestow
a guttural blessing on you as you pass.

One sees the walls of old places hard to be distinguished from the rocks themselves, as if growing
out of them, while he goes by or over the sterile hills
of Theokasto and Krotoni. The modern road is well
made and passes rivers and profound ravines on solid
stone causeways and bridges, as in Switzerland.

As you travel further on, the country grows more

pleasing and open with now and then a farm-house guarded by surly dogs, until the village of Nea-Epidauros is reached, situated rather high on the side of a hill and surrounded by lemon groves. Some five miles on is Epidavros, or ancient Epidauros, in the neighborhood of which are the ruins of the Hieron of Epidauros, which have been, and are now, the scene of active exploration by the Archæological Society of Greece, under the superintendence of Kabbadias, general director of antiquities, who has published a learned work entitled "*Fouilles d'Epidaure.*"

Epidauros is one of the loveliest hill-girt spots in Greece, a mountain shrine, having a quiet charm without a shadow of the modern, and remains in the memory a pure Hellenic picture, as if painted on a Greek vase, or carved on the front of a white marble temple, with a sunny sky above and a "sea of beauty" around.

Epidauros lies at the base, or in the hollow, of a semi-circle of gray mountains that catch each passing delicate tint of color, and in an inner fold of the mountains, as it were, and nowhere, as I have said, in Greece, is there a scene more thoroughly permeated with the quiet past, as if it were a poem of Alkman, who wrote in a tranquil historic period. It is not rugged and defiant, like warlike Mycenæ, but peaceful as the home of a benificent power, for this was the seat of the worship of the gentle Asklepios, as was Argos, of Hera, and Nauplia, of Poseidon ; and here came the sick of the whole Greek world to be healed, and it impressed me that it must have been the healthiness of the place itself, near the sea and yet among hills, which suggested it, and drew the people to it.

Through the valley runs a little brook where the nymphs might have bathed and played, and great

12

fragments of half-sunk polygonal wall here and there
show the hoar antiquity of some of the remains, while
the highest mountain of the Argive peninsula, Mt.
Arachnæon (now Arna) rises bare and stony-faced in
front.

The cult of Asklepios at Epidauros and other places,
putting him at the head of the Pantheon, calling him
on inscriptions lately discovered μέγας, σώτηρ, κύριος,
even Zeus, show how much the Greeks thought of
this divinity.* It shows, too, how much they thought
of vigorous health, and physical culture, how they
loved the priceless boon of a sound mind in a sound
body ; and when one comes to see the beautiful things
that are and were in this spot, he perceives that Greek
art was healthy art, and was a product of the cheerful
Greek spirit, that its root was in joy, that it sprang
from the poetry born in the hearts of the people.
There was nothing sickly or false in sentiment. It
was virile and strong. It was, for the most part, for
the invigoration and the elevation of the mind in what
was beautiful in nature and thought.

There was also in this spot among the springs of
the hills an abundance of pure water, and great use
was evidently made of bathing, as seen from the great
cisterns that are found—no bad therapeutics ; and
that much vigorous open-air exercise was prescribed,
the ruins of the gymnasium and the stadion, and the
extensive walks about the ample grounds, testify ;
but it was held that the cures were effected by no
human means, or prescriptions (though the old Greeks
understood well for their day the science of medicine)
but by supernatural power. "Science," as another
says, "was subordinated to religion." Having offered
the sacrifices to Asklepios, and having performed all

* New Chapters in Greek History.

the prescribed religious rites, the patient lay down in one of the splendid porticos of the temple, and was hushed by the temple-attendant to sleep through all the ''holy night,'' in whose still hours, under the golden stars raining their happy influences, it was hoped and believed he would be visited in his dreams by the kindly god himself, who would tell him what to do for his recovery. A number of inscriptions have been dug up attesting to such miraculous cures ; but if no cure was made no pay was asked for, and how would this rule work now-a-days, when the patient not only has to pay for the drugs, but is not permitted to return the visits ?

There was another odd pagan practice, that no patient was allowed to die on the premises, and the poor dying man was hurried off to some other vicinity to perform that last act. Yet it was, on the whole, a humane institution, and through the force of imagination, or the medical skill of the priests, an alleviation of human suffering and disease was undoubtedly effected. Lavish offerings were made to the shrine by grateful patients, who went away leaping and joyful from this Greek pool of Siloam ; and many bas-relief *ex-votos* in the style of a good period of art are discovered, portraying the exact kind and manner of the healing that was wrought. I copy from a recent English author this translation of a cure of dyspepsia recently found at Epidauros : '' never to give way to anger, to submit to a special diet of bread and cheese, of parsley and lettuce, of lemon boiled in water, and milk with honey in it, to run in the gymnasium, to swing on the upper walk of the sanctuary, to rub the body with sand, to walk barefoot before bathing, to take a warm bath with wine in it, to rub oneself with salt and mustard, to gargle the throat and tonsils with cold water, finally, and this is all-important, to sacrifice to Asklepios and not to forget to pay the prescribed fees. This treatment was to be tried for nine days." But this is all introductory to the fact that here was another famous seat and center of Greek art.

Asklepios was held to be the son of Apollo, and, as one tradition has it, of a human mother, Koronis, and a touch of humanity was thus attached to him in the view of the ancients, and he was looked upon as a human god, as a mediating power to whom men might go without fear for aid and healing. His central Hieron was at Epidauros, and other shrines were subordinate to this, for here was the place of his birth, and one writer thus describes its situation : "Suppose we have landed at ancient Epidauros, and are bound for this beautiful upland health resort. First our course lies southward till, at half a mile's distance, the inland road turns to cross the fertile but narrow Epidaurian plain, which is about a quarter of a mile in width. The way then follows a mountain torrent for a time, and goes inland two miles more.

"At this point the pilgrim to the shrine of Esculapius leaves the high road to ascend the side and cross the shoulder of Mt. Tithion, on which Esculapius was born. Two downward miles and you are at last on the consecrated ground. A semicircle of gentle and for those parts well-wooded slopes hems in the Hieron to the northward, southward and eastward, while towards the north-west the valley leans into a wider valley through which extends the road that goes to Nauplia."

This was the road by which I had approached the Hieron, and in its immediate vicinity it passes through a level valley with shrubs and trees under the shadow of Mt. Tithion till it reaches the Hieron itself. Many delightful hours were spent in examining the rich remains, and in looking at the cheerful toils of the swarthy peasant laborers—men, women, girls and boys—who were engaged in excavating the lower lying portions of the ruins, and who sang and leaped as they stepped along under their basket burdens like the old Greek dithyrambic dancers. The dance and leap were in their blood.

The beautiful and symmetric theatre is situated a little higher up on a spur of Mt. Kynostion, now called Charani, and on the other extreme to the east are remains of reservoirs with the huge cisterns, showing that water was freely used, and that it was, in truth, a sort of water-cure establishment.

The Hieron, or sacred enclosure, with its clustered buildings, stood in the middle space, and consisted of the Temple of Asklepios, the Tholos of Polykleitos, the stadion, and the gymnasium. Of the ruins of the small peripteral temple of Asklepios, eighty-one feet long and forty broad, there is not much now standing, but its pediments were once carved with sculptures, some of which are in the Museum at Athens, representing on the eastern pediment a battle of Centaurs, and on the western a fight of Greeks with Amazons; and there were figures of Nereids and Victories; but the most remarkable building of all was the Tholos of Polykleitos, a circular structure one hundred and seven feet in diameter, of which the substructure is seen. This served as the base of two concentric rings of columns, the exterior ring being Doric and the interior a combination of Doric and Corinthian, that must have had an elegant effect. These pillars have disappeared excepting some capitals and other sculpture details now in the museums.

The edifices were evidently splendid, adorned with

relief-carvings portraying, as has been said, animated conflicts of Centaurs and Lapiths, and Greeks and Amazons, recalling the reliefs of the Temple of the Wingless Victory on the Acropolis, and those of the Temple of Zeus at Olympia. There were also round sculptures of Asklepios, Hekate, Hygeia and Aphrodite. Here Thrasymedes, a scholar of Skopas, is said to have wrought with something of his master's free skill. The statue of Asklepios found at Epidauros is in the National Museum, and the mild benignant countenance and symbolic curling snake, denote the healing divinity. There is also in the National Museum a statue of Aphrodite, found in the Temple of Asklepios, which is a Venus Genetrix, bearing a sword in one hand and an apple in the other. The Victory discovered in the Sanctuary at Epidauros, is like the Victory of Paionios at Olympia, and was probably an acroteria of the temple of Artemis. The Asklepios enthroned, in the National Museum, is from the Epidaurian sanctuary, a reminder of the similar chryselephantine statue by Thrasymedes of Paros. He sits receiving the long line of his patients, but the finest sculpture of all is the Amazon on horseback, from the rear front of the temple. This statue, of spirited action and the bèst style of Greek art, is a noteworthy addition to the Greek art found on Greek soil. Such works, with the more recent discovery of the interesting bronze quadriga at Delphi, which I omitted to speak of, are the invaluable things that archæology is bringing to light.

There is, likewise, in the Athens Museum a Corinthian capital from the Tholos, which is a masterpiece of architectural carving. The composition is of acanthus leaves, crisp and elegant, the upper portions so arranged as to make a play of light and shade, producing a lovely effect.

THEATRE OF EPIDAUROS

The head of a lion forming a gargoyle, from the temple of Asklepios, is an admirable specimen of architectural decoration, and but very little conventionalized, the head fiercely grinning, the crinkled skin, the rough hair, affording a fine contrast to the exquisite flower ornamentation that curves and blossoms at its sides ; and how powerful is the carving in every stroke, though the lower jaw is gone, which would have given it still more grip and character !

The Theatre constructed by Polykleitos, at Epidauros, is one of the best preserved theatres in Greece, and decidedly the most beautiful of all.

Pausanias wrote of it, " Roman theatres may be finer, and those of latter days in Greece may be larger, but the Epidaurian theatre is peerless for harmony of proportion and charm of aspect." It is a rare pleasure to be able to confirm by one's own eyesight an old critic's opinion, as if it had been expressed to-day, and to confirm it in every particular.

The Epidaurian theatre is, in point of fact, in all its lines, almost in a perfect state, and its concentric rows of seats could be occupied to the very top by thronging crowds at this moment. In our great political meetings I have longed for such grand audience rooms. The theatre opens to the northwest, and is divided half way up by a broad passage into thirty-two lower rows of seats and an upper section of twenty rows. These are apportioned into wedge-like divisions, ascended by flights of steps for the convenience of seating the audience. To show the size and scope of the auditorium, the upper seats are one hundred and three feet above the orchestra, and behind them there is the boundary wall of the building. I tried the acoustic properties, and one could be heard from below at the topmost seat with perfect distinctness without straining the voice. The circular floor of the orchestra, surrounded by a stone parapet, is not flagged like the Dionysiac theatre at Athens, and in the middle of it is a cyclindrical stone where stood an altar.

The stage, whose foundation walls have been cleared, once held an ornate building, or scenic palace, with fourteen Ionic columns, standing back of the proscenium, and at this part of the structure were side-entrances to the orchestra—a sunny scene and spot with groupings of picturesque sharp-pointed though low hills beyond, hemming it in like a secluded niche, away in the mountains consecrated to silence, health and repose.

In the small stone museum near by, where you walk about undisturbed, are preserved fragments of considerable interest, pedestals with inscriptions in honor of Asklepios, and commemorative of cures wrought by his power, pieces of pillars combining the Ionic and Corinthian styles, and ornamental slabs from the frieze of the Tholos, honeysuckle patterns, interlacing vines and hints from nature crystallized into stone, that show a most delightful fancifulness of poetic art.

Epidauros will always be to me a rare poem of the beautiful Greek land, most peaceful and pleasant, and though real, yet more like a dream of the classic age over which bends the deep blue sky of Hellas.

CHAPTER XIV.

OLYMPIA.

I made the journey from Athens to Olympia
smoothly enough by rail, and quite differently from the
old times when one went on horseback through the
rough stony defiles of the Peloponnesian hills, by
narrow and tortuous paths; and how different from
the classic days, when the Greeks made this journey
to Olympia the event of their lives, in order to attend
the great games!

Having already spoken of Corinth, one passes next
after leaving Corinth through a cultivated littoral
country sloping to the Gulf, and delightfully green
with vineyards, though crossing the frequent sandy
beds of dry torrents, until he comes to the site of
Sikyon, which was the seat of a famous school of
sculpture, as also of painting on wood. This is in
the land of the Achaian League, where the last
gleam of freedom fell on Greece.

Opposite, across the Gulf, stand the mountains of
Kithæron and Helicon, the sapphire sea rolling
between; and in truth, this ride from Corinth to
Patras, is one of the most beautiful in the world (the
Riviera not excepted), from the noble forms of mountains, the coloring of water and sky, and the glorious
historic associations. There are, at Sikyon, remains
of a stadion, and of a theatre, which the American
school have excavated. The low conical coast-hills,
cultivated to the top and backed by the higher range
of Kyllene, afford a constant variety of scenery; and

I was struck with the evident truth of Col. Leake's
remark, that the soil of the southern hilly coast of
the Corinthian Gulf, had been formed by the wash-
ings of the loftier Peloponnesian mountains. Crossing the river Asopos, you reach the plain of Ægion,
traversed by numerous streams and dotted with
cypress groves, and pale ashy green olive-trees, that
give the local coloring in Greece, so that one " sees
grey," until near the bay of Itea, the snow-capped
escarped summits of Mt. Parnassos (when that mountain chooses to unveil itself) come in view. Parnassos
is a truly majestic object seen directly in front, from
this side of the Gulf, and its highest crest is almost
always covered with snow, forming the central,
craggy white throne of Greece. Diakóptika, I
remember as a place where the road passes over one
of those deep ravines or cuts in the hills made by
mountain torrents, so characteristic of the scenery.
Ægion, is, for this region, a large town, consisting of
two parts, the upper and lower, and was known by
the name of Vostizza to Col. Leake, and it bore this
name when I saw it first. In ancient times it was
the most important city of Achaia, the hills rising
finely at its back, and walling in the plain which
smiles with plantations of currants and vineyards that
grow more rich and cultivated as one approaches
Patras, though the mountains run down nearer the
sea ; but the most striking object of all, continually
drawing attention to it, is the emerald sea itself, that
spreads out, in the middle regions of the Gulf, into
broader dimensions, and which is of a glancing sap-
phire-blue, changing to a greenish yellow, or lemon,
color, closer in to the shore ; and now and then it is
enlivened by the sail of a Greek bark, which the distance leaves us free to imagine to be antique or

modern, the water dancing and sparkling with its γέλασμα of sunny waves, though in fierce moods roughened by white-caps.

You look across to Mesolonghi, which has its associations of Botsares, and of bloody siege and defeat turned into victory. On the 17th of March, 1824, Mesolonghi gave the freedom of the city in terms of grateful praise to Lord Byron, who afterwards died there, telling the Greeks with his last breath that nothing was left for them but to fight. This was three years before "the happy blunder" of Navarino, and when the outlook was gloomiest, and the unaided hand-to-hand struggle against the Turks was going on. Now this is changed, and Greece if not a great, is a free country, and is waiting its chance to become strong and self-supporting. This depends, in a large measure, on its agricultural resources and development, for Greece is capable of producing a great variety of products, that might become, by intelligent and systematic labor, of the highest value. It is a land of fruits and flowers. The laurels and roses by the roadside, and at the railway stations, make a variegated bordering to the way, though some parts of the route are monotonous, even as an old Greek dramatist says that there must be in every journey, and also in every discourse, some dull place.

At Patras, the inn was far from clean or comfortable, and the dogs yelled awfully in the streets all night. Early the next morning of May 29, 1895, I set forth from Patras for Olympia, a journey of five and a half hours by rail, or seventy-four miles, a soft cooling breeze from the sea circulating through the railway carriage, so that one was tempted to sit bareheaded and enjoy it. There was, indeed, a great deal to enjoy by the way, which lay along the pleas-

ant coast of the Bay of Patras, planted on hillside and
in valley with currant gardens—the currant (derived
from " Corinth ") being a small kind of grape, and not
the currant-berry as we know it. On the opposite
Ætolian coast are the almost mathematically pyramidal rocks, towering darkly, while inland to the
south, the range of Panachaikon runs nearly down
to the sea, until the narrow plain of Kato-Achaia is
reached, dotted with oak trees like a park, and we
here arrive at the boundary line between Achaia and
sacred Elis. In the distance are the higher Arcadian mountains, and Mt. Erýmanthos renowned in
fable. Wild red geraniums here skirt the roadside,
and the blue of the sea with its snowy foam-line is
ever a lovely sight.

In the neighborhood of Pyrgos, the island of Zante,
blue and ethereal in the distance, with its peak of
Mt. Skopos, comes into view, and this sight of Mt.
Skopos accompanies us the rest of the way. Two or
three days previous to this, there had been seven considerable earthquake-shocks felt at Zante, lovely
Zante, for these beautiful lands are precarious lands
to live in, so that we might say that they have the
fatal gift of beauty. Pyrgos, a place of 12,000 inhabitants, is the largest town on the road, and a busy
mart of the currant trade ; and hereabouts, the railway turns more inland, and, going over the little
river Enipeus, runs into the valley of the Alpheios,
until it reaches Olympia.

In the fifteen minutes' walk from the little station
of Olympia to the inn which is situated near the foot
of the hill of Drouva, one crosses a small bridge over
the Kladeos, an impetuous and turbid stream, which
has worn for itself a channel thirty or forty feet deep,

cutting the earth away nearer and nearer to the ancient wall that surrounds the ruins, so that if it be not curbed at some time by artificial means, its current may be joined by the overflowings of the larger river, Alpheios, which with the Kladeos surrounds the plain of Olympia, and there will then be danger of the submerging once more of the whole plain and its classic ruins. Olympia, in this way, with the concurrence of land-slides from the neighboring hills, was buried under an alluvium deposited by the Kladeos, which had left its channel and passed across the plain, the destruction being completed by the larger stream of the Alpheios, whose embankments were broken down.

Olympia, which had stood comparatively undisturbed even down to Christian times, became sealed up for a thousand years, until it occurred to the German art-critic, Winckelmann (with whose name we began this Greek story), that there must be rich remains of antiquity here, and this idea was enthusiastically caught up by French writers, and was discussed both in France and Germany, until the French government sent a scientific expedition to Greece in 1829, which made some superficial explorations; but the matter then rather rested until, in 1874, a treaty with the Greek government was negotiated, by which the sole control of the enterprise was given to Germany, and the scholar, Ernst Curtius, was appointed to carry out the work.

This work of excavation was done successfully in the space of six years at the cost of two hundred thousand dollars, so that the great rectangle of the Altis, six hundred and fifty feet long by five hundred and seventy-five broad, was uncovered, with the exception of the stadion, and a small portion of the

northwest corner. The earth had lain upon the
plain to the depth of from sixteen to twenty-three
feet, but this immense undertaking was rewarded by
the discovery of some one hundred and thirty marble
statues, thirteen thousand objects in bronze, and four
hundred inscriptions, while the whole plan and story
of this renowned precinct was laid bare to modern
eyes. Alas, Christian hands had already destroyed
the temples and numberless works of art !

The natural aspects of the spot, where was centred
so much of ancient Hellas, are not disappointing.
Nature, as at Delphi, and Marathon, has done all to
make it a marked scene. The vale of Olympia has,
indeed, the reputation, in modern times as in ancient,
of being a very hot region, a place of warm damp
climate almost unbearable, but, fortunately, I found
the atmosphere there delightful, with a clear sky and
a cool breeze to temper the heat.

The area of the Altis, which once was filled with
oak-groves, and with an almost tropical vegetation, is
now a waste spot and left to its memories, and where
one can wander about at will with none to interfere
with him, among fallen columns and sweet-scented
blossoming weeds and wild-flowers, under the shadow
of Mt. Kronion, a hill of four hundred feet high.

This hill of Kronion though small, is a notable
feature, thickly overgrown with low trees and bushes,
from the top of which can be seen the whole topog-
raphy of the Olympic plain, that is like a round
amphitheatre circled by low hills, open only to the
west where the valley of the Alpheios trends toward
the sea. The river Alpheios to the northward, rims
in the plain like a silver ribbon running about it,
with gently outlined hills beyond. You see also the
torrent of the Kladeos, and how it has sheared down

OLYMPIA AND THE ALPHEIOS

its banks, and at the point of junction of these two
streams, lies the sacred enclosure of the Altis.

In visiting the ruins from the inn, you repass the
small bridge over the Kladeos, near the remains of
the wall of the Altis, and come first upon the ground
where was formerly situated the Large Gymnasium,
surrounded by porticos, and a part of which formed
the Palæstra. You see also the ruins of the Theok-
leion, or the house of the priests, and the Byzantine
church built over what is supposed to have been the
studio of Pheidias where he wrought the statue of
Olympian Zeus. After these are the remains of the
Leonidæon, formerly the largest building in Olympia,
and of the Boulouterion, or council hall, a Doric
building, the foundations of whose long south portico
have been uncovered, and where the athletes took
their oath. Following around the bend of the river
you come to the Stadion, as yet unexcavated, and
which, in the ancient days, was six hundred and
thirty feet long. The triumphal arch leading up to
it, built in Roman times, and now half in ruins and
overgrown with weeds, is a picturesque object that
you are tempted to sketch, but which seems out of
place on this Hellenic ground. Then come, one
after another, a number of curious little stone treas-
ure-houses, crowded in at the foot of Mt. Krónion,
then the bases of statues of Zeus called the Zanes;
the Metroön, or temple of the mother of the gods;
the circular Ionic edifice of the Philippeion built after
the battle of Cheronæa, in which were golden statues
of Philip II and Alexander; the Prytancion; the
Herodes Exedra; the Agora where were many altars;
the spot, too, on which once was the tomb of Pelops;
and so we are brought round to the place from which
we started, and to the Heræon, or the old sanctuary

of Hera.   In the centre of all this sacred area, and
the centre of all interest, amid the thick oak-groves
of the Altis, stood the great temple of Panhellenic
Zeus, the broad stylobate of which remains, and in
front of which was the Festal Square, where congre-
gated the concourse of Hellenes who came to Olympia
from all parts of Greece, and from the golden Cher-
sonese, the African Cyrene, and Halicarnassos and
Syracuse, every four years, in the ''Peace of God.''

The temple of Zeus, thrown down by earthquakes
in the sixth century A.D., was a Doric hexastyle
peripteros, with thirteen columns on each side, built
of a kind of shell-conglomerate limestone, coated with
stucco, and was erected by an Eleian architect named
Libon, in 570 B. C., out of spoils taken from the
Pisans.   It was a Doric temple, but of coarser work
than the Parthenon.

Immense capitals lie about, half covered with earth,
that give one an impression of great antiquity, and,
in the pronaos, is still some rude mosaic ; the cella
was divided in three sections, in one of which (the
marble partition walls of it you can now see) were
paintings of Paionios.

The color used on these temple walls, and on the
walls of other Greek temples, must have made their
appearance quite different from our common notions
of them.   They shone in strong positive colors.
Under the brilliant heavens of Greece, these structures
responded to the warm sky-tints, and the lively imag-
inations of the people.   The primitive colors were
employed in mural painting—red, yellow, blue, black,
and sometimes violet—but in a variety of lines and
decorative patterns, combined also with gold and
bronze ornamentation.   The use of color on statues
was, undoubtedly, more modified, but, one may be

sure, that the painting which was laid on the most beautiful marble statues, was sparing, and without injury to them, with a chaste and exquisite taste that did not merge into the coarsely realistic.

In the third section of the temple, at the rear of the sanctuary, was the still more famous ivory and gold statue of Olympian Zeus, held to be the last and master work of Pheidias. It was acknowledged to be the true image of his form, when, at the artist's prayer, Zeus hurled a thunderbolt shattering a hydria that stood in front of the statue. What is odd enough, undoubted fragments of the black limestone pedestal of this statue, at least of the pavement where it stood, lie scattered about, so that you can pick up a piece and put it in your pocket. The figure of the enthroned divinity was forty feet high, so that, as an old writer said, if he should rise he would take the roof off. He held a sceptre in one hand and a Victory in the other, as representing the supreme judge of the sacred games given in his honor. The upper part of the body was represented as nude, carved in broad ivory plates resembling white flesh, and the lower part was clothed with simple drapery made of gold of different tints. The head, majestic and mild, like the Otricoli bust, that, however, lacked in power and was but a faint type, was crowned with bronze sprigs of olive. The throne was decorated with elaborate painted bas-relief. It was Pheidias' masterpiece. An old coin of Elis has been supposed to be a copy of the statue, but this is conjecture, since the coin-image is stiffly archaic, and yet the pose of the figure is of a serious majesty, and the countenance has strongly marked brows, as in the original. Such was the Greek conception of him who came nearest in their idea to the All-Father. Zeus was worshiped at

13

Olympia not as a local divinity, but as a universal power, and his was the common shrine of the Hellenes from all the provinces, and the Greek who had not seen this benignant powerful statue of Olympian Zeus was thought to have lived in vain.

In front of the temple there were statues of the nine great Homeric heroes, carved by Onatas, and also bronzes of athletes, of which scattered about the whole area there were some three thousand, commemorating the victors of different periods and cities. I will speak of the Greek games in the succeeding chapter.

To the east of the temple is still to be seen the tall triangular base, on which once stood the Nike of Paionios. All the paths tended to this central spot, and were arranged for the easy circulation of vast multitudes.

At the foot of bosky Mt. Kronion, was the Heræon, the oldest temple in Olympia, differing from the rest, and, at present, most of its half-broken pillars, not uniform in style, are standing. The peculiarities of this edifice go to prove the theory of the development of the Doric order from buildings of wood-construction; but here,—and this is its distinction, was found the Hermes of Praxiteles, the base of which statue now is seen inside of the temple, where Pausanias said it stood. The sculpture was discovered lying in front of the pedestral imbedded in a deposit of gravel and clay, which, in a wonderful manner, preserved it. The Heræon is not far from the Palæstra, to which I found myself returning, as to a spot which seemed to conserve the classic memories of the place. The pavement on the Palæstra, or a part of it, artificially prepared for the better hold in boxing and wrestling, still remains.

Here, as I came more than once, and seated myself
on a base of a broken pillar, under the blue sky, with
a soft breeze that gently swayed the purple weeds
and flowers, the Alpheios shining in the distance
like silver as it sweeps around the borders of the
plain shut in by low hills, and the brightness, and the
silence, in which only great memories stirred, these
made it a place where one could feel the very *geist* of
the old Greek life, which was a life of heroic effort,
of strength that came through struggle, of aiming
after, even if it could not attain, that which is higher
than life—ideal beauty and perfection.

We have to recross the bridge over the Kladeos to
go up to the Museum, where so much of the real life
of Olympia still survives in its art.   The Olympian
museum was designed by the German architect Adler
with the aid of Dr. Doerpfeld, and is the third of
those solid galleries which show such good taste and
such artistic knowledge, and which are among the
chief attractions of modern Greece ; and it holds
the gem of them all, itself worth a pilgrimage to
Greece.   The edifice is an attempt to represent the
size and plan of the old temple of Zeus from which
the sculptures it contains were mainly taken.

On either side of the entrance are two Doric columns
that reproduce those of the temple, and the central
hall corresponds to that of the original temple, while
around it are grouped the fragments of sculptures
that adorned the pediments and walls of the sanctuary.   At one end, between the doors, as if flying, is
the colossal Nike of Paionios, or what remains of that
bold and beautiful statue that stood near the temple
of Zeus on a pedestal still there, with its extended
wings, the tips of the toes touching a piece of stone
painted blue as symbolizing the sky.   The inscrip-

tion on this pedestal runs thus : "Messenians and Naupactians have consecrated this image to the Olympic Zeus from a tenth of the booty taken in war. Paionios, the Mendean made it, who also carried off the prize for the acroteria placed upon the temple." An *æstrus* of inspiration fills it with a rushing movement, in which its ample robe is caught and swelled outward. The long extended form clad in Doric chiton appears to float in the air; and yet the figure is too robust for highest beauty, as if it were, in truth, an *athletic* victory with all the energy of Olympian Zeus in its body. Noble as it is, it does not equal the grandeur and flying movement of the Nike of Samothrake, now in the Louvre, with its broad magnificent wings, and which combines the same abounding bodily vigor, with an ethereal power of heaven-sent angelic victory.

On the sides of the hall are arranged the sculptures of the two pediments, and, first on the left as you enter, is *The Preparation of Pelops for the chariot race*, usually ascribed to Alkamenes, and which stood at the east end of the temple. This has been pieced together from a great many fragments, so that you cannot be grateful enough to the archæologic skill that accomplished such a difficult work. At the apex is the imposing form of Zeus whose head is lacking, but the wide chest and drapery flowing over the lower limbs, present a mighty personality. Oinomaos, the father, on the left of Zeus, holding a staff, is also a powerful form, by whom stands Sterope, his wife, the best-preserved figure. The tall young hero Pelops, in whom the interest centres, and his bride Hippodameia, are on the right of Zeus, the female holding a veil above her head. Two four-horse-chariots stand on each side of the group, with their charioteers, that tell the story of the contest; the horse of each, in the outer row, is of round sculpture, while the other horses are in high relief-sculpture. A bald-headed man with meditative and prophetic look, a sitting boy, a strong youthful figure of the river Kladeos, a kneeling girl, and the still more vigorous recumbent river-god Alpheios, with one or two other fragmentary figures, complete the composition, which is of a severe archaic style, the forms though symmetric, unbending and vertical, varied only by numerous actors and surveyors of the coming strife.

It has been remarked that the contemplative baldhead bears a strong resemblance to Garibaldi; and from this a prophetic analogy of future empire in Greece and Italy, might be tortured by the ingenious mind.

On the opposite, or right hand of the hall, is the more crowded composition of the west pediment, which has been commonly ascribed to Paionios, who was, perhaps, one of those universal geniuses like da Vinci, who could do anything, and it represents *The Fight of the Lapithæ and the Centaurs.* This is as full of action as the other is of quiet preparation. It portrays a violent interruption of the marriage banquet of Perithoös. The centaurs excited by wine, attempt to carry off bride and maidens. Theseus and the Lapithæ resist them. A centaur has laid his brutal grasp on a woman, and at the same time defends himself against the enraged bridegroom who swings a battle-axe. Another centaur seizes a maiden who struggles with him though with calm face. Other struggling groups and deadly wounded forms, are seen. Bestial passions let loose contend with principles of law and order. Over all, in the centre, stands erect a youth of powerful beauty, who stretches

out his right arm to quell the storm of passion.   This
is Apollo, the god of harmony and light.   He merely
stands quietly as a Greek personation of law and civilized rule.   His head and the style of the hair recall
the ephebos of the Acropolis museum.   One of the
finest faces of this stormy scene, all unagitated by it,
is that of the woman on whom a centaur has laid his
grasp ; and it is hard to explain this on the simple
principle of repose in Greek art, where, in this case,
the provocation and action are so great.   Two recumbent female figures at the extremities of the pediment,
view the furious battle also with undisturbed gaze—
river-nymphs who are able to keep cool.   At the
ends of the hall are the metropes which delineate
The Labors of Herakles, and these are but fragments
like the one of Herakles and of the Nemæan Lion,
the lion being represented by a plaster-cast of the
original which is in the Louvre.   This, with Herakles presenting Athene a Stymphalian bird, are on
the south end.   One of the most simply conceived of
these groups is Herakles winning the apples of the
Hesperides.   The hero (kindly foresight of the Hesperid nymph) has a cushion on his head while supporting the weight of the world, and while Atlas
brings to him the golden apples he has run to fetch ;
the gentle Hesperid meanwhile standing by clad in
Doric peplos.   But why did Atlas resume the burden
of the world when he had a good chance to throw it
off ?   This is a piece of *naïve* honesty in the thought
of a subtle Greek artist and poet that is hard to solve.
The nude male forms are knotted and powerful to do
their mighty tasks, but they are robust figures, with
squares of coarse flesh and muscle, without the ideal
beauty of the divinely strong Pheidian figures of gods
and heroes.   They are more hasty productions of the

chisel, yet among these ruder forms occur some of exquisite Greek delicacy, and these singular inconsistencies have been attempted to be explained by the fact that in the decorative work of the temple of Zeus at Olympia, distinguished Attic masters were employed, as was Pheidias himself a little later, to design the sculptures, but it was left almost entirely to local and inferior artists to carry out these designs, thus producing inequality in conception and execution.

In the side-rooms, grouped about the main hall, is a great number of interesting marbles and bronzes found at Olympia, as for example, part of a brazen bull famous in antiquity, swords, lances, helms, discs, an archaic head of Hera, but, above all, the sculptured marble-reliefs from the Treasury of Megara, representing the gigantomachia, and which are among the very earliest specimens of pedimental carving.

These are but preludes to the greater work that lies beyond, or to which they serve as an avenue of ruder forms of approach. It is curious to read now the following passage from a modern writer :

"If the traveler is disappointed at the little of antiquity that remains either here (Elis) or at Olympia, or indeed upon any of the Hellenic sites of this province, it may be some consolation to him to consider, that a soil, subject like that of the Eleia, to alluvial changes, was the best adapted to conceal, and may still therefore preserve some of the works of art which survived the fury of the persecutors of idolatry, whether Christian or Mohammedan, and that if there is less above ground in the Eleia than in any of the provinces of Greece, there may be more below the surface." *   May be indeed ! It was beyond the

* Leake's Morea, v. ii, p. 219.

bounds of poetic, to say nothing of archæologic, vision, to have foretold or imagined the discovery of such a transcendent work as the Hermes, described though it may have been by Pausanias centuries before ; and why should it not be so ? Who could have dreamed that two incomparable sculptures, like the Hermes and the Venus of Milo, would be reserved for our generation, as the first among moderns, to see ?

Praxiteles was the second of the great masters of Greek sculpture. Religious and political changes had come over the Greek world between the times of Pheidias and Praxiteles, that brought about a corresponding change in art, somewhat like that which separated the style of Michel Angelo from the style of Raphael, in which art grew less divine but more human, so that new possibilities were opened ; it became less objective but more subjective, less sublime but more attractive, since freer play was given to the emotions. The age of faith, of Æschylos and the older poets, had passed away, and the age of skepticism, of Euripides, Aristophanes and the sophists, had succeeded, and while the divinities were portrayed in marble, they were copies of beautiful humanity. There was a lowering of the ideal, but a heightening of the loveliness of Greek art.

The date of the Hermes is, probably, the second half of the fourth century B. C., so that Praxiteles had Pheidias and Polykleitos to precede and teach him, but his exquisite genius created the new art, transfiguring the old into a loveliness caught from nature and the softer passions of the heart. There was a fascinating grace in his Apollos, Eroses and Fauns, that had never before been seen in Greek sculpture ; and even later reproductions in Roman times of his Thespian Eros, his Apollo Sauroctonos,

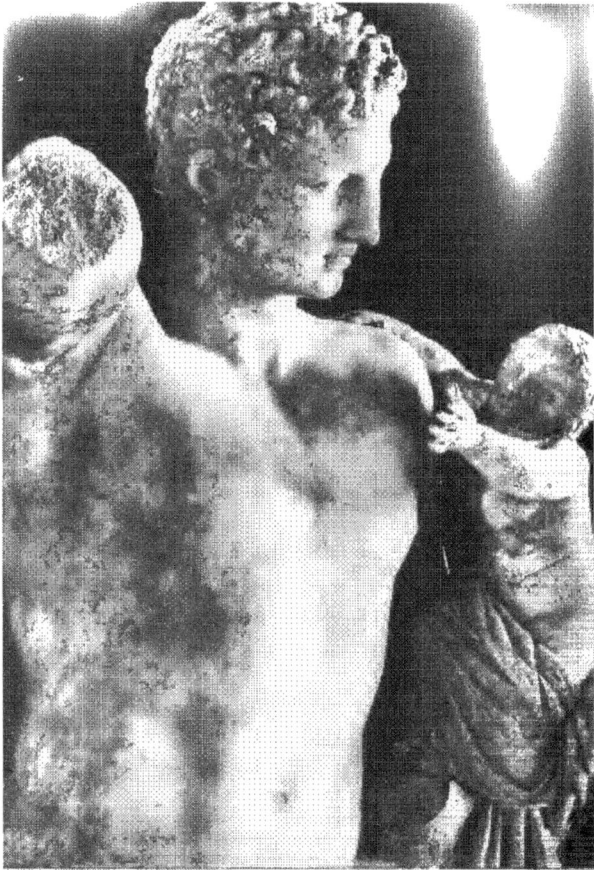

THE HERMES OF PRAXITELES

and the Satyr of the Capitol called "The Marble Faun," give us intimations of the greater loveliness of their originals. The superb bronze Narkissos, with rich buskins, now at Naples, is of the Praxitelean school, as seen in its graceful indolent poise and the charm of youthful bloom. The Aphrodite of Cnidos, carved by Praxiteles, was said to be worth a journey from Rome to see, and, to judge of it by its supposed copy in the Capitoline Venus, the saying was true. The Capitoline Venus is a statue of nobler type than the Venus de Medici, and until the original Cnidian Aphrodite by Praxiteles is found, the Venus of Milo itself must be held to be of inferior beauty.

Softly enchanting as were the creations of Praxiteles and fixed forever in their youthful prime, full of pleasing grace, they were not effeminate, but they combined mind with matter, a thoughtful sentiment with the passion of love ; and, in Praxiteles, Greek art had not lost, as it did lose afterwards in his successors, an iota of its vigor and purity ; and this may be seen, at this day, in the relief-sculptures of the contest of Apollo with Marsyas found at Mantinea, of which I have spoken, and in the celestial grace of the Venus of Arles, that, in all likelihood, was of the Praxitilean type. The ancients said that " Praxiteles excelled in fidelity to nature without falling into realism, and that he permeated his marble with moods of his own soul ;" and this virile quality of moderation, always characteristic of the best Greek art, is, more than in any other work that we know, to be found in the Hermes at Olympia.

That this sculpture-piece which now stands in the north central room of the Olympia Museum, the only object in the room, is a work of Praxiteles's hand, is proved not only by its intrinsic merit and by all the

marks of an original work, but by the words of
Pausanias who, when he came to Olympia, went into
the temple of Hera, and, among other observations
concerning his visit to their temple, left this simple
and indubitable record: "In later times, other
works were also consecrated in the Heræon—a Hermes of marble; he carries the babe Dionosos, and is
the work of Praxiteles." After lying eleven centuries under heaps of rubbish exposed to the ravages of
frost, rain and time until May 8th, 1877, this work
was found in the Heræon where the careful Pausanias
said it was, but fallen and covered up, lying on its
face in the cella of the temple, and with the exception of its legs and its broken arm, in perfect condition.

The motive of this composition was not for the first
time used by Praxiteles, but by his father, Kephisodo-
tos, in the group of Eirene and the infant Ploutos
(sometimes called Leukothea), and this adds interest
and sentiment to the work, which, in the Hermes,
was improved by the more delicate genius of the son
and relieved of its baldness. The mantle of the
Hermes, it has been remarked by Brunn, has been
treated in a subtle manner, with its heavy folds
broken up by small lines showing a surplus of labor
that betokens a feeling after something more complete.

The severity of archaic art had vanished. The
charm and perfection of the new art, that, alas, foretold also its approaching decay, had come. But the
old force was there. This is seen, for example, in
the treatment of the rich curly locks made with "a
free use of the drill," not with artificial fineness but
with bold deep strokes of the chisel. The form, too,
of manly beauty and size, the wide breast, the broad
shoulders with their loaded muscles and the thin

flanks, have the ease of absolute power. It is young manhood in its primeal bloom. It is a son of Zeus, strong and swift messenger of the gods, and this is not all. A sweetness of expression lights up the face, and there is a contemplative look as into futurity, which is linked with a benignity that seems to express a consciousness of present care and duty. His right hand may have once held a bunch of grapes that he shows and will give to the child. It is love blended with power. There is "a soulful interest in the whole," a stamp of mind and character on the broad but indented arch of the brow, in the wide-apart eyes which have such calm sweetness, in the heroic dignity of the figure.

It is not alone the harmony of the lines, the perfect poise of the body deviating from the vertical and bearing its weight with careless grace on the right leg and partly on the left arm as "sweeping around a pivot," every token of stiffness gone, nor is it the discrimination of bone and muscle as in the real body, "the undulating curves of the flesh receding and subsiding into each other like waves of the sea "— this, even, is not all, but there is a living spirit in it, while it stands in breathing repose and immortal beauty.

I do not think the words I have written are extravagant. The statue is, perhaps, the most perfect work of plastic art. The impression of its beauty was, to myself, confirmed by its sight. Its artistic perfection, however, is not increased by a modern restoration of the legs, though skillfully done by Professor Schaper. The lower portions of the legs and the left foot are new, the right foot with an elegant sandal having still some trace of gilding and color, being antique. At the same time it may be said

that it is now seen in its bodily entireness, and
thus less is left to the imagination. The lower part
of the body is a little in advance of the rest. The
Parian marble of which the statue is made, the
rounded limbs, the deep central division line of the
breast, the right arm raised so as to bring out the
muscles of the shoulder, the feet long and straight,
the hand resting on the hip, the strong knee-joints,
the small Greek head and oval face, the sweetness of
the eyes, the character so noble and pure, and the
divine serenity of the whole figure, these are features
of a work which could not by any possibility be
created now, because sculpture has no more real but
only imitated gods.

The ideal of Christian art has been raised into the
spiritual sphere, but with Pheidias and Praxiteles,
power and beauty in the human form, were themselves divine. Yet the sense of divinity in the Hermes is not unnatural or overpowering, and there is
even the suspicion of a playful smile on the face. It
is human. The statue, however, is grander and more
powerful than I had supposed.

"The sculptor sure was of a strong spirit."

The face is slightly stained by rust though not
seriously so, and the smooth polished marble itself is
one of its marvels. All rough lines of labor are
swept out of it, and it stands in its splendor like a
god, yet with all the gentleness of a loving and lovely
humanity.

It was hard to leave this great work of art so
authentic in its antiquity and so genuine in its beauty,
and to see the last of it ; and, as I turned to go out
of the room the statue caught a ray of the setting sun
which seemed to warm, etherealize and give it a
higher life. Nature aided the impression of art.

Outside of the museum the natural scene itself was truly a remarkable one, for the sun, which, during the afternoon, had been partially obscured, came out of the clouds and lighted up the whole region, a delicate rainbow spanned for a moment the plain from mountain to mountain, and then, as if by magic, a golden mist of Zeus whirling up from the west and from the sea, like the drop of a great curtain, shut out from sight the vale of Olympia, and the theatre of the old religion, art and glory of Greece.

CHAPTER XV

THE GREEK GAMES.

The chief interest attached to the athletic games of the Greeks is the influence they had to foster the heroic spirit, proving not only that it was a heroic nation that established them, but that they tended to make the nation heroic. The heroic element shows itself early in Greek art and literature, yet is hardly ever without certain childish features and accompaniments that are, indeed, to be found in the sagas of all Oriental races, Indian, Hebrew and Arabian, as well as Greek, and which is an evidence of the simplicity of the poems of earlier nations. Even the Homeric heroes exhibit traits of weakness, and they were not all of them anxious to go to the big wars, and tried hard to bribe Agamemnon to except them from military service, the wily Odysseus feigning madness to escape the draft although his device was detected and he finally joined the army with an effective contingent. When the Trojans got among the ships of the allies, the Greeks cried like children because they fancied that they were fated to destruction ; and this sensitiveness in regard to death, which the heroes nevertheless fearlessly met, is manifested in the scene where the inspired horses of Achilles, shedding tears as if human, foretold his early doom.

The heroic Greek character was crystallized in the strong Doric race and type ; but, singularly enough for a Greek, Xenophanes of Colophon, the founder of the Eleatic school of philosophy, decries heroic qualities and the athletic games ; and he says : "Whoever wins in a foot race, boxing, wrestling or chariot race, receives all kinds of honors, precedence at festivals, a purse of money and public support. This is his reward, even if the horses have done it. Yet he is of less valor than I ; my wisdom is better than the strength of horses or men. All this is foolish ; it is not proper to prefer strength to wisdom. Of what use is all this physical skill? It secures no better government, and the delight of winning a contest is a brief one, in no way helping to fill the granaries of a city."

The vigorous life which sprung up after the first Persian wars gave an additional impulse to the athletic games, as tending to keep alive the heroic spirit that had been kindled in the strife of a small but free people against innumerable foes combined by a cohesive rather than organic unity, and urged to a compelled valor, whereas the heroic spirit is bred from a deeper race-principle ; as, for example, Sir Philip Sidney was a courtier and poet, spending much of his time in composing euphuistic phrases and "rustical roundelays" in praise of Queen Elizabeth, and yet he lived a perfectly heroic life ; and Gen. Gordon, it is said, was more like a quiet citizen than a soldier in appearance and habits, who, nevertheless, was a hero if such ever existed ; but the Greeks found one of the chief means of nourishing and perpetuating this spirit in the agonistic games.

The great athletic games were held every four years at Olympia in Elis, during the month of the sacred truce, and they constituted, perhaps, more than anything else, the symbol and realization of Hellenic unity.

The wonderful scene which presented itself to the

eye at one of those great Olympic festivals, was that of
a whole nation met for an inspiring and joyful purpose ;
and it offered just "that mixture of uniformity and
variety most stimulating to the observant faculties of
a man of genius," who, at the same time if he sought
to communicate his impressions or to act upon this
mingled audience, composed of such diverse charac-
ters—soldiers, legislators, orators, writers, poets,
sailors, wealthy men and vine dressers, princes and
demagogues—he was forced to shake off what was
peculiar to himself and to his little town and community, and to put forth matters in harmony with
the feelings of all, and in this way mutual interest
and competition was excited, and the *human* element
came into Greek life and drama, and was the most
important feature of Greek art and the secret of its
expression, variety and power.   In the vast crowd of
spectators brought together from every part of Greece
and her remotest colonies—from swarthy African
Cyrene to the borders of snowy Scythia—do you
think that the artist was not there?   Do you think
that he neglected such an opportunity to study human
nature ?

And the contests themselves were not confined to
simple athletism, but were combined with philosophy, history, the drama, music and sculpture ; and
the wreaths of wild parsley, olive and pine showed
the essentially heroic character of the games appealing to an ideal motive, while the combats of youths
in the *palæstra*, inspired by ancestral heroic tradition, served to build up a splendid manhood ; and
yet after a time, and almost of necessity, there came
about a degeneration of the sports, and the professional
athlete made his appearance on the scene, who was
not regarded with the highest respect, since the Greeks
did not glory in mere brawn and muscle.

The forms represented in Greek heroic sculpture prove that they were not of men who made a business of being athletes, but of the choice youth ; there is in them the light and grace of something more than physical power, for, though the statues of Greek athletes betoken a complete development of physical strength, compared with which Michael Angelo's models were porters and draymen, they manifest muscular force combined with fineness of proportion, and a beauty and simplicity, that show the sincere but unconscious enthusiasm for honorable things which belongs to a youth who might have gone from the most exciting race that strained every nerve, or the most violent wrestling match, to sit at the feet of Plato.

Yet it is to be noticed, as proving the finer character or training of the Greeks, that even in the professional athlete and gladiator of later Roman times, the Greeks still showed the touch of a superior race, as illustrated in what Plutarch relates of the sanguinary athletic exhibitions in his day, that at the last banquet which was commonly given to those who were about to die, while Roman and Thracian gladiators gave way to excessive feasting, the Greeks spent the precious moments in taking leave of their families and giving advice to those who would hear them no more.

Athletic training in Greece, it should be remarked, aimed at the development of power combined with harmony of action ; and the athlete exercised himself not only in the arena but in the choruses of singing and processional dances, that induced rhythmic grace, and for this purpose music of the flute, harp and lyre contributed to bring his nature into agreement with musical measure and tone, which, combined with the study of rhetoric and philosophy, produced, in its

14

best examples, the result of the heroic spirit, beautiful action and lofty thought. The life evidenced the
training, and there are, indeed, relations that nature
has established between the body and mind, a mysterious interdependence of the faculties, that cannot be
overlooked if broad and healthful intellectual results
are to be sought for, so that even the reign of intellect-
ualism is a short one which neglects those bodily conditions under which it can only exist at its best ; and
I think, therefore, that the gymnastic training in our
universities might derive, through the study of Greek
sculpture and the methods and discipline of the Greek
gymnasia, much valuable aid, and that, by this, the
athletic training of the university would tend to
become more earnestly practiced and more generally diffused, and it would be regarded as an element
of education, or as forming a part of that culture
which would modify and enlarge the whole system.

In order rightly to understand the Greek athletic
games and their influence on art, we must go behind
the games to the gymnasia. The gymnasia (from
γυμνός, naked) were the local training schools for the
great games ; but the gymnasia belonged to the system of education of which Greek philosophy, literature and art formed the consummate flower.
Education was held to be the most important of the
state's functions, so that Aristotle laid down the
principle that the state was justly compelled to
assume its control, and that any occupation, art or
science which rendered the body or soul of the freeman less fit for the practice of virtue, should be prohibited as vulgar ; wherefore all arts and occupations
that have an influence to deform the body or the mind
were not only not to be encouraged, but forbidden ;
since it must be confessed, that the Greeks, for free

citizens of democratic communities, were, in many respects, rank aristocrats, and they held a lower opinion of honest work than we do, or than is just and right, esteeming manual labor fit only for slaves, which sentiment, with other similar ideas, finally brought about the overthrow of Athens and Greece; but should we judge this bright and noble nation too harshly, and refuse to learn from them what was really beautiful in their life and example?

Aristotle likewise said that "gymnastic exercises tended to infuse courage, while drawing and art were fitted to make pupils judges of the beautiful; for to be always seeking the useful does not become free souls."

The gymnasia might be called the universities of Greece, and they exerted a direct influence on the art of Greece, because there was in them just this mingling of the physical and intellectual; and springing as they did from the needs of the state to train young men for civic virtue and for war, that demanded the best disciplined strength (as in those warring communities to exist was to contend), it came about in a natural way that the whole man received discipline, and even the highest, for these contests had a higher side, because, since they were held to be instituted by heroes and demi-gods, no one could contend in the games who had disgraced himself by a dishonorable act or been guilty of sacrilege.

The games were, in fact, a part of popular education, and formed, as it were, its summit; and education was not a creature of accident, fashion or custom, since the Greeks believed in compulsory education, and thought that it could not be left to loose ends; for Greek education, whatever it was, was not superficial; and while it doubtless had its faults, it was founded, as I

have said before, on a philosophical basis, or on the
nurture of the soul as a living organism that was contained in a body which needed careful training. The
passions were to be regulated but not repressed ; and
even in nature, the higher element, the spirit, was to
be cultivated ; and this cultivation of the spirit was
the work of the gymnasium, as Plato remarked, that
a man could be best judged by the manner in which
he bore himself in the gymnasium—meaning probably his patience, self-collectedness and courage. The
true object was self-training. This was that hard
element of human nature, which, if rightly nourished,
becomes bravery, but if it be exclusively encouraged,
degenerates into brutality.

Then followed the culture of the imagination and
tastes, and, above all, of the rational soul, which
needs philosophy.

The three great divisions of Greek education were
"Gymnastic," "Music," and "Philosophy ;" and
"Gymnastic" was by no means considered to be the
least of these, for though it was bodily training, it
was not to end in the body but the soul, in a spiritual
discipline which made one hardy, self-centred, endowed
with manliness, another name for the perfection of
all the powers, and the full development of mind and
body. This made the heroic man. It was inward
more than outward, but it was the outward in combination with the spirit and acting upon it.

At first gymnastic exercises were held wherever
there was convenient open ground; but as they
acquired more importance the state provided places
and erected buildings, and as these required room,
the gymnasium usually covered a large area ; and
Athens had three such great training schools—the
Kynosarges, the Lykeion and the Akademeia, of

which the last, situated in a dell and surrounded by a grove, was a resort of the best citizens. Indeed, the spaces devoted to the gymnasia were of such size that the whole arms-bearing population of the city could exercise in them. In the special building, or gymnasium proper, parts of it were used for dressing rooms, and for anointing the body with oil and sanding it, and for cleansing the body with the ' strigil ;' and other chambers were employed for cold and hot baths, fires and lodgings. To these were added porticos for the assemblage and conversation of the Ephebi, colonnades and halls, walks, gardens and copses of trees ; and, as the gymnasium was dedicated to some divinity, altars, statues and religious symbolic adornments were not wanting.

The exercises of the Greek gymnasium were quite simple when compared with the modern elaborate system, and consisted, originally, of the *Pentathlon*, or five contests, to which the horse-race and other contests were afterwards added.

The *Pentathlon*, in a word, was made up of the combined exercises of running, leaping, throwing the javelin, casting the diskos and wrestling with boxing ; though running or the foot race (*diaulos*) in which the stadium was traversed twice, seems to have been the principal of the sports, and the Greeks carried it to an astonishing pitch of perfection. The course was usually of deep sand, where the foot took no firm hold, and the runners were naked, but sometimes were armed in complete armor, or, it might be, with shield and helm only.

'' The length of a long course was 24 stadia (about three miles, and that the runners who were trained for special emergencies were of extraordinary speed and endurance is shown by the story of the Platæan

Euchidas, who on being sent after the battle of Salamis to fetch fire from Apollo's altar, made in one day the distance between Platæa and Delphi and back—a thousand stadia (about 100 miles)—but the exertion cost him his life.''

The exercise of leaping, both the high and distant leap, was practiced by the simple spring of the muscles, though sometimes weights (*halteres*) were held in the hand and swung to give impetus. The javelin sport consisted in the flinging of a light lance covered with a thong to make it revolve, and both accuracy and distance were striven for.

Casting the diskos was of very ancient date, as Homer teaches. The diskos was a heavy circular plate of bronze or iron, about eight inches in diameter, which was grasped by the whole hand, and swung round to give it a rotary motion. Before the throw it was carried in the left hand so as not to tire the right ; and both positions are illustrated in the two well-known statues of the Diskoboloi.

Wrestling was developed to an art ; and the victory did not depend on strength alone; there were rules, sleights and advantages of various kinds in which the wrestler was instructed, so that scientific skill not seldom bore off the prize from sheer strength.

If gymnastics were universal in Greece so also was the enthusiasm felt in these contests, which were regarded as national affairs, and at which every free man of Hellenic blood had a birthright to be present and to participate in them. The greatest were not too great to enter them, although a youthful Alexander, flushed with power and victory, had to prove his claim to Hellenic blood, before he could take a share in the contests.

It is worth considering what a stimulating effect

these games must have had on the art of sculpture, and what a concentration of popular sentiment was brought to bear on them. That the sculptor made use of the study of the nude of which the games afforded opportunity, numberless Greek statues and bas-reliefs of heroes, fighters and victors testify, in which there is a force, a *technique*, a close imitation of nature, a freedom of composition, a truth without exaggeration or violence in the rendering of the muscular system, a beauty springing from full and exact knowledge, which could only come from daily, yearly, life-long sight and study, and an actual mingling in the contests themselves where every power was tried, every muscle developed and every energetic and beautiful attitude that the human frame is capable of, was presented. I fear we can never have such sculptors again, certainly not without a revival of a system similar to that which produced them ; though, indeed, it is said that in the wrestling matches on the village green in Cumberlandshire, England, fine models for the sculptor may yet be found, because athletic sports have been kept up for centuries by a hardy mountaineer race. But our sculptors copy from the Greeks, while their sculptors copied from nature ; and they had models as nearly perfect as humanity, perhaps, ever afforded.

Looked at artistically, the main effect of the public games upon sculpture was in the opportunity presented for artistic study of the human form ; and I have translated this short passage bearing on the subject from the French of Duval :

"There would seem to be a contradiction between these two facts, viz : that while Greek artists have on their part shown in their works the most vigorous anatomical exactitude, on the other hand neither they

nor their contemporaries, the physicians, studied
anatomy by dissection. But this contradiction dis-
appears when one examines the conditions whereby
artists were permitted to have incessantly under their
eyes the human form in movement, which set them to
analyze these forms, and to acquire, through the
mechanism of their active changes, empirical ideas as
precise as those demanded to-day by the scientific
study of physiology.

"The artist was privileged to study his model
before exercising, while anointing himself; then during the course, or leap, which showed the muscles of
the lower limbs ; then at the play of the diskos which
brought in relief the contractions of the great deltoid
muscles of the shoulder ; and during the wrestle,
which successively, according to the numberless variety of efforts, threw into play all the muscular system.
Why need we be astonished that when antique life
was given up, images deprived of the movement of
life, and that satisfied the religious sentiment only,
succeeded those reproductions of the man in action,
those statues which inspire the beholder with the
force and beauty drawn from the living plastique of
the Greek gymnast ? In point of fact, the decadence
of the art of sculpture proceeds parallel with the
abandonment of gymnastic exercises ; later, in the
Middle Ages, art returns to the producing of sculptures without living force, which, however, express
the mystic aspirations of the epoch, but have nothing
in common with the real representation of the human
form well developed and active."

It is a valuable idea for the student of art to obtain,
that Greek sculpture was a genuine product of the
national mind, and that it had an object which called
it into being and dignified it ; that it was to set forth

real deeds, and was commemorative of actual struggle and caught the breath of popular life. A statue was not made, as nowadays, to be put in a palace or museum and admired as a work of art, but it carved a man in full life, as like him as could be and be beautiful, and bade it live with the spirit which inspired him and his act. Thus alone sculpture could be great and have a purpose which was vital, nay, religious, springing from man's deepest impulse.

Greek sculpture was stimulated by the athletic games, not only from the fact that artists had a chance to study the human frame and compare form with form, thus idealizing the forms of gods who presented the sum of perfection, but that the greatest sculptors were employed to make statues of victors to be placed in the Altis, or sacred enclosure of Olympia.

The public games gave a *raison d'etre* to sculpture and a practical aim to artistic effort, and, combined with the motive of religious cult, this influence wrought mightily on the various schools of sculpture. The custom of commemorating successful athletes by setting up statues to them, arose about 600 B. C. and signs of progress appear as early as the 50th Olympiad (544); but when the usage became more general of thus dedicating the statues to victors, sculptors were obliged to study their subjects carefully, since an accurate resemblance to all parts of the body was demanded, and this led the way to the vigorous marbles of Ægina, the lifelike statues of Myron, and the ideal forms of Pheidias. It was building on nature and knowledge which is art's inexorable condition of progress; and many of the statues we are now so familiar with in the European galleries, were probably these very statues of athletes that were erected in the consecrated places.

The immense antiquity of the games, which, tradition says, were instituted by the Idaean Herakles, is evinced by pictures painted on vases of extreme antiquity representing wrestling matches ; and the influence of the athletic sports on archaic Greek sculpture is seen in the combats carved on the tympana of the old Doric temple of Ægina, older than the Parthenon, and that are of the purely heroic type. The people of the island of Ægina were renowned athletes. In the forty-five odes of Pindar which have reached us, there are but four odes commemorative of victors in the games from his own city of Thebes, four from Agrigentum, two from Athens, and still fewer from other cities whose praises he celebrates, while he sings of eleven who belonged to Ægina ; and the first victor honored by a statue in the Altis of Olympia, was an Æginetan. These Æginetan groups represent real fighters, forms taken directly from the *palæstra*, correct in physique, regular in movement, of terrible because disciplined energy, yet wanting the grace, life and poetic touch of Pheidian sculpture. It was the realistic period of sculpture, but was on the way to something higher.

Herakles, the heroic ideal of the Greeks, as represented in the familiar statue of what is called the "Farnese Hercules" now at the Naples Museum, is a noble, but unnaturally exaggerated, example of the school of heroic art, which, in the Græco-Roman time, had lost its idealism and gloried in enormous exuberance of muscular development to express utmost physical force.

The so-called "Apoxyomenos " is an older and more simply natural statue of very easy attitude, being a marble copy of the bronze original by Lysippos, and now stands in the *Braccio Nuovo* of the Vatican. It illustrates the use of the "strigil" after the athletic contest, and it is a trivial but curious fact that among the remaining evidences of Alexander's remote conquests, the use of the "strigil" for cleansing the body of oil and sand still survives in India; for the Greeks carried their athletism everywhere, to India, Syria, Egypt, Spain; and Pausanias said that a Greek city could be told at once by its *palæstra*.

The "Diskobolos," the work of Myron, was celebrated even in antiquity—Lucian wrote of it:

"You speak of the diskos-thrower, who stoops preparatory to the throw, with the face towards the hands holding the disc, and with one leg bent, as though he meant to rise again after the throw." This sculpture is now in the *Palazzo Massimi* at Rome, and its original was, also, probably of bronze. It has a vigorous swing as if the whole force was thrown into it, while the beauty and manly modesty of the face show one bred to hardship yet retaining the sweetness of youth. The "Diskobolos in repose," sometimes ascribed to Alkamenes, illustrates what I said of the athlete's holding the diskos in the left hand when at rest. The so-called "Fighting Gladiator," by Agasias of Ephesos, giving the whole stretch of a powerful human frame, is really an athlete in the games contending as an armed hoplite, probably against a horseman, and may have been one of these public statues of victors.

The group, too, of the "Wrestlers," is a fruit of the effect of the public games on sculpture; and its anatomy will bear the most scientific criticism. All scientists say that the free range of movement of the shoulder is one of the most striking and beautiful arrangements of the human form, so that the arm can be moved around in every direction through space;

and when we examine this carving, we can have no
doubt that the physical fact, or contrivance, of bone
and muscle in the shoulder, has been closely studied
by the artist.

We see in this sculpture-piece that subtle quality,
or device, sometimes employed with great effect in the
most thoughtful art—of suspense—or of suspended
action.   In the movement of the figures and the expression of the faces, there is a prolongation of the
action after the moment of the act seized upon has
really ceased, and we feel that it is by no means certain that he who now has the upper hand will have it
at the end ; when his determined antagonist who has
evidently bated no jot or tittle of courage will have
painfully regained his equality of position, or may
even suddenly turn the tables on his somewhat more
youthful rival.

The 'Borghese Achilles' of the Louvre, represents
the hero as an athlete, nude though wearing a helm,
and resting from combat, with a melancholy expression
as if thinking of his great grief and loss.   The sculpture of the 'Diadumenos,' after Polykleitos, is a young
athlete binding the fillet of victory on his forehead,
with a placid expression.   It is the *palmam non sine
pulvere*, but with a lofty peace that fills his soul.

By way of comparison, or it might be said, contrast,
there are some modern sculptures of athletes, such as
the 'boxers' of Canova, illustrating the story of
Creugas and Damoxenos.   While these have undoubted vigor, they are results of study rather than
of nature, and are barbarians, absolute savages, when
compared with the Greek.   The simple nobility of
youth, the repose in the midst of action, the classic
facial expression of a high type of race, the even
health and unconquerable spirit of the young Greek

athlete—in fact the heroic element which is chiefly
spiritual—is not in them. The harmonious pose of
body and mind is absent, and, in their place, only
agitating passions. The gladiator ' Spartacus ' of the
Louvre, by the French sculptor, Barrias, is spirited
but too academic to be great, and lacks the freedom
and nature of the antique.

Taken as a whole, one of the most charming, shining, and admirable ancient statues of a Greek athlete
is the ' Hermes of the Vatican,' carved as a runner·
resting himself, while the trunk of the palm on which
he leans signifies that he has conquered in the race.
The mirror-like polish of the statue is retained. It
shows in its natural force and grace, that the Greeks
studied the living body before putting it into the
marble, thus lending it life without affectation, and
repose without weariness. Take for another example
the wonderful fragment of the ' Belvedere torso '
which Michel Angelo called his 'master,' and its
anatomy, the magnificent arch of the chest, the great
hollow of the pelvis and the mighty legs, could only
have been produced by an artist who knew the human
form thoroughly by a life-long study in the arena.
In its pathetically broken condition, what veritable
flesh and blood, what breathing powerful life !

The Greeks regarded the public games in a peculiar
light, for they were looked upon as an inheritance
from the immortals, since a perfect human body was,
in some sense, the most sacred of objects, enshrining
the soul as in a temple, and associating it with the
divine. To contend in the games was a religious
aspiration, a lofty endeavor, a striving for the perfect,
even as antiquity, or the best antiquity, was full of
the idea of struggle, of bringing forth the perfect
through contention ; and we can probably have no con-

ception of the earnestness thrown into these games when a nation was looking on, when it was sometimes the whole aim of a life to conquer, when it was a religious consecration. The fine statue now in Berlin of the "Praying Boy" has been supposed by some to be that of a youth consecrating himself to the gods before or after the Olympic games.

The relation then of the athletic games to the art of sculpture was mainly three-fold :

1. They kept alive the heroic spirit.

2. They brought to the front the best artists to carve iconic statues of victors erected in the sacred enclosures.

3. They gave opportunity for constant and accurate study of the human form in every attitude, and of the most perfect specimens of the human body developed by training and under circumstances that tended to ennoble rather than debase it ; since athletic discipline was one part of the system of physical, intellectual and religious education.

The games had a wide influence on the national character. The sacred truce which accompanied and made possible their celebration promoted both national unity and the interests of a higher civilization. Every peaceful art received an impulse. There was healthful competition in all. The artists exhibited their freshest works. The dramatists recited their newest plays and poems. The familiar tradition, not fully substantiated, of Herodotus having read his history to the assembled Greeks at Olympia, does not stand alone. Even commerce and agriculture had their markets. There was an interchange of thought and ideas, and knowledge was more freely diffused among the people. If, indeed, this fusion of minds and interests, and this unity of feeling among the different states and provinces of Greece, brought about by the great games, and aided by such institutions as the Amphictyonic Council and the Achaian League, had not been interrupted and weakened by other political causes, there would have been reared up a free empire that would have stood against Rome, and that power while yet in its infancy could not have triumphed as it did; whether this would have operated for or against the general welfare of the world, is a question very difficult for us at the present time to decide.

In view of what has been said of the athletic system under the Greeks, and its importance in many ways, I venture to remark that modern athletism, especially at the university, might be also regarded from many interesting points of view other than the training of the physical powers for athletic contest and competition, although this is a great object, and I doubt if the athletic system could be maintained without it, as was demonstrated by the Greeks themselves in the games, bringing young men up to a high pitch of physical power and skill, and making them ready to contend for the prize with any foe however formidable ; but that, with this, it should fit in with the training of other powers, and not aim at the discipline of the body only, but of the soul, in order to give it its fullest efficiency in our university life. A high tone of manly character, a friendly spirit among the students of different colleges rising above all jealousies and rivalries, a patriotic union of minds for the good of the common country, a widening out of the great republic of letters, would be inevitably promoted.

The best period of athletic practice among the Greeks before its degeneration in the Alexandrian and Roman days, was when a great deal was still left to nature, when it was a real joy and inspiration to contend in the games, as well as a hard struggle, when it was healthy sport and had not yet become a rigid system of overtraining and sheer muscularity, but continued to be a means of healthier, happier and more beautiful life.   This rare combination of athletics and art in Greece meant a great deal, and was a most happy and pregnant circumstance.   The close connection that existed between the agonistic games and sculpture, though at first sight there would seem to be no connection between them, brought into the games the æsthetic, and, I might say, the poetic, element, and gave to them a higher meaning and glory.   The Greek's genuine love of the beautiful and his earnest conception of the state, and its demand upon him for the best he could give it, for all the power of body and mind he was capable of, ennobled everything he did.   The Greek sought instinctively the ideal, the perfect, development.   Beauty with him was no mere sentiment, but was another name for perfection.   He understood, as far as he went, the working principles of a true education, which aspired not to knowledge merely, but also to culture, and that belonged not to the few highly trained men only, but to the entire educational system, serving the purposes both of living and art, and tending to create a healthy nature and heroic spirit in the best youth of the land.

APPENDIX.

Having alluded in one of the foregoing chapters, in a few words, to the theory of art, or to its fundamental idea, I desire to add some remarks better considered, in order more carefully to amplify the thought there expressed.

Æsthetics, from a Greek word of subtle meaning, was first used comparatively recently in Germany to signify the philosophic classification of those mental faculties with which we perceive and are pleasurably affected by the beauty of the world, and was thus made to comprise more than the term fairly means, viz., the whole theory, production and criticism of art ; and yet this word, æsthetics, happily emphasizes one important element of art—feeling, or the sense of delight in the perception of beauty—for art springs chiefly from the emotions, just as in the "terribleness" of Michael Angelo's nature averse to delights there was one spring of joy—the love of art ; and so, too, after the influence of the sceptical philosophy of the early part of the eighteenth century, that dried up the spiritual emotions, the new feeling for the beautiful, opened by the movement of romantic literature, produced such works as *Faust* and *Wallenstein.*

The philosopher, Hegel, in treating æsthetics as a branch of psychology, set to work to explore the laws of spirit which constitute mind and to construe nature and art by means of universal ideas, on the principal assumed by the German transcendental philosophy of the subjectivity of all knowledge, regarding nature as the unconscious realization of

15

spirit in time and space, and, in the same way, viewing the genesis of every human institution, science
and art as spiritual expressions. He sought to trace
through its various stages the philosophy of culture,
and to develop *a priori* the history of human consciousness, in its growth from the first crude ideas to the
most advanced theories that shape our modern civilization.   Civilization, in his application of philosophic
analysis, is the mind realizing itself. Human consciousness perceives the ideal form which measures
and moulds the phenomenal world, although this consciousness is not awaked at once, and only gradually
awakes to find itself contemplating its ideal prototype,
its absolute personality, which thus becomes self-
consciousness ; and this rousing of self-consciousness
constitutes the intellectual progress of the race.   It
sees its ideas realized, or reflected, in art as well as
nature, and makes at each step an advance in civilization.   Hegel's philosophy was the revelation, in
the world of time and space, of self-consciousness, of
the personality of the absolute, of the advancement
of humanity in the consciousness of its unity and perfection, of the gradual merging of the individual into
the universal, which universal consciousness is the
progress of thought from nature to spirit, from the
sensual to the ideal, from the objective to the subjective ; and, under this system, art is an expression
of the spiritual, a manifestation, more or less clear, of
the eternal idea which measures the outer and phenomenal, recognizing in the external world the image
of itself and comparing all things to this inner form,
this self-determined and abiding idea, which is the
absolute, the ego, the rational totality of the race,
the spiritual personality.   The reality of things—art
among them—is in the idea, while all else is show

and changing phenomena. "The real world," says an Hegelian writer, "is the spiritual world; things exist because spirits experience them, and spirits experience them because, as parts of the complete life, it is their interest to be as manifold and wealthy in their self-realization as possible."

In a word, idealism, in which the world of nature and art is the evolution of spiritual existence—this is the basis, the road-bed, so to speak, in which Hegel's æsthetics is planted; and it must be confessed that it is an admirable foundation of art, the Greek foundation, going beneath the superficial theories now prevailing, most of which regard art as a mere fashion to catch, like a mirror, the flitting reflections of the outward, and to decorate life and amuse the senses; and also going beneath that false realism which lies in the physical merely, and not in the mind that contains the unchangeable types of beauty. Art, according to Hegel, is the discovery of the type-ideas upon which nature and all things are formed and which must be sought within, not without, so that self-apprehension is the artist's highest law, and that by which he seizes the universal, the absolute beauty. Nature acts as a medium of the manifestation of the ideas, or idea, of beauty, and is the objective form of a subjective fact. The artist studies nature, viewing it as an intermediary of the spiritual perfect truth, and not as perfect in itself; for perfection is in the idea consciously apprehended.

Mr. Stillman, in an article in the *Atlantic Monthly* entitled "The Revival of Art," has favored this Hegelian theory of art, carrying it, however, so far as to make the artist wholly an idealist inspired by that beauty which he sees in his mind, and he seems to give but little value to the inspiration and study of nature, quoting Turner's saying that "nature puts him out."

The truth, I believe, would hold nature as that which mediates between and unites the ideal and the real, the subjective and the objective. The true idealist is he who has the deepest knowledge of nature and who can use this knowledge in the formulation of his own conceptions.

But, even before Hegel, Schelling attempted to construct an æsthetic philosophy. His poetic temperament led him to look on nature as unconscious art, and to believe that material forms symbolize spiritual processes, so that in nature our ideals are expressed. He said that "artists were often unconscious philosophers and that the greatest philosophers were consummate artists."

Singularly enough, too, the pessimistic philosopher, Schopenhauer, set forth one of the most consistent, if but partial, theories of æsthetics of any of the school of the German idealists; for while himself belonging to this school, in place of Hegel's ego, or spiritual personality representing the absolute, he regarded the "world-will," or concentrated power of all world-activities, as the capricious and accidental but real creator of the phenomenal world of nature, which "world-will" and its ideas we interpret by experience. Our intelligence, as also a creature of the *Weltgeist* or *Weltwille*, penetrates to the inner will of nature, and "reaches its perfection in the power of contemplation that sinks into the depths of nature, and which belongs, above all, to the temperament of the productive artist." Art, then, according to Schopenhauer, is "the embodiment of the essence of the 'world-will,' as seen or interpreted, by the artist's intelligence. The world-will has fashions of expressing itself, kinds and degrees of self-objectification, and these, in so far as contemplation can seize them, are ultimate types or ideas exemplified in space and time by individual objects." They are the embodiments of the world's desire, of the world's passion and longing, the forms of the whole world's will that exist. Art grasps these world-forms, these types of creation, action and desire, and exhibits them in artistic forms; for an example, architecture (as a commentator of this philosophy says) "portrays the blind nature-forces or longings of weight and resistance;" or, as I venture to add, the harmonious arrangement of matter and mass, paralleled by the scientific theory of the rhythmical disposal of molecular atoms. Art is the universal appreciation of the essence of the "world-will" from the point of view of an intelligent on-looker, above all, artist; and thus art, while embodying the world's desire, or will, is not itself the victim of passion. Of all the arts, according to Schopenhauer, "music most universally and many-sidedly portrays the essence of the world-will, the soul of desire, the heart of this passionate, world-making, incomprehensible inner nature;" and, listening to the longing and oft abrupt strains of Wagner's music, I have been sometimes startlingly reminded of Schopenhauer's "world-will," or desire, so wistful, passionate, objectless and chaotic, and finding its utterance in those weird and changeful harmonies. "The opposition between will and contemplation" reaches, indeed, its most systematic statement in the philosophy of Schopenhauer; but the difficulty remains, that the "world-will" of Schopenhauer is at best "a simple desire and selfish striving," and the longing after perfection even, is only an accidental and changing will; whereas human life has a spiritual

centre (ψῡχή), as the material universe has a physical
centre, from which ever-recurring influences and
attractions spring, that tend to the recognition of
unchangeable and eternal ideas of beauty—a will
lying back of the phenomenal world in the spiritual ;
and in this Hegel is truer in his æsthetic philosophy,
than Schopenhauer.

Leaving these speculations of the German idealists,
let me offer a few thoughts, imperfect though they may
be. This is a good theme to theorize a little upon,
and such speculations tend to promote the interests
of art, that is assuming, together with physical science and literature, its own place in modern civilization as well as in modern education ; and I would
follow out here for a moment this suggestion in regard
to education.

It might be taken for granted that the training of
the knowing powers makes education mean nothing
unless it mean the development of the intellectual
faculties ; but this surely is not all in education.
There is still left a portion of the being which is
more peculiarly the region of æsthetic power, and in
which are the sources of the beautiful ; and how
broad a region, and how narrow the view which would
suffer this part of our nature, the truly human part,
to lie barren ! It is the æsthetic power that reconstructs and makes all new ; it is the creative power.
It is that which gives one man's speech a freshness
that another's of equal force of thought does not possess. Æsthetic culture should be introduced into
education also, because art comprises so great a portion of the life of mind. It needed mind to build St.
Peter's dome and to compose the music of Sebastian
Bach, as truly as to compose the *Principia* or the
Mechanique Celeste ; and we are not confined to archi-

tects, musicians, painters and sculptors, but may reckon in as artists the poets who body forth ideas of beauty reflecting spiritual types. It is the province, too, of education to bring out the lovely perfection of truth, so that it shall meet the desires of the mind and be followed freely ; yet as a people we have freedom much on our tongue, but not so much in our spirit. We have brought down everything to the dead level of the actual. It is the thing which answers the present use, the present success, and not the thing which should be, or the ideal ; and while we would not weaken this noble, practical, American quality, we would counteract its current towards an utterly earthly conception of life and thought ; and art would help in this struggle to deliver ourselves from the crass bondage of materialism and to give play to spiritual ideas. Art would likewise afford a counterpoise to certain narrowing tendencies in education by presenting truth in more natural and vital forms. The purely scientific process, it is true, comes first. The mind must learn to investigate and reason. First fact, then beauty. But the scientific process has its dangers unless guarded against, dealing as it does almost entirely with analysis, and may tend to lose the living synthesis of truth, and not to come, after all, to the unity of knowledge and the perfection of truth. Art through its intuition arrives often at truth's wholeness when science sees but in part. Art aims at unity, the beautiful whole, the perfect form of nature and spirit, and its influence is towards the introduction of a living variety into educational processes, so that young men may come out of the university not mere scholars, but men of broad, alert and independent minds, with the eye open to see the beauty and glory of the universe.

This is exemplified in Goethe, who took art out of the false sphere of dilletantism, and gave it its place among great things. He looked at art as a high study, and one valuable in the development and civilization of humanity. As an artist, in the technical sense, he did not do much, or profess to do much, although, for myself, I was surprised to find in his house at Weimar, so large a collection of drawings and paintings by his own hand, done mostly in his Italian tours. They seemed too poetic and lacking in what is the chief charm of his writings—reality. He had a supreme love of and devotion to nature. He sought power in the laws and principles of nature. His works, his dramas and poems, spring from the depths of nature—as do his thoughts of endless variety on art and its philosopy. He loved Greek art, though from his study of nature he avoided the narrowness of theoretic classicism. The principles of his artistic culture were laid broadly in nature. He tells us little or nothing of his feelings, but lets his personalities live out their lives before us naturally, as an artist should do, suffering his own individuality to be lost. Goethe was not a slave of nature though her servant, for he was not wholly a realist in art. "Two things" he said "are required of the poet and artist, that he should rise above reality, while he yet remained in the sphere of the sensuous." From the natural he rose into the poetic, or that beauty which is beyond nature in the mind. Another principle upon which Goethe as artist founded himself was truth. "He was driven to be original, and thus driven he became the avowed enemy of the conventional in style—'the mortal enemy'—as he loved to say, of all artificialness. It is not enough for him that a poem is eloquent, or that it is popular; for, according to him, poetry, and every artistic production must be true, or wrought from the original comtemplation of nature, and an earnest work. He is always so near reality, and examines it with such a penetrating eye, that it is a problem how he can remain a poet, and yet he remains a poet to the last." Faust is all compact with imaginative power, yet it is based on a substratum of facts, hard fact not fancy, and on the realness of human life, as much so as any work of Shakspeare's, and resembling Shakspeare in this respect. But Goethe comes nearest the Greek artists and dramatists of any modern mind. In regard to poetry he said. "I have never affected anything. I have never uttered anything which I have not experienced, and which has not urged me to production. I have composed love-songs when I have loved—and how could I write songs of hatred when I did not have the feeling of hatred." He soon got past the artificialities of the romantic school of literature in which he started forth, and came to repudiate "The Sorrows of Werther," and wrought upon simpler principles of truth in art, so that Schiller said of him "I am but a bungler in poetic art compared with Goethe." Schiller may have been the nobler man in his moral perceptions, yet he was not so great a poet as Goethe, who represented a world with its heights and depths, comprehending life, and striving to express the complete whole. His art, like that of the Greeks, was healthy, springing from truth, full of hope, not abnormal or sickly, and he recognized the law of sympathy which runs through the universe ; and though at times he burst wildly from the bonds of custom which knit society together—and I would not for one moment defend the immoral *tendenz* of some of his writings, nor the cold selfishness of spirit he seemed to display in times of the throes of agony in which Germany writhed, yet he did not ever forget the principle he laid down in Faust, that it was through law man comes into freedom, and that he himself had a great work to do as a teacher of true culture. But to return from this digression.

We sometimes hear it said that man is a religious animal, and yet it might just as well be said that man is an artistic animal—artistic in the constitution of his mind. Metaphysicians commonly divide mental faculties into reason, sensibility and will. This metaphysics—whose tendency is to view mind by sections, as it were, or as a congeries of faculties, each distinct from each, and which assigns its own value to different powers, giving to some an undue value—is apt to make the so-called intellectual faculty an exclusive object of consideration, losing sight of the truth that the mind is one and indivisible, that it acts as a whole, and that, in every act, all its energies enter, some more and some less ; that there is a vital interplay of functions in mental acts, intellect in feeling and feeling in intellect, the rational nature resting on the moral and the moral moved to activity and choice by the sensibilities and imagination, so that, however convenient this metaphysical classification may be for the analysis and study of philosophical concepts, you cannot erect such distinctions in the inner spiritual substance of the mind, and to do this sometimes leads to grave errors ; for you cannot really say that any one part of the mind is of more value than another and that any part of the mind can be ignored, or affirm that it does not belong to mind as mind, and therefore deserves no special attention. Shall we neglect that rich domain where lie the springs of feeling for the beautiful, the productive powers in the achievements of art? In this realm, called, in metaphysical language, the sensibility, is found mainly the domain of art, though it is by no means confined to this, since all the faculties are involved in art—reason, invention, will, the use of the intellectual and logical faculty that pervades a work of art, the judgment as well as feeling. But there is, nevertheless, a quality of sensibility, of emotional susceptivity, which is the mind's power of receiving impressions from the outward world and its beauty.

This feeling is not a mere excitation of the senses, the sensual nature, but it is a mental susceptibility, which not only feels but acts, and, when roused to act by impressions from objects, it becomes a power of self-differentiation, or a power of contemplating itself, a power capable of recognizing its own acts and impressions made on it, and of reproducing these impressions, being the correspondent within to the nature without; and it is thus a permanent quality, to which we give, with other elements combined, the name of *the æsthetic sense*, or, from the faculty through which this instinct chiefly operates, the perception or sense of the imagination. The imagination is the idealizing, the image-making power—the power that receives and communicates the form of things (*form-sinn*, as the Germans name it), even as the intellectual faculty receives and communicates the truth of things.

This æsthetic power of the imagination, when acted upon by correspondent objects in nature that are sympathetic to man's spiritual conditions, seeks to reproduce the essential form of these objects, since they exist in the mind only in their forms— some philosophers deny any other real existence

to objective matter—and on seeking thus to reproduce the forms of things, by a law of the mind it
strives to reproduce the perfect form in which the
mind delights and was made to delight. The mind's
susceptibility to be impressed by the world of nature
through the organ of the imagination, which not only
receives but imparts impressions of objects, since it is
full of energy and creative power, is the mind's function of form, and, necessarily, in a rational nature, of
perfect form or beauty, and here dwell the ideas of
beauty in the mind, say, above all, the mind of a
Pheidias. If the imagination works simply in order
to body forth the form of things as an "idealized imitation," to interpret nature in all its forms, it works
artistically and its products are what are termed
"art." The artist, in fact, is the poet ; he is poet of
another sort, who tells in line, form and color, as the
poet in words, what nature tells him ; and this is the
more important because we ourselves are parts of this
nature, inframed in her subtle organism. The artist,
by his imaginative or *quasi* creative power, reconstructs nature, becomes nature's interpreter, and finds
in nature the responsive image of the soul. Art is
poetry, mainly poetry—I believe this.

   We see thus in all mind, though in a less degree in
most men, but especially, and sometimes supremely,
in the artist, this æsthetic power, this artistic faculty,
by which it must and will express itself in the sphere
of art as surely as the mind must and will express
itself in the sphere of knowledge, and, indeed, so
related are the mental powers that, as we cannot keep
out any of them from the æsthetic faculty, so we cannot keep out the æsthetic sense from any of these,
and we cannot say—in the investigation of truth, the
highest truth, which is moral—that the imagination,

which is the organ of the sensibility, can be excluded, for here dwell the forms of truth and beauty.   I am a Platonist.   I believe art belongs to the spiritual powers, and is, in some sense, spontaneous—a law to itself.   Schiller says : "The artist (meaning the poet or creator) is no doubt the son of his time.   But ill is it for him if he be also its pupil or darling.   A beneficent divinity snatches the suckling in time from his mother's breast, nourishes him on the milk of a better age and lets him ripen under distant Greek heavens to his maturity.   Then, when he has grown into manhood, he returns to his own country in the image of a stranger, not always to please it by his presence, but, terrible as the son of Agamemnon, to purify it. The substance of his work he will take from the present, but the form of it from a nobler time, yea, from beyond all time, out of the essential, invariable individuality of his own being."*

The highest conception of art is that it is the interpretation of the spirit in its varied forms, feelings and experiences, and of those eternal ideas of beauty that are in the soul and belong to absolute mind ; but this admits, of course, of modification, when other faculties and qualities of our nature—above all, the sensuous— come into view.   The senses play their part in art, and a great deal of art is on this lower and not unnatural plane.   What a world, that of color !   Color has a strong, sensuous appeal, as in nature, but is sometimes too pronounced in art, as in the luxurious warmth of Rubens, the fiery tones of Raphael's greatest pupil, Giulio Romano, the violent contrasts of the Spanish school of painters.

Now, more directly, What is art?   But we can only approximate to a definition.   It is impossible to

* *Æsthetic Education of Mankind* (ninth letter).

give a rigid definition of art. It bursts from our formulas like an uncontrolled spring. It is indefinable because it is a truth rather than a term ; and yet we may do something towards a definition by separating art from truths closely akin to it. Art, for example, is not nature, while it is nothing without nature. Nature, in a general way, is all that is not art—all that is created, not made. Nature is the substance, physical and spiritual, out of whose depths art arises like an exhalation of beauty. It comprises the forces at work to produce the phenomena of the world and their laws outside of human agency. Those phenomena in ourselves and the world " which we do not originate but find " represent nature ; those " which we do not find but originate " represent art. Thus the human element comes into art to mold nature to its purposes. Art, too, is not science. Science concerns itself with knowledge and the investigation of truth, and it may be said to be the law of knowing, dealing with the facts of the universe, its chief instrument being the reason whose special function is analysis. Art has also to do with knowledge, and art may aid in the search of truth ; but it does not end in knowing. Art is, in fact, a science as far as its methods of *technique* are concerned, and it applies science to its own methods, but its end is farther on in the perfect and joy-giving work touching profounder emotions, rather than in scientific knowledge of the technical process. Art, in like manner, is not philosophy, nor religion, nor morality ; and it does not pretend to overtop, oppose, usurp or meddle with these while keeping to its own sphere, and much confusion has been caused (and no one has done more of this than Mr. Ruskin) by mixing these ; but the difference in such cases is obvious. Art, however, is no negative thing, but is a most positive reality, in that it implies the existence of natural material on which to work and out of which to create its results, requiring at the same time a principle of susceptive thought that understands and orders nature for its conscious ends. In every work of art, as, for instance, the Hermes of Praxiteles, its original material of nature, the subjective idea which calls it forth, and the form which is complete in itself like a divine creation, are comprehended. This applies to all forms of art, even the most mechanical ; and, first, the term doubtless meant the arts of bare existence, first of all, probably, the art of agriculture—the "coarse arts" as Emerson called them in contradistinction to the "fine arts"—so that the useful was the first idea, and, indeed, what is not intrinsically useful is worthless now in art, in the highest art, which belongs to the highest needs of being, and compared with which its commoner uses are as earth and clay. But as new methods of civilization arose, art came up into its more spiritual spheres. Nature was studied ; her subtle laws of working were lovingly observed ; finer natures were touched to finer issues ; and the arts which have in them a thoughtful element, which spring from an idea, succeeded the arts of mere existence, until "art" won a peculiar meaning, limited to the production which has in it the love of perfect creation, of beauty, which Plato says is the most manifest and desirable of things. But while the artist represents the beautiful object that he sees in his mind's eye, and paints from this mental image, art is never simply a mental act. Hegel contended for this. Art, without the mediation of objective form, he said, was an empty thing. "The art-idea is not a mere conception—'ist niemals ein

Begriff'—inasmuch as the latter is a frame into which different phenomena may fit, whereas the artistic idea must stand in the most intimate agreement with the particular form of the work." The subject must be conceived in the object ; there must be the manifestation of the idea, which is its expression, as in nature, and which expression must accompany the conception.

It can hardly be said that the power of vision in the artist is ever unaccompanied by the power of expression, though the two may be unequally distributed. The bas reliefs on the pediment of the temple of Zeus, at Olympia, which Pausanias ascribes to the Attic sculptors, Alkamenes and Paionios, are conceived with the utmost dramatic power, but are stiffly and rudely executed ; probably the conception was that of the great artist, and the work that of the local artist. What wonderful power of expression, for another example, is in Rembrandt's painting of " Abraham's Sacrifice," now in the Hermitage, at St. Petersburg—the obedience of a servant, the heart-rending grief of a father, the mysterious awe which the celestial messenger inspires ! Here the great artist is seen, and great artists exist because they cannot help being so any more than the roots of a willow-tree can help running to the water. Da Vinci and Correggio were predestined artists as truly as Isaiah and Martin Luther were predestined prophets, and Dante and Tennyson predestined poets ; for the spiritual conceptions and yearnings in them, the strivings for universal beauty, found their only expression in art-forms.

Art, therefore, if we should attempt to define the indefinable, might at least be described in its works as the power of representing, like a new creation, in form, line and color, the object presented to the mind, or, more specifically, to the imagination, which is awakened to act by a joyful and loving sympathy with nature in all her forms—it may be ugly as well as beautiful—but more especially with what is beautiful and perfect in nature, as that for which the mind was originally made or adapted.

1. Art, though having to do with the perceptive faculties and the senses, is spiritual in its essence, and has its foundation in an inner susceptibility of the soul which corresponds to outward forms. There is a power in the mind of receiving impressions corresponding to the power that impresses. There is more than this. The mind contains the very ideas, in their conceptual mold, in which the forms of natural objects are cast, and is fitted to comprehend them, so that art is the condition under which the sensibility for impression is excited when the object and subject become identified. The German philosopher, Lotze, indeed says that "the impression of beauty cannot be referred to a uniform standard in us, to a spiritual organization actually existing in all individuals, but to one that has first to be realized in each person by means of development, and realized in each only in an imperfect and one-sided way;" but, though this opinion of Lotze's may be true, that the perfect standard is not realized in every mind, or in the artist himself, yet for it to be realized at all, there must be the organization, the susceptibility in every mind as mind, and the imperfection of its development does not militate against the truth that there is an ideal condition, like the plate delicately prepared to receive impressions of objects, and without which the actualization of any form of beauty would be lost and objects would remain without form and void. A mountain is a pile of rocky matter of a certain geol-

16

ogic period, as science teaches, until thoughts of
majesty, unity, power, are developed in its impinge-
ment on the ideal sense.   The beauty of nature is
only to him who appreciates it ; but we are all of us
inframed in this natural kosmos as an organism itself
designed to be that through which the soul realizes
its ideas, and without which the mind could not
formulate them, and this is the most important part
nature plays in art.   In like manner the ethical sense
is a permanent condition of the soul, but the ideas of
justice, right, duty, are not developed except in the
actual relations of our natural life.

Call the beautiful an intuition or not, man, I contend, has an æsthetic sense, the outcome of whose
formulated ideas is art, and which is capable of recognizing and expressing the objective view and beauty
of the universe.   We are subjects of impressions which
do not always find expression, and only do so when
they impress with sufficient power to form distinct
conceptions.

3. Art finds its laws and principles primarily in
nature.   It cannot go a step independently of these
and remain art.   Michael Angelo seemed to lose his
creative power, and virtue went out of him the moment
he left nature and began to work from a dry scheme
of abstract form.

There is, for instance, the fundamental law of truth,
which involves the idea upon which the universe was
built.   There must be a sensitive relation in the artist's
mind to this law, without which art is artifice or sham.
But art, as has been said, is not nature, nor does the
artist, in Coleridge's words, " pick nature's pockets."
Nature is inimitable ; for how can a little square of
painted canvas convey the infinitude of mountain
scenery whose power is revealed like a divine inspira-

tion? Yet nature in her commoner moods, if still inimitable, is genial and accessible. She is odd and humorous at times, with a fancifulness full of grotesque irony. She does not hide her winsome face. She invites us to sit at her feet and learn of her. She will herself teach us. We cannot follow her instructions too closely, nor imitate her too minutely. Not a leaf but is a map of the boldest and most complicated pattern. Nature furnished the originals of Greek forms of every sort. But the artist must go beneath the surface of things to the plastic laws of these forms, else imitation would be untrue. He must discover, as it were, nature's own law of creation. A picture is an illusion, but it is not a delusion, for its end is not imitation, which would be something unreal and an absurdity, but it is the production of similar effects of nature's beauty and power so as to speak to the mind in some sense as nature speaks. While the artist is not to leave nature and lapse into a dreamland of his own, while he is to seek truth, yet by his thought, by separating the natural object from its accidental circumstances and conceiving it as a whole, by so painting the tree, the flower, the man, that the true form is seen, that the type is brought out in which the properties of the species are developed and in which it is best fitted to discharge the functions for which it was made—this shows the highest skill ; for here is the action of the artist's soul which gives to his works the appearance of fresh creations. This is the ideal in art. This is the law of mental selection and probably was coeval with the law of imitation even, and accompanied the earliest art, savage and archaic art, since no art, even the most primitive, could have been entirely imitative.

"In the effort to imitate the human figure the process of thought and sympathy becomes apparent ; and where this process of controlling power begins there the ideal in art begins. Whenever this isolated position, or scene, or action of nature is taken, it cannot be truly represented unless by an act of thought it is connected with the whole. The idea, or the whole, to which it belongs as a part, must enter into it and transfuse it.''*

Yet be it noted that the ideal does not exist without the real passing into it like a life, even as mind works on facts and molds them, and this might be called ''the idealized real.'' The real is the working basis of the ideal, even as the sculptor puts his thought first into a clay model and works from that. The poetic superstructure is grounded in the soil of the actual. ''The beautiful is the real,'' was the Florentine sculptor Dupré's motto. Imitation is not the object of art, or is, at best, a low idea of it ; yet how can a picture or sculpture be too true to nature? Were the best Greek sculptures? You may be sure that it was not the close imitation only in the old familiar story of the grapes that made the birds peck at them, but it was chiefly the truth. It was the real life of natural objects that the artist of poetic genius had caught. It was a picture and not a copy. A portrait—what is it worth if it be not real and rugged as life is ; otherwise it would become like the many unauthentic portraits of Columbus—a specimen of what has been called ''artistic subjectivity?'' This realness is the test of artistic excellence. ''The more nearly and truly a picture approaches the exact colors and forms of nature, the greater will be the effect.'' There is no excuse for false drawing. The healthy tendency of art, then, is to become more and more

* A. S. Murray, *Hist. Gr. Sculpture.*

real, which is in the true line of progress. The vigorous revival of art in the Netherlands in the first half
of the seventeenth century, which created the Flemish
and Dutch schools, to which the names of Rembrandt,
Franz Hals, Terburg, Jan Steen belong, was nothing
more than a return to realistic art from the feeble con-
ventionalism of decadent Italian classic art. But rash-
ness in theory makes a one-sided development, and
the attitude of the artistic mind should be ever that
of a thoughtful receptivity. All great painters have
been realistic painters, but that is not all that they
were. They painted from an idea. Velazquez, the
greatest of artists both in technique and expression,
did not paint the architecture of a face, but its character, its character drawn from his creative conception
of a man. So art must continue to have in it these
two elements of the real and the ideal, or it will run
into something analogous to that coarse realism in
literature, whose works, viewed as works of art, are
only pieces of loose real life, without unity and plan ;
or, on the other hand, that subjective school of poets
illustrated by Dante Gabriel Rossetti, ravishing as it
is, but neither of them complete in itself. Art would
die out, since some essential quality of life would be
lost. It would either drop the element of truth to
nature or the element of thought. The canons of
universal art must not be swamped in the turbid deluge
of a coarse realism ; though in regard to *impressionism*,
which is the tendency of modern art, when not carried to an extreme, I have a good word, as infusing
new life into painting, catching the light and atmosphere of heaven, penetrating into the mystery of color,
and promising a true advance in landscape art. But
it is well to remember, in this realistic age, that art
has a spiritual side allying it with poetry and with the

loftiest achievements of the mind, in which the beauty
that lives in the idea and in the universal and spiritual
is expressed.   All true art in every age catches a
spark of this unfading glory of the beautiful ; and yet
I do not say that there is no true art which does not
aim so high as this, as witnessed in the hundred forms
of unambitious art, the crude but honest efforts of be-
ginners, the drawing which aims only at correct imitation, the pictures of many realistic artists painting
nature as it is and not so much in minute detail as in
whole true impressions, the graphic illustrations of
literature carried to such excellence at the present
time, the rich field of decorative design which is
mainly scientific—all this is pleasing and laudable
and having its genuine place in art, but I speak now
of art in its enduring forms, which, like the best
poetry, is of "imagination all compact," and must
spring from the love and idea of beauty.   This innate
sensitiveness of the Greek mind to *beauty* made it to
differ from Egyptian, Roman, and almost every other
national art, and constituted it the standard of art
for all time.   But the Greek sense of beauty was a
thoughtful quality of a thoughtful people ; since the
sensual, strong in the Greek, was subordinated to the
intellectual and moral in this finely attempered race.
"Beauty with the Greek," says an English writer,
"was neither little nor voluptuous ; the soul's energies were not relaxed but exalted by its contemplation.
The service of beauty was a service comprehending
all idealisms in one, demanding the self-effacement of
a laborious preparation, the self-restraint of a gradual
achievement.   They who pitched the goal of their
aspiration so high knew that the paths leading up
to it were rough, steep and long ; they felt that perfect workmanship and perfect taste, being supremely

precious, must be supremely difficult as well.''* Thus beauty, with the Greeks, was the manifestation of their ideal self-development, the working out of a profound principle of culture, and this made their art so noble ; and it is this by which, in presence of their serious sculptures, our spirits grow calm, and we feel the truth and moral power of the Greek conception of beauty, raising us above our littleness into a region of higher thought and feeling.

So there are other laws of nature besides truth which enter into art, such, for example, as order, which belongs not only to the structure of the world, but of the mind and its structures ; as unity, or that consistency of parts with the whole which gives delight in a beautiful object ; as proportion, which is the outcome of a symmetric mind ; moderation, which is the continence of conscious spiritual strength ; grace, which flows from inward sympathy and freedom ; character, or individuality, or expression, so variously named, which, indeed, is much the same as ideality, by which the artist expresses his own thought and personality, and by which also a distinctive spirit of the period and history of the work is stamped on it ; and not to mention more of these laws, above all, the great law of form, to which everything in art comes, which is the highest intellectual expression of art, so that sculpture, perhaps, is the purest art manifestation ; and it is by studying these laws that we come at the principles of art criticism, and through the ignorance of which there is often shown a want of judgment in matters of art, betokening false standards drawn, it may be, from metaphysics or political economy rather than nature, making to be measures of art productions such qualities as logic, difficulty, cost, pretti-

* *Westminster Review.*

ness, melodramatic effect, bulk, warm coloring, elaborate though senseless detail—instead of the true and invariable standards of nature, by a return to which through the clear instinct of æsthetic genius lies the only road to reform and advancement.

4. Art in its source is divine. The divine ideal has not been perfectly attained, but ever beckons on like a star. Nature is a projection of divine ideas of beauty into time and space; and the human mind, which could know nothing objectively unless the same existed subjectively in itself, can read these types of beauty, or, as Ruskin calls them, "the eternal canons of loveliness," in its consciousness. Ruskin classes among spiritual ideas typical of divine attributes such purely æsthetic conceptions as unity, perfection, infinity, order, repose, moderation, purity, truth. These are moral as well as æsthetic qualities; and I was greatly pleased to come across this passage spoken to the students of Johns Hopkins University, from a poetic point of view, by an American poet—poet of the salt-sea marshes—Sidney Lanier: "Cannot one say to the young artist, whether working in stone, in color, in tone, or in character-forms of the novel: So far from dreading that your moral purpose will interfere with your beautiful creation, go forward in the clear conviction that unless you are suffused—soul and body, one might say—with that moral purpose that finds its largest expression in love; that is, the love of all things in their proper relation; unless you are suffused with this love, do not dare to meddle with beauty; in a word, unless you are suffused with true wisdom, goodness and love, abandon the hope that the ages will accept you as an artist." We cannot help wishing that Lanier could have lived longer to carry out his own noble theory of art.

ADDITIONAL NOTES.

P. 20.—*Wunderthätige Bilder sind meist nur schlechte Gemälde.*

P. 25.—The crescent and star adopted by the Turks after the capture of Constantinople, to be their banner-device, was originally upon old coins of Greek Byzantium, commemorating the light of Torch-bearing Hekate, that shone in the heavens on a dark night revealing the Macedonians who were on the point of seizing the town, so that this came also from the Greeks.

P. 56.—The Cotylos belonging to the National Museum at Athens (No. 3442) is a vase of very fine clay. The figures stand out in pale red upon a beautiful black varnished surface, their only accessory decoration being a wreath running around the middle of the vase and with palms under the handles.

On the first face is the figure of a Bacchante with a tambourine, dancing on the tips of her toes. She is clad in a robe and a short chiton without sleeves, cut close to the shape. In most of the representations of the Dionysiac dances, as that of the Crater of Boulogne and of an Apulian vase of the Jatta collection, there is a violent expression of ecstatic fury. Here, on the contrary, notwithstanding the unbound hair floating on the shoulders, the dance is placid and graceful, and the physiognomy earnest and sweet. On the reverse of

P.   56.—*Continued*.

the vase, a young girl, clothed in the same style
of dress, but with her hair tied *en corymbe*,
marches or dances, holding with her two hands,
suspended by the feet, a kid, doubtless dead.
Skopas has long been supposed to be the inven-
tor of the type of the Bacchante in delirium,
tearing the kid.   In recent years M. Winter
has published the account of a bas-relief of the
Esquiline, which represents the same subject ;
the invention of the type is thus carried back
to the anonymous author of the bas-relief.
However this may be, all representations of
the motive, in sculpture at least, occur after the
Vth century, and are therefore derived from
the bas-relief or the statue of Skopas.   The
paintings on vases do not allow us to go back
further than the second half of the Vth century ;
the most antique of these Bacchantes, represented as swinging the mutilated limbs of a
fawn, is that of a figure on an amphora now in
Munich.

But the examination of the most ancient
vase-paintings leads us to conclude that the
classic type comes from the combination of
many anterior types.   It is evident that different motives entered into the formation of the
classic type, which art has definitely fixed
as belonging to the IVth century.   What
approached nearest to the style of Skopas is
precisely that of the second figure on the
Cotylos.   The dancer has a quiet and graceful
movement which does not recall the furies of
Bacchic intoxication, and seems to be swayed
by the gentle animation of the dance alone.

P. 56.—*Continued*.

She is not excited by swinging the mutilated fragments of the animal that she carries with its head downward, and with both hands, as if it would need a strong effort to rend it asunder. But in the excitation of the dance, that grows more and more violent, she tears the kid in pieces : the classic type is fixed.—*Bulletin de Correspondance Hellenique*.

P. 181.—The design of the Tholos of Epidauros has ever been a difficult problem. M. Defrasse and myself have always believed that the fact of a well, or spring, the sacred spring of Asklepios, whose source is now dried up, should be taken into account. Pausanias, in the rapid enumeration which he made of the monuments of the *Hieron*, cites separately the Tholos and a spring, κρήνη, "remarkable for the roof which covers it, and above all for its decoration." But neither the spring, which ought to be, according to the context, in the neighborhood of the stadion, nor the ruins of the structure that covered it, have been found, while the description that Pausanias gives of it applies exactly to the Tholos. Therefore it seems to me that the Tholos and κρήνη are one and the same monuments, even if Pausanias does not give them as identical. But this is only an hypothesis. The testimony of the traveler Desmonceaux is of importance in regard to a subterranean *central* of the edifice in question. This subterranean *central* was divided interiorly by concentric walls which served to sustain the *dallage*, a natural arangement. This, indeed, accounts for the employ-

P. 181.—*Continued.*

ment of concentric walls. But here is the difficulty. The said concentric walls are not continuous; they are every one pierced with a door, or opening, and these openings make a communication with all the interior circles; besides that, these circles are barred each with a little transverse wall; in fine, the respective disposition of the transverse walls and the doors are such, that if one starts from the centre, he must necessarily follow each of the three circles to the end of each, and when he returns on his steps, he must follow the same inverse order, without which there is no possibility of shortening the course. This singular arrangement constitutes the originality of the subterranean *central* which is yet to be explained. The fact that the upper courses of the walls below the *dallage* having disappeared, does not militate against their having once existed.—HENRI LECHAT, in the *Revue Archéologique.* March, 1896.

P. 182.—The discovery of the bronze quadriga occurred in this way. About May 1, 1896, members of the French Archæological Society who were exploring at Delphi, found between two retaining walls, in a kind of pocket, a life-sized bronze statue (whose color is wonderfully kept), in the style of the early part of the Vth century B. C. The statue is that of a youthful but bearded victor of the Pythian games. The height is 1.78 metres. From head to foot it is well-preserved, excepting that the left arm is lost and the head is in two pieces. The hair is in long locks daintily arranged. About the

P. 182.—*Continued.*

forehead is a fillet or garland. The garment reaches to the feet, with regular folds, and is gathered in at the waist by a girdle. The statue once stood on a chariot, and in the right hand are remains of reins. Only small fragments of the chariot and horses are left. The pupil and apple of the eyes and the eyelashes are of some encaustic material. Homolle identified this at once as Onatas's statue of Hiero of Syracuse, victor in the race 472 B. C. (Pindar's first Pythian Ode). Near by was found the base of a monument large enough to hold a chariot, and bearing an almost indecipherable inscription O N A (Ἱέρωνα) and also Polyzelos brother of Hiero.

A polychrome statue of a female figure has lately been found by the French School at Delos. A brief notice of this appears in the *Bulletin de Correspondance Hellenique.* It is in a perfect state, a little over life-size, height 1ᵐ 80. The body rests on the left limb, the right foot thrown back just touching the ground. The left arm hangs down, while the right is placed across the breast and raised to the shoulder. The costume is composed of a tunic and peplos, the tunic falling in large folds to the feet which it covers almost completely. The peplos is thrown about the form nearly concealing the tunic except the lower portion, and one of its ends is wrapped around the left wrist. The sandal of the right foot which is partially seen, has a triple sole and is ornamented with red and gilded fillets. In the

P. 182.—*Continued.*

decoration of the cloak there is blue color with broidery of rose-violet. The robe is adorned with bands on which are figured scrolls of white and gold upon a ground of clear blue. Though somewhat in the conventional style of such statues, the face is lovely. If a portrait, which it might be, it is idealized in that charming manner of Hellenic art of the third and second centuries B. C., free reproductions of the fourth age of Praxitelean forms. The style of the hair is peculiarly elegant and at the same time simpler than in examples known of the same period, being in undulating bands like that of the Nymphs of the Vienna bas-relief. It is what we find in the little figures of Tanagra and Myrina ; and the analogy with these is more striking inasmuch as the hair is tinted red. The features are fine and regular, the eyes are cast down, and the oval face is a little elongated, delicately narrowing toward the chin. The neck is straight and long. The expression is sweet, but it would be considered cold, were it not for a smile hardly indicated yet sufficient to animate the countenance.

It resembles a Muse, Mnémosyne, perhaps, from its thoughtful character.

Such a work, brought to light from the oblivion of the past, expressive of that Hellenic beauty to which art, even if in modern times it may have added some new elements of nature and realness, must ever return for its renewal, is enough to reward the attention and labor given to exploration in Greece.

www.ingramcontent.com/pod-product-compliance
Lightning Source LLC
Chambersburg PA
CBHW030337270326
41926CB00009B/869